ROBERT F.
KENNEDY
RIPPLES
OF HOPE

ROBERT F. KENNEDY

RIPPLES OF HOPE

—⁓—

Kerry Kennedy in Conversation with
Heads of State, Business Leaders, Influencers, and
Activists about Her Father's Impact on Their Lives

—⁓—

KERRY KENNEDY

CENTER
STREET.

New York   Nashville

Center Street

Hachette Book Group

1290 Avenue of the Americas, New York, NY 10104

centerstreet.com

twitter.com/centerstreet

First Edition: June 2018

Center Street is a division of Hachette Book Group, Inc. The Center Street name and logo are trademarks of Hachette Book Group, Inc.

The publisher is not responsible for websites (or their content) that are not owned by the publisher.

The Hachette Speakers Bureau provides a wide range of authors for speaking events. To find out more, go to www.HachetteSpeakersBureau.com or call (866) 376-6591.

Book design by Timothy Shaner, NightandDayDesign.biz

Library of Congress Cataloging-in-Publication Data has been applied for.

ISBNs: 978-1-4789-1824-0 (hardcover), 978-1-5460-8294-1 (large print), 978-1-4789-1826-4 (ebook)

Printed in the United States of America

LSC-C

10 9 8 7 6 5 4 3 2 1

*For my mother, Ethel Kennedy, who raised
eleven children with undaunted courage,
deep faith, and rollicking adventure.*

*For the board of directors and my colleagues at
Robert F. Kennedy Human Rights, who carry
forward Daddy's unfinished work on social
justice and inspire me daily; and,*

*For Cara, Mariah, and Michaela, who seek a newer
world and fill my days with wonder and love.*

CONTENTS

FOREWORD by Thurston Clarke 1

PREFACE by Kerry Kennedy 13

Harry Belafonte 33

Tony Bennett 49

Joe Biden 59

Bono 67

Bill Clinton 75

George Clooney 95

Tim Cook 99

Marian Wright Edelman 111

Al Gore 123

LaDonna Harris 133

Dolores Huerta 145

Van Jones 157

John Lewis 171

Portrait of RFK by Aaron A. Shikler, 1975, based on photo by Paul Slade. On view at the Department of Justice, Washington, DC (US Department of Justice)

CONTENTS

STEFAN LÖFVEN 185

SHIRLEY MACLAINE 195

CHRIS MATTHEWS 199

GAVIN NEWSOM 211

BARACK OBAMA 219

SOLEDAD O'BRIEN 229

MATTEO RENZI 241

JEFFREY SACHS 247

JOE SCARBOROUGH 255

HOWARD SCHULTZ 267

MARTIN SHEEN 275

ROBERT FREDERICK SMITH 287

GLORIA STEINEM 295

ALFRE WOODARD 307

VICTORIA WRIGHT 315

ACKNOWLEDGMENTS 321

ABOUT THE AUTHOR 324

"Each time a man stands up for an ideal, or acts to improve the lot of others, or strikes out against injustice, he sends forth a tiny ripple of hope, and crossing each other from a million different centers of energy and daring, those ripples build a current that can sweep down the mightiest walls of oppression and resistance."

—Robert F. Kennedy

ROBERT F.
KENNEDY

RIPPLES
of HOPE

FOREWORD

BY THURSTON CLARKE

One of the passengers on the train bringing Bobby Kennedy's body from his funeral in New York to his burial at Arlington National Cemetery looked out a window at the mourners lining the tracks and asked herself, "What did he have that he could do this to people?"

It's a question that I tried to answer in my book about his 1968 campaign.

It's also a question we might ask ourselves in 2018, fifty years after his assassination: What did Robert Kennedy have, for example, that has brought us all together tonight, almost fifty years after his death, in this place, at a conference bearing his name?

It's a question whose answer may help you make decisions that take into account justice, human rights, the environment, and poverty.

I came across the question at the archives of the JFK Library in Boston while reading a collection of oral interviews conducted with passengers on that twenty-one-car funeral train bound for Arlington on June 8, 1968.

Passengers on that train looked out and saw what may have been the most dramatic and moving display of public grief ever displayed for an

Crowd reaching out, California, 1968 (Steve Schapiro/ Fahey Klein Gallery)

American never elected to the presidency. Trains carrying the remains of presidents Abraham Lincoln and Franklin Roosevelt had traveled at a slow and mournful pace, but Kennedy's train had been scheduled to travel nonstop and a normal rate of speed. Crowds were expected, but no one had imagined that on a steamy Saturday afternoon in early June two million people would spontaneously head for the tracks between New York and Washington, wading through marshes, hiking into meadows, filling tenement balconies, climbing onto factory roofs, standing in junkyards and cemeteries, looking down from bridges, and creating a 226-mile-long chain of grief and despair.

Once the train emerged from the Hudson River tunnel into New Jersey, it encountered so many people jamming station platforms and spilling onto the northbound tracks that the engineer had to reduce speed, and reduce it even more after a tragic accident in Elizabeth, New Jersey, when those in the train could look out the windows and see their grief reflected in the faces of mourners lining the tracks.

They saw men in suits, sport shirts, uniforms, and undershirts, crying, saluting, standing at attention, hands over hearts. They saw women in madras shorts and Sunday dresses weeping, kneeling, covering their faces, and holding up their children.

They saw American flags dipped by American Legion honor guards and waved by Cub Scouts, and because anyone with a uniform seemed to have decided to wear it, they saw policemen in gold braid and white gloves, fire companies standing at attention next to their trucks, and veterans in overseas caps snapping salutes.

They saw the kind of white working-class voters who had supported the 1964 candidacy of Alabama governor George Wallace for the Democratic nomination, and who might vote again for Wallace or Richard Nixon in November, although until four days earlier many had been planning to vote for Kennedy, even though he was an acknowledged champion of black Americans and had condemned an American war as "deeply wrong."

The NBC commentator David Brinkley had called Kennedy "the only white politician who could talk to both races," and compared his assassination to Lincoln's. So the passengers saw black Americans who had embraced Kennedy more passionately and completely than any white politician since Abraham Lincoln, and who sang the "Battle Hymn of the Republic" as the train passed through Philadelphia and Baltimore.

The passengers remembered five nuns standing on tiptoes in a yellow pickup truck, black militants holding up clenched fists, a white policeman cradling a black child in his arms, and a line of Little Leaguers standing at attention along the baselines, heads bowed and caps held over hearts.

A *Life* magazine reporter, Sylvia Wright, saw a wedding party standing close to the tracks in a Delaware meadow. The bridesmaids were holding up the hems of their pink and green dresses in one hand and their bouquets in the other. As the last car carrying Kennedy's coffin approached, they extended their arms and threw their bouquets against its side. After seeing this Wright asked herself the question that has become the descant of much that has been said and written about Bobby Kennedy since, "What did he have that he could do this to people?"

I think that the best way to answer it is to examine Bobby's 1968 campaign, one that a reporter covering it called a "huge, joyous adventure." It was that, and more, and no presidential candidate since has run so passionately—or, if you will, recklessly—or put poverty, justice, and human rights so squarely at the center of a campaign, or criticized the American people so brazenly.

Try to imagine a politician now saying, as Kennedy did in a *New York Times* essay shortly before he announced his candidacy, "Once we thought, with Jefferson, that we were the best hope of all mankind. But now we seem to rely only on our wealth and power." Or say, as Kennedy did on *Meet the Press*, "I am dissatisfied with our society. I suppose I am dissatisfied with my country."

He delivered the first speech of his campaign on March 18 at the Kansas State University field house, to a record-setting audience of 14,500 students at a conservative university in a conservative heartland state. He was nervous about kicking off his campaign there, but before deciding to run he had agreed to deliver a speech commemorating the Kansas governor and former presidential candidate Alf Landon. The night before, he told Kansas governor Robert Docking, "What I'm going to say isn't very popular." Quite a statement for a candidate for the presidency to make on the eve of launching his campaign.

He told these supposedly conservative students that America was "deep in a malaise of the spirit," and suffering from "a deep crisis of confidence." He admitted his own complicity in the Vietnam War, saying, "I was involved in many of the early decisions on Vietnam, decisions which helped set us on our present path," adding, "I am willing to bear my share of the responsibility before history and before my fellow citizens." He closed by saying, "Our country is in danger: not just from foreign enemies; but above all, from our own misguided policies—and what they can do to the nation that Thomas Jefferson once told us was the last best hope of mankind."

The students rushed the stage, cheering, weeping, tipping over chairs, grabbing at his hands and shirtsleeves. Stanley Tretick of *Look* magazine stood on the platform, photographing the melee and shouting, "This is Kansas, effing Kansas! He's going all the way. He's going all the effing way." A reporter called Kennedy's speech and the students' reaction to it "the first indication that we were about to embark on something unlike anything we had ever experienced."

Three days later, Kennedy embarked on a ten-day, thirteen state cross-country tour. His first stop was at the University of Alabama in Tuscaloosa, where as attorney general he had sent in federal marshals to enforce the registration of black students. Going there was courageous, or foolhardy, perhaps both. He told students he had come because he believed, "any who seek higher office this year must go before all Americans: not just those who agree with them, but those who disagree; recognizing that it is not just our supporters who we must lead in the difficult years ahead." And he said that he would count his campaign a failure if it left Americans as divided as when he began it.

This would be one of many things that he said during his campaign that seem to reach across the five since decades and speak to us today.

He flew to California and demonstrated that his appeal went beyond the nation's college campuses. The crowd at the Stockton courthouse contained a large contingent of Hispanics, many of them farmworkers. Kennedy told them that "Decency is the heart of this whole campaign," and that "poverty is indecent. Illiteracy is indecent. The death, the maiming of brave young men in the swamps of Vietnam, that is also indecent. And it is indecent for a man to work with his back and his hands in the valleys of California without ever having hope of sending his son on to college. This is also indecent."

He did not tailor his message to an audience. Later that afternoon he spoke at a shopping center in Sacramento and said the same thing to a white, middle-class audience, telling them, "It is indecent for a man on the streets of New York City or Cleveland or Detroit or Watts to surrender the only life that he has to despair and hopelessness."

Nor did he pander to black audiences, and when he drove through Watts several days later in a motorcade that the *Los Angeles Times* called "uproarious, shrieking and frenzied" and "a spectacle without parallel in the American experience," he told one of many street-corner audiences that he addressed, "And I tell you here in California the same thing I told those in Alabama with whom I talked. The gulf between our people will not be bridged by those who preach violence, or by those who burn or loot."

His first primary would be in Indiana, and no northern state seemed less promising for a politician campaigning on racial justice and the indecency of poverty. It had cities with large white ethnic blue-collar populations who felt threatened by black progress and had given George

Wallace 30 percent of the vote in the 1964 Democratic primary. Yet Kennedy launched his campaign there with a speech at Notre Dame containing nothing to appeal to backlash whites. He said, 'in the midst of our great affluence, children—American children—are hungry, some to the point where their minds and bodies are damaged beyond repair." During the question period he returned to his continuing theme of national redemption through good works, of healing the wounds that Vietnam had inflicted on the national psyche by eliminating hunger and poverty, and asked, "What other reason do we have really for our existence as human beings unless we've made some other contribution to somebody else to improve their own lives?"

While he was flying to Indianapolis afterward in a small chartered plane, Martin Luther King Jr. was assassinated in Memphis. Kennedy was scheduled to address a crowd in a black neighborhood. The police chief met him at the airport and urged him to cancel the rally, telling him, "It's not safe for you to go there." He went anyway and delivered the finest speech of his campaign, perhaps the finest extemporaneous speech ever delivered by an American politician. All he had was a few notes scribbled on a sheet of yellow legal paper.

The atmosphere at the small neighborhood park in the black neighborhood was electric, and edgy. The organizers were afraid Kennedy would be attacked and had told some men to climb trees and look for snipers in the surrounding buildings.

Kennedy did not discount the importance of physical courage. He had copied Emerson's line "Always do what you are afraid to do" in his daybook and had rafted through treacherous waters and climbed challenging mountains. Even so, he considered moral courage more difficult to demonstrate. In 1966 he had told students in South Africa that moral courage was "a rarer commodity than bravery in battle or great intelligence," and extolled it as "the one essential, vital quality of those who seek to change a world."

In Indianapolis he demonstrated the physical courage to address a black audience two hours after a white man had murdered the most beloved black leader in US history, the moral courage to announce his death to this crowd (and many in it would hear the news for the first time from Kennedy) and then deliver a speech offering comfort and hope. He also demonstrated the same political courage that had led him to speak in Kansas, the University of Alabama, and other potentially hostile venues, because if a riot had broken out during or after his speech he would have been blamed for causing it.

Because of his courage, Indianapolis would be the only major American city to escape the riots and violence that wracked 119 others in the wake of the King assassination.

He spoke haltingly at first, repeating phrases and words, groping for the right ones. Pausing after each sentence to compose the next. His voice was hollow, close to breaking, and tears welled in his eyes. The spotlights made him look pallid and haunted.

He demonstrated more physical, moral, and political courage the next day. He was driving into Cleveland in a white convertible when an aide with a mobile phone reported that the police believed that a sniper was hiding in a steeple overlooking the hotel where he was about to address an audience of business and civic leaders and suggested he wait by the side of the road.

Kennedy said, "No. We'll never stop for that kind of threat" and continued into town with the top down. One day after King's assassination, when riots were continuing in dozens of American cities, he told these 2,200 civic leaders that white Americans bore some responsibility for the violence. He was solemn and muted, as if delivering a eulogy, as he said, "Some who accuse others of inciting riots have by their own conduct invited them," adding, "violence breeds violence, repression brings retaliation, and only a cleansing of our whole society can remove this sickness from our soul." He followed this with what were, even for

1968, profoundly radical words. He told these pillars of the Cleveland establishment that their own public and private institutions had contributed to the unrest that had roiled their city after Dr. King's assassination. "For there is another kind of violence, slower but just as deadly as the shot or the bombing in the night," he said. "This is the violence of institutions; indifference and inaction, and slow decay. This is the violence that afflicts the poor."

Two days later he demonstrated more courage by walking through the riot zone in Washington, DC. Fires were still smoldering and National Guard troops were on the streets. The crowd following him grew so large that guardsmen at first mistook it for a gang of looters. A woman stared at Kennedy in disbelief and asked "Is that you?" When she saw it was, she said, "I knew you'd be the first to come here, darling."

On April 16 he visited the Pine Ridge reservation in South Dakota. Of the approximately seventy events that he attended during the first month of his campaign, ten were on Native American reservations or in Native American schools in the Southwest and Midwest. His aides thought he was wasting his time and tried to remove these appearances from his schedule. He called these aides "callous sons of bitches" and put them back. He had two days to campaign in South Dakota before its primary and elected to spend most of one of them on Pine Ridge, a Connecticut-size reservation with only sixty miles of paved roads and not a single bank, supermarket, or library.

He stopped in a one-room shack that was home to nine people, including Christopher Pretty Boy, a ten-year-old Lakota Sioux whose parents had died in an automobile accident the week before. A photograph taken by a Jesuit father from the local mission (because Kennedy had asked reporters and news photographers to remain outside) shows Kennedy, hand jammed into his trouser pockets and smiling, as if there was nowhere else he would rather be than sitting on a worn blanket with a heartbroken orphan in a shack in Calico, one of the poorest communities on the poorest reservation in North America.

When Kennedy emerged from the shack he was holding Pretty Boy's hand. The two remained together all day, and Kennedy frequently leaned down to talk to him. While Kennedy was flying to Rapid City he told an aide to call the Holy Rosary Mission and tell the fathers that he had invited Pretty Boy and his sister to spend the summer with his family in Hyannis. Pretty Boy died before he could go there. Some on Pine Ridge told me he died in a car accident, others that he had killed himself, although he would have been younger than most of those who committed suicide on the reservation.

The invitation to Pretty Boy was a predictable result of Kennedy's lively moral imagination—his ability to imagine himself, or his children, orphaned and living in Calico; to imagine himself being a migrant farmworker, a disadvantaged urban African American, a Nebraskan farmer, or a child in Washington, DC, who lacked a playground in his neighborhood. While driving through a poor neighborhood there with his children, he said, "Look, there are no playgrounds. There's no place for these kids to play. They're just like you; they have the same wants and needs." Then he raised money to build a playground there and brought some of his children to the opening ceremony.

His brother's assassination and his experiences among the poor had deepened Kennedy's moral imagination, so that when he spoke to members of these aggrieved communities they sensed a communion and intimacy that went beyond politics or pity; they sensed a man who understood them, and felt their suffering as if it was his own. His moral imagination was the silent heartbeat of his campaign. It explained why black Americans called him their "blue-eyed soul brother," why a former Wallace supporter told a reporter, "I like him. I don't know why, but I like him."

Telling an audience the opposite of what they probably wanted to hear, or making members of a sympathetic audience ashamed of themselves is a risky political strategy, but Kennedy pursued it throughout his campaign. He told an audience of aerospace workers in California, "We should slow down the race to the moon." When a bellicose student in Oregon demanded that the government mount a military action against North Korea, Kennedy replied, "It's not too late to enlist." When whites in West Virginia complained about being unemployed and with nothing to do he said, "Well, you could remove those wrecked cars from the side of the road." He defended a new open-housing law to a luncheon meeting of the Indianapolis Real Estate Board, saying, "I think if you are asking people to go fight for us 12,500 miles away and tell them 'You can die for us but you can't buy a home' seems rather inequitable. Don't you think?" His statement was reportedly met with only "mild applause."

There was of course much more to his campaign. There was a twelve-hour, five-hundred-mile whistle-stop across Nebraska when he converted crowd after crowd of initially skeptical farmers. His speechwriter Jeff Greenfield remembered it as a revelation for Kennedy's staff and the press, demonstrating, Greenfield said, his "ability to relate to people who had nothing in common with him at all."

There was his nine-hour, one-hundred-mile motorcade across northern Indiana that the reporter Jules Witcover would call "one of the most incredible outpourings of sentiment for a political candidate in all of the annals of American campaigning."

There was his two-hour May 29 motorcade through black and Hispanic neighborhoods in Los Angeles, with people screaming his name, slowing his car to a crawl, grabbing at his hands and arms. As they cheered, he pumped his fist in the air and shouted, "These are my people!"

So, what did he have that he could do this to people? Why did those bridesmaids and their bride wait for hours in that field on a hot day so they could toss their bouquets at his funeral train?

What did he have in 1968 that we need now, in 2018, a time that finds Americans more divided, angry, than 1968?

What did he have that might guide you in your decisions? That might guide all of us?

He had courage: moral, physical, and political courage that he demonstrated again and again throughout his campaign.

And perhaps most important, for a leader seeking to unite a bitterly divided people, he had a lively moral imagination. The ability to imagine what it would be like to be an orphaned Indian boy, or child bitten by rats in a Harlem tenement, or a hungry child in a sharecropper's shack in Mississippi, or a Nebraskan farmer, a farmworker, or a blue-collar worker in a Midwestern city.

And he not only had this moral imagination, he acted on it. He raised money to build playgrounds for children in Washington, DC. He invited Christopher Pretty Boy to spend a summer in this lovely place where we are tonight.

Congressman John Lewis served on Bobby Kennedy's campaign staff in 1968. When I spoke with him about Kennedy he told me that before he is about to cast a difficult vote in the House of Representatives he often asks himself, "What would Bobby do?"

It's a good question, and not just for a politician, but for anyone faced with a decision that has a moral dimension and requires courage.

"What would Bobby do?"

Good question. I hope you ask it of yourselves.

—Thurston Clarke, historian, author, and journalist, from his June 2017 speech at the Kennedy Compound, adapted from his book The *Last Campaign: Robert F. Kennedy and 82 Days that Inspired America*

PREFACE

BY KERRY KENNEDY

Think of John Kennedy, Lyndon Johnson, or Richard Nixon. Each, in his own way, is firmly set in a certain era of American history. Yet as vibrant as they all were at the peak of their power and influence, none of these men could easily slip into the contemporary political world. Their leadership was unique to their time and place.

That conclusion does not ring true for my father, Robert Kennedy. His appearance is ever modern: the shaggy hair, the skinny ties, the suit jacket off, the shirtsleeves rolled. Beyond appearances, what is striking about RFK are the themes he returned to again and again—themes that still energize debate and resonate in our own time and place.

Think of the headlines over the past few years, and it is easy to hear Robert Kennedy's voice speaking out in our country as he did fifty years ago—on the madness of gun violence, the shame of police brutality, the need for compassion in welcoming immigrants and refugees, the defiance of the easy call to war, and, where war has broken out, the moral necessity of seeking peace. One imagines him urging us to focus not only on stopping terrorism but also on understanding and addressing its root causes. He would encourage us to focus on the destructive force of hate, the disillusionment of young people, the inherent injustice of a criminal

Robert Kennedy and Kerry Kennedy, Snake River, Idaho (Harry Benson)

13

justice system that discriminates based on race and class and in which thousands go to jail simply because they are too poor to make bail—the New Jim Crow. And it is easy to think of RFK reminding us of the duty to address the struggles of those who are not in the headlines, the most vulnerable among us: farmworkers, small farmers, factory workers, people who have seen the jobs that supported them replaced by cheap labor or technology. He would also remember our duty to Native Americans and those suffering in the hollows of Appalachia, on the Mississippi Delta, and in the most destitute slums of our great cities.

Bobby Kennedy's presence was grounded not only in policy, but most especially in values, values that never wavered, values that stand in high contrast to too much of our political leadership today: integrity, courage, faith, humanism, patriotism, all tempered by curiosity, children and dogs, laughter, fun, and, most especially, love.

Jeff Greenfield, RFK's speechwriter, and Frank Mankiewicz, his press secretary, posited that Kennedy's credo was "Get your boot off his neck." Indeed, Robert Kennedy stood up to bullies throughout his life. As a grade school student he disdained gossip and meanness. As a member of the Harvard football team he refused to play away games unless the African American student on the team was allowed to stay in the same hotel as the rest of the squad. He bravely took on Father Leonard J. Feeney, the anti-Semitic chaplain at Harvard who spewed hate, for insisting there is no salvation outside the Catholic church. Feeney was later excommunicated. Kennedy traveled to Israel in 1948 and advocated for US support for the new and beleaguered nation surrounded by enemies. As a law student he invited Ralph Bunche, the first African American to win the Nobel Peace Prize, to speak at the segregated University of Virginia—and then successfully petitioned the UVA Law School to allow Bunche to speak before a mixed-race crowd. Unable to find a hotel in the area that would take Bunche, Bobby and Ethel invited Bunche to stay in their tiny home, where they endured a night of white supremacists hurling racist epithets and Molotov cocktails.

In the 1950s Kennedy worked for the Senate Committee on Investigations—for five months—during which he focused on how US allies were benefiting financially by selling goods to China, which, in turn, was using those goods to create the machinery of war and use it against US soldiers in Korea. His report was lauded as exemplary and as the only usable intelligence to come out of the committee chaired by Senator Joe McCarthy. When he wasn't conducting his China research, Kennedy spent the remainder of his time on the committee fighting the excesses of the chairman and Roy Cohn, describing the senator's insatiable need for publicity as though McCarthy were on a wild toboggan ride, addicted to the adrenaline rush, unaware and uncaring about the tree at the end of the hill. Kennedy later exposed the excesses that caused Cohn's resignation and led to the end of McCarthy's reign of terror. Asked a decade later by Peter Maas how he could have worked for Senator McCarthy, Kennedy responded, "At the time, I thought there was a serious internal security threat to the United States . . . and Joe McCarthy seemed to be the only one doing anything about it. I was wrong."

Kennedy joined the Rackets Committee and pursued union bosses like Dave Beck and Jimmy Hoffa who were stealing from the rank and file. As attorney general, he stood up to Bull Connor, Governor John Patterson, Governor George Wallace, and other white supremacists on behalf of civil rights activists. When Prince Edward County, Virginia, sought to avoid desegregation by closing all its public schools, Kennedy opened the Prince Edward County Free Schools, imported volunteer teachers from across the country, and made sure that the African American kids would receive an excellent education while the case wended its way through the courts.

Whereas J. Edgar Hoover renounced arrested teenagers as "delinquents" and jettisoned them to jail, Kennedy saw children, mostly of color, were often the victims of a cruel structure that condemned them to life-destroying prison terms for petty crimes with little or no access to defense council. Kennedy obtained legislation to reform the juvenile justice system. His focus on poverty and his establishment, at the DOJ, of the Juvenile Delinquency Committee, as Arthur M. Schlesinger wrote in *Robert F. Kennedy and His Times*, the most insightful and well-researched biography of RFK, led to the establishment of "VISTA, Legal Aid, mental health centers, youth development projects, neighborhood services, and the foundation for what would become the War on Poverty." For the first time in history, Kennedy ordered the Justice Department to resolve Indian land claims rather than fight them. As senator, his first act gained Puerto Ricans in New York access to the vote by offering voter registration forms in Spanish. He came to the aid of farmworkers in California, miners in West Virginia, African Americans in Bedford-Stuyvesant, and Native Americans across the country.

But to leave it at stopping the bullies would not do justice to Kennedy. On that terrible night when he told a crowd in downtown Indianapolis that their leader, Martin Luther King Jr., had been murdered, he included in his remarks a quote from Aeschylus: "To tame the savageness of man and make gentle the life of the world." Indeed, Kennedy focused much of his life on taming the savageness, *and* he also made gentle the life of the world.

I DID NOT SET OUT to pen a biography of Robert Kennedy. Many have been published, and there are more on the way. Instead, I sought to write a book not so much about Bobby Kennedy in history, but about people who, inspired by him, are influencing our world, fifty years after his death. Some knew him and worked closely with him. Others were not born when he died in 1968. But he touched all their lives in profound ways. They are women and men, white, black, brown, and mixed, they grew up in wealth and in poverty, in cities and on farms, in the Northeast, the Midwest, the South, the Southwest, the West, the West Coast, and abroad. They include four heads of state, actors, students, politicians of both parties, business leaders, television personalities, feminists, and leaders of women, Native Americans, farmworkers, and civil rights activists. They range in age from eighteen to ninety. Each has made a mark on our country or our world, and all consider Bobby Kennedy a profound source of inspiration.

Hillary Clinton famously compared herself to a Rorsach test, in which what you see tells you more about yourself than it does about her. In many ways that is true as well of Robert Kennedy. In our interviews, John Lewis described his empathy, Shirley MacLaine talked about his joy for life, and Marian Wright Edelman spoke about his tenderness with starving children.

The people I interviewed saw Kennedy through the lens of their own experiences, and the issues that are dearest to their hearts. Some of these issues were not on the front burner in the 1960s, yet Kennedy's presence is nonetheless strongly felt by the leaders on these topics today: Al Gore on climate change, Gloria Steinem on the future of feminism, Tim Cook on the use of technology to address overwhelming social needs.

Others spoke about their lives in ways that were not directly involved with RFK, but which paralleled his values, and spoke to their own commitments for a more just and peaceful world. Tony Bennett told about being a pacifist who was drafted into the army in World War II, and found himself in a firefight during the Battle of the Bulge, refusing to shoot. Afterward, he and his companions marched into a nearby town where they emancipated prisoners from a Nazi concentration camp. Years later, while performing at the Super Bowl, Bennett refused to sing the "Star-Spangled Banner," which he considered a tribute to war, and instead intoned "America the Beautiful."

Stefan Löfven, the prime minister of Sweden, grew up in the remote reaches of the country. His father disappeared before he was born, and his mother, unable to care for him but unwilling to give him up, placed Löfven in foster care but would not allow him to be adopted. He was raised by a loving couple, the mother a caretaker for the elderly and the father a lumberjack. After completing two years of college, he decided on a career as a steelworker, joined the union, and rose quickly to its presidency, where upon his political career was launched. Within six years, he was prime minister. Löfven spoke about the importance of creating a world in which ordinary, common people are treated with dignity in their working environments and are not abused by powers beyond their influence—a vision shared and championed by his hero, RFK. Soledad O'Brien spoke about growing up the daughter of immigrants, her father Australian and her mother Puerto Rican of Afro-Cuban descent. Her parents lived in Maryland, right across the Potomac from Virginia, where Mildred Loving (who was black) and Richard Loving (who was white) had been recently arrested and sentenced to a year in prison under antimiscegenation laws. Unable to lawfully marry in their own state, O'Brien's parents were wed in Washington, DC, and moved to Long Island to raise their children. Having produced award-winning documentaries on being Latino in America and black in America, O'Brien spoke about the future of race in our country, and the all-important overlay of class when addressing racial justice issues—all topics of deep and abiding concern to RFK.

VIEWING PHOTOGRAPHS AND FILMS from Daddy's 1968 presidential campaign fifty years ago brings back a flood of memories: images of people reaching out to him, almost desperate to touch him, while powerful men—professional football players and Olympic athletes—hold him back with all their might as crowds mobbed him, pulled him closer, insatiable. In defiance of gravity, he leaned over, leaned in, reached out with his full body, light, sinewy, muscular, as if to say with a full heart, "I am yours, we are one." He never seemed frightened or ill at ease among the throng; he was just there, in the moment. The images also remind me of the aftermath: Daddy returning home, his fingers red and swollen, cuff links missing because of all the hands grabbing his, wanting to be part of him.

Since then, I've heard literally thousands of stories from people around the world, all saying what Robert Kennedy meant to them. Each story is different, but there is one common thread that made RFK so special: he reached deeply into the hearts of his audiences, and what he touched was the noble soul in each of them, and in us.

Robert Kennedy was a presidential candidate, a senator, the attorney general, his brother's confidant and campaign manager, a prosecutor, a lawyer, a husband, a son, a brother, an uncle, and a friend. But his most important role, as far as I was concerned, was that of father, to his brood of what would become eleven children, seven boys and four girls, spanning sixteen years.

As kids, my father made us read an hour a day. He loved poetry, and he read it aloud on campaign trips. We would memorize the lines and recite them Sunday nights around the dinner table: Kipling's "If," Robert Service's "The Cremation of Sam McGee," Tennyson's "Ulysses."

Books were everywhere in our home: floors, ceilings, shelves, bathrooms, closets, the attic, the basement, and every coffee table. The breakfast table was covered with daily newspapers: the *Washington Post*, the *Washington Sun*, the *New York Times*, the *Daily News*, the *Wall Street Journal*, the *New York Post*. We subscribed to *Time, Life, Look, Newsweek, US News & World Report, National Geographic, Harper's*, the *Village Voice*—and a strange magazine with a 3-D cover called *Venture*. *WWD* and *Vogue* occasionally found their way into the mix as well.

Perhaps the importance of current events in our house, Hickory Hill, was most reflected in the first room on the left as you walked into the large center hall colonial where we lived in McLean, Virginia. It was dominated by an RCA Victor and known as "the TV room." With all those children, rules were important. Whoever turned on the TV first decided what channel to watch. But any program, at any time, could be trumped by the news. As a result, the news was almost always on.

While breakfast was for reading the papers, dinner was all about content. Daddy would go around the table, asking each of us to tell one thing we read in the paper that day. Seating became strategic, as no one was permitted to repeat an article previously cited. Next came a discussion on the issues, when Daddy would ask our opinions and a lively debate would ensue. The only one I recall in detail was, if he ran for president, should we abandon Hickory Hill in favor of the White House—at eight years old, I was fine with the campaign but firmly against the move. Current events were followed by educational games—Botticelli, a history game, and Ghost, a spelling game, were standards. Then, after dessert—and there was always dessert (usually vanilla ice cream with hot fudge sauce)—Daddy took down the Children's Bible and read aloud from the Old Testament. After dinner we played games: hall hockey in the front hall or freeze tag on the staircase landing. Before bedtime, we gathered in front of the lighted crucifix or around our parents king-size bed, recited the Rosary, and went off to sleep.

Many children of politicians dislike the campaign trail, but we loved campaigning because Daddy made it fun. He took us to the Bronx Zoo, where we fed the elephant, then rafting on the headwaters of the Hudson River, ice-skating at Rockefeller Center, and, later, to Bedford-Stuyvesant, where we played with neighborhood kids, and to the World's Fair in Queens. When Daddy ran for president, he took us to Disneyland—every kid's dream! There's a great photo of Chris and Max on a rocket ship ride with Daddy and John Glenn—who else!

Most of my memories with Daddy involved exercise. In Virginia, we rode horses from Hickory Hill onto trails in back of the CIA, played chase-one-chase-all on the roof of the barn, kick-the-can with a tree for base, had relay races in the pool, round robins on the tennis court, and, nearly every day, played football. When Daddy was quarterback, the girls had actual roles in the game, and were not consigned to the usual hike-the-ball and flood-the-zone.

Winter found us skiing in Waterville Valley, New Hampshire; Stowe, Vermont; and Sun Valley, Idaho. I remember coming up to the top of Bald Mountain on the Warm Springs chairlift, the wind howling, the woolen blanket frozen to my stretch pants, crying for hot chocolate. And Daddy patiently removing my leather lace-up boots, pulling off my two pairs of woolen socks, slipping off the stockings beneath, and carefully, lovingly taking my frostbitten toes between his warm hands and rubbing until I was warm enough to put it all back together, ski down the mountain, and then repeat the process.

One time we went skiing in Lake Placid. As usual there was a large entourage, all the more so with skis, boots, poles, and the accoutrements of the sport. In addition, our family had a habit of sleeping with all the windows open and a large three-foot fan at the foot of the bed, so there were a half-dozen large fans added to the luggage. Soon after we had sorted rooms, unpacked the bags, and gone off to sleep, Daddy learned that the hotel enforced restrictions based on race. We stuffed our gear back in place, buttoned our parkas over our pajamas, then drove through a blinding blizzard to the only hotel that could accommodate our brood and was free of Jim Crow. After a brutal day of campaigning and travel, and in the face of a snowstorm, it would have been easy for Daddy to let it go, just for the night—but his integrity never wavered. And rather than making the move feel like an enormous burden (which it must have been, on some level, with all those kids), Daddy transformed the evening into a great adventure, full of fun.

Summers we were based in Hyannis Port. My earliest memories are of that sweet anticipation, waiting for the air force helicopter to land on Grandpa's lawn, then racing down the hill with a flood of siblings and cousins, jumping into Daddy's outstretched arms while the Shrivers ran for Sarge and Caroline ran to Uncle Jack, Kara and Teddy ran for Uncle Teddy and Steven ran to Uncle Steve. Daddy always took us for a dip in the ocean before breakfast. We swam, sailed, raced, and dragged in a long line knotted with orange life preservers behind the *Resolute*, our Wianno Senior. We dug for clams on Egg Island, climbed the break wall, fished for scup off the pier, and picnicked on the beach. Grandpa was bedridden in those years after a series of massive strokes. We spent weeks creating and practicing plays for his birthday and, despite the fact that we had no acting talent and couldn't possibly carry a tune, Daddy always seemed delighted by the results.

The highlight of the summers were the rafting trips out west. We rode horses at dude ranches and then ran the rapids on the Green, the Yampa, the Snake, and the Colorado Rivers. Daddy read poetry around the campfire and calmed my fears that bats would make nests in my hair as we slept beneath the stars. After downing our lunch of hot dogs and potato chips, Daddy took us to find a cliff and we would all jump off—an early lesson in mustering the courage to overcome fear. He taught us to fish and kayak, and he encouraged us to float down the river in life preservers, bobbing along like so many rubber ducklings.

One day we heard a mournful whine high up on a cliff in the Grand Canyon. Daddy scaled a ridge and rescued the ugliest, mangiest starving chihuahua mutt on earth. The poor thing had fallen off a raft days earlier and had been left to fend for itself. Daddy carefully wrapped the shaking, biting, barking mongrel in a towel and gave her carefully to me. From that day forward, "Rocky the Rockhound" never left my side.

People sometimes ask if I felt forced to work on social justice. Daddy made everything he did so much of an adventure, we didn't see his work as a duty. Daddy didn't press us to take up causes. That's why one dinner stands out. Mummy and all the kids were sitting around the table at Hickory Hill, eating what we wanted and passing around second helpings. Meanwhile, Daddy had been on a trip to the Mississippi Delta for the Hunger Committee of the US Senate. Suddenly he appeared in the doorway, and the room became silent. He said "I've just been to a part of this country where three families live in a room this size—we've got to help those children." He then went to the secretary of agriculture, held hearings, worked with Marian Wright, and expanded the food stamp program.

When he wasn't playing with us, Daddy sat upstairs in his study, working in the one room of our sprawling house that none of his children could storm into unless it was a matter of utmost urgency. I now know that his big brown desk was where he wrote his books, important speeches, and legislation.

One particular day is etched in my memory. All I knew was that I needed my father's immediate attention. My brother Michael and I were reenacting World War II in the ancient magnolia tree that dominated the sloping backyard of Hickory Hill. As usual, Michael demanded he be the victorious American, whereas I, eighteen months younger, weaker, and not nearly as good a shot, was again assigned the lesser role of the doomed German. The branches were so perfectly spaced that we boasted not one but two tree houses, with the Americans holding the more elaborate fort dominating the top branches. I vainly scaled upward as my brother lobbed down volley upon volley of magnolia pods, which eerily resembled hand grenades but felt more like boulders as they bounced off my head. After taking one direct hit too many, I scrambled out of the tree and ran for the house, bounding up the red-carpeted stairs and bursting into my father's study without even pausing to knock. Tears were streaming down my face and the white satin bow atop my platinum curls, a daily fixture, was hopelessly askew.

My father turned from the desk as I tumbled into his arms. He hugged and kissed me, and told me he loved me. As I recounted my woes, Daddy wiped away the tears and told me to go fetch Michael. I knew right then I'd be saved from this horrendous assault, and that justice would prevail. After all, my father was always fair, not to mention having been attorney general of the United States. When we returned, Daddy told me I could not interrupt while Michael gave his side of the story. Then Michael had to listen while I told my side. These many years later the details are fuzzy, but I know it was hard and irritating. Even at age five or six, however, I was forced to accept that I wasn't all right, just as my brother was not all wrong. Ultimately, Daddy made us kiss and make up, and he sent us to our rooms to read for an hour.

As an adult, I recognize the lessons my father taught us as children mirrored the very beliefs he wanted the entire nation to embrace: we must build a system of justice that enjoys the confidence of all sides; that peace is not just something to pray for, but something each of us has the responsibility to create, daily; and that we must muster the courage to face the truth about ourselves as well as about those we perceive as enemies.

I think there was no quality my father admired more than courage, save perhaps love. I remember after dinner one night my father picked up the battered poetry book that was always somewhere by his side and read aloud Tennyson's poem "The Charge of the Light Brigade." We listened aghast to the story of a group of soldiers whose commanding officer orders them to ride into an ambush, knowing they will be slaughtered—yet they still obey the command. My father then explained that he and my mother were going on a trip and challenged us to a contest to see who could best memorize the poem while they were away. I did not win that contest—Courtney did—but four lines still remain with me:

Theirs not to reason why,
Theirs but to do and die,
Into the valley of Death
Rode the six hundred.

Why would a father ask his ever-expanding brood of what became eleven children to memorize a poem about war and slaughter? I think there were three reasons: He wanted to share with us his love of literature. He wanted us to embrace challenges that appear daunting. But most of all, he believed it was imperative for us to question authority, and to learn how those who fail that lesson do so at their own peril. Now, coming upon fifty years after Robert Kennedy's last campaign, those are also among the lessons I think he would have liked to impart to all Americans. We face daunting challenges both nationally and globally. But we must rise to those tasks armed with courage, faith, love, and an abiding commitment to justice, yet girded with a healthy sense of skepticism.

So how did Daddy influence the work I do today? My parents didn't separate their home life from Daddy's work. There were always Justice Department lawyers, administration officials, and social justice activists at Hickory Hill to see Daddy, for parties, and to play with us, especially on weekends. The civil rights movement was in full swing when I was a little girl, and when I learned to tie my shoes, I was careful to make sure that if I put on the left one first, I would tie the right one first, because I didn't want anything to be unfair. I think growing up with three sisters and seven brothers, and being the seventh down the line, makes one appreciate human rights at a very young age. My mother used to pile six or seven of us into her convertible, along with a football and a few dogs, and we would often go visit my father at the Justice Department. I had a special affinity for his office, as my godfather, Carmine Bellino, and my godmother, Angie Novello, worked with Daddy, and I especially loved to see them. After one visit, Daddy wrote me a letter:

Dear Kerry,

Today was an historic day, not just because of your visit, but because, over the objections of Governor Wallace, two negroes registered at the University of Alabama. It happened just a few minutes ago. I hope these events are long past by the time you get your pretty little head to college.

Love and Kisses,
Daddy

Imagine the idealism of a man who, having sent in the National Guard in order to protect James Meredith, could declare, only five years later, with heartfelt conviction, "Forty years from now we will have an African American president of the United States." In some measure because of the tenacity and daring of his work at the Department of Justice, that prediction came true when Barack Obama was sworn in as president.

Between the time Daddy wrote me that letter and the time I went to college, many events had passed. In almost every way I had an ideal childhood. But it was punctuated by a series of horrors that threw my world into chaos again and again.

When I was three, Uncle Jack was assassinated. Five years later, Martin Luther King was killed, and then a few short months later my father was taken from us. I am grateful to the many people who took up his cause, but some work cannot be done by others. The death of a parent leaves the work of love undone.

When I was in fifth grade my friend told me her father was beating up her mother. I didn't know what to do. I didn't know if it was a secret or if I should tell my mother. I didn't know how to protect my friend or her mother whom I loved. And I didn't know how to think about her father, whom I loved as well.

These were grim times.

Then, in high school, two friends were raped by men they had recently met. Again, I felt unmoored by the violence, the secrecy, the impossibility of stopping the perpetrators, the injustice. Shortly later, one of my best friends from high school was among the earliest known victims of HIV/AIDS in the United States. He was gay but was not out of the closet because he knew he would be ostracized and hated simply because of the people he loved.

All these things made no sense to me—they caused pandemonium in my life.

Still, I understood, even in the midst of the bedlam, that everyone has these stories—that I had far more resources than most, that none of us escape suffering, and that I was blessed to have family and friends who showed me, in those awful times, an abundance of love.

As a college student I interned at Amnesty International and read the Universal Declaration of Human Rights.

I realized all the crazy challenges in my life had one thing in common: they were all abuses of human rights—political assassinations, violence against women and sexual minorities, impunity and violations of due process. Uncle Teddy brought home stories about Refusniks in Russia, anti-apartheid leaders in South Africa, the mothers of the disappeared in Chile. Amnesty showed me a whole world full of brilliant, strategic activists who were using the Universal Declaration of Human Rights to right the wrongs. I realized I could learn from colleagues and join them in the struggle to stop the horrors. That realization changed my life.

It wasn't a stretch to connect the dots from upholding international human rights to my father's efforts on civil rights and poverty, and on aligning our country with liberation movements abroad.

When I graduated from law school I went to work at the organization now known as Robert F. Kennedy Human Rights. Since then I've spent my career partnering with the bravest people on earth across the world—people who face imprisonment, torture, and death for basic rights. They embody Bobby Kennedy's admiration for courage, and share his vision of a just and peaceful world.

Speaking to university students in Cape Town, South Africa, in 1966, Bobby Kennedy spoke about the power of the next generation. He said, "It is a revolutionary world that we all live in; and, it is the young people who must take the lead."

I wanted to help students feel empowered to change the course of their lives, even if that meant changing the course of their communities. The RFK human rights curriculum—known as RFK Speak Truth to Power—teaches students about the Universal Declaration of Human Rights and then helps them use it to create change. Participating in the lesson plans transforms the way students see themselves from passive bystanders to human rights defenders. Our attitude is, "You are valuable; you have something to contribute; you can create a better world—a more just and peaceful world—and we are going to work with you to decide what is important to you and help you do it."

Even if both governments and corporations comply with human rights norms, our accomplishments will be short-lived unless we train the next generation of human rights defenders.

Bobby Kennedy said, "I think there are injustices and unfairnesses in my own country and around the world. I think if one feels involved in it, that one should *try to do something about it.*"

In our country and around the world, Robert F. Kennedy Human Rights speaks out against injustice—and *does something about it.*

Robert Kennedy believed that long-term transformation would not happen without changing laws. Today, RFK Human Rights holds governments accountable for human rights violations through advocacy and litigation of emblematic cases including sexual minorities in Uganda, children's advocates in Egypt, families of femicide victims in Guatemala and Mexico, and, in New York, reforming the bail system and closing Riker's Island. I think my father, who always aimed to win, would be proud to know our team has never lost a case.

Bobby Kennedy spoke of the central role of private enterprise in addressing our most pressing issues, and engaged the largest corporations, IBM and Mobil, when he set out to transform Bedford Stuyvesant, Brooklyn. Of the 100 largest economies on earth today, fifty percent are corporations. Human rights work can no longer be confined to addressing government action—we must find new and effective ways to engage the business community. At RFK Human Rights, we expanded our work to hold corporations accountable through the investors who own them—often pension plans which invest the savings of the very workers at the bottom of the supply chain most at risk. We work to assure that the pension plans' investments are aligned with the needs of the pensioners whom they represent. (Consider, for instance, that the pension plans of the teacher's union at Sandy Hook and Parkland were both invested in the company which sold the assault weapons used to murder their teachers and students.)

RFK HUMAN RIGHTS is not about *process*—it is about *progress*. We do not just advocate for legal change—we support social movements that sustain civil society and transform our global community.

That's how I have taken the lessons of my dad's life and put them to work. I am well aware that mine is only one of many ways to learn those lessons. I draw inspiration daily from my daughters, my mother, my siblings, nieces and nephews, who are all engaged in social justice, if not professionally, then as volunteers. I look at the many people in this book—politicians, journalists, actors, business leaders, students, activists, and more—and how they draw from Daddy's speeches and life to inform their decisions about how to create a better world. I think of, and am grateful to, the thousands of people who, throughout my life, have told me what Daddy meant to them.

The pages of this book are filled with people inspired by Robert Kennedy to stand up when it was easier to stay seated. Each has sent forth his or her own ripples of hope. Just as Daddy inspired them, I hope their stories will inspire others, so that, together, we will sweep down the mightiest walls of oppression and resistance.

> *Each time a man stands up for an ideal, or acts to improve the lot of others, or strikes out against injustice, he sends forth a tiny ripple of hope, and crossing each other from a million different centers of energy and daring, those ripples build a current that will sweep down the mightiest walls of oppression and resistance.*
> —Robert F Kennedy
> South Africa, 1966

---------⸎---------

*"What other reason do we have
really for our existence as human
beings unless we've made some
other contribution to somebody else
to improve their own lives?"*

—ROBERT F. KENNEDY

---------⸎---------

Civil rights demonstration in Washington, DC, Attorney General Robert F. Kennedy
speaking to crowd, June 14, 1963 (Warren K. Leffler, Library of Congress)

---∞---

"It is not enough to allow dissent.
We must demand it. For there is
much to dissent from."

—ROBERT F. KENNEDY

---∞---

HARRY BELAFONTE

✦

Harry Belafonte has been known for over sixty years as a theatrical performer and movie star, but his first calling has always been the fight for civil rights and freedom for oppressed people in the United States and around the world. He was born in Harlem, spent his early years in Jamaica, was the first African American singer to sell a million copies of a record album, and walked with Martin Luther King in the March on Washington in 1963. Mentored by Eleanor Roosevelt, he has worked on civil rights, nuclear disarmament, the anti–apartheid movement, AIDS, cancer, Haiti, and more. He was an honorary chair of the Women's March in 2017, and he remains active in the struggle.

M r. B. has served on the board of RFK Human Rights for decades. He is a constant source of inspiration, a moral voice urging us to press forward ever harder. In 2017, he won the RFK Ripple of Hope Award. We met in my dining room along with Harry's mighty and generous wife, Pamela. Candid, outspoken, controversial, Mr. B. stands strong so others may rise.

Harry Belafonte: I'm ninety now, and I feel the biological process, which is very disturbing when you first encounter it. Then you realize there's absolutely nothing you can do about it: it's the process of nature. So I make an accommodation: if it aches over here, I'll wait for it to go over there.

During my very long life, a lot of people have asked me, "What motivates you? What made you become an activist?" The answer is very simple. It's called poverty. I had to get out of it. I was born in Harlem. I saw poverty strangle the people in my community.

My mother was an undereducated immigrant woman. I admired her courage. I admired her dignity. I admired her feistiness. She was a domestic worker; she used to go out for day work. She'd stand in line in certain locations in Harlem and downtown, where employers would come and go down the line and pick who they'd give work to for that day. She came home on this particular day, and she was despondent. She took her hat off, stuck a pin in it, sat on the bed—we lived in one room—and she just looked at the wall for the longest time and said nothing. I said, "What's the matter, Mom?" She said, "Harry"—she had this wonderful accent— "Harry, I want you to promise me something: that as you go through life, you will never see an injustice you don't stop and try to fix."

I didn't quite understand what that meant—I realized it was huge— but as time unfolded her counsel stayed in my mind. No matter what I did, no matter how much good fortune came my way, there was never a day when I saw injustice and didn't try to fix it. That gave me my place in the world. There's always injustice, and I was never intimidated. What happened in my life, the position I was in, offered me power I could use.

Kerry Kennedy: *There were other people who had power they didn't use.*

HB: That's probably because they weren't driven by the conditions of poverty. People act based on what they experience on their journey. My family came from the Caribbean, and there's a distinct difference between Africans of Caribbean descent and Africans who are entirely formed by the American experience. Although I was born in New York, my mother took me back when I was a year and a half old to grow up with my grandmother. My grandmother was from Scotland; she was as white as you can get, and she came from just outside Glasgow. She came to Jamaica, met her love, and married. She was a woman of enormous generosity; she cared for the community, she cared for everybody. In the Caribbean, race didn't have the same dynamic it has in America. Although we were under British rule and there were certain rules, Jamaica didn't have the severe racial laws you would face in America. Out of the independence and respect I experienced in the first twelve years of my life under my grandmother's protection, I developed enough personal esteem that when I came back to America and there were all these racial rules and attitudes, I rejected them. I had lived in an interracial community in Jamaica. Nobody was at anyone else's throat. As a matter of fact, the black population of America is unlike the black population of almost anywhere else in the world. We are the only country that never went through an armed rebellion, except the Civil War. But black people in America didn't rebel against the racial rules of the state. In Haiti they did. In Brazil they did. In Jamaica they did. In Africa they did.

When I came back to America, I brought this sense of independence, which got activated here when I faced "You can't go here," and "You can't do this." There was no reason for those injunctions except race, and if race was the reason, then it was unacceptable. I was ready to challenge the system, because if you didn't challenge the system you would have to exist in the status quo, and that wasn't acceptable to a person raised as I had been.

I dropped out of school in the ninth grade. I had dyslexia, I had medical disorders, I had a lot of environmental pressures. My father was an alcoholic and very violent. My mother's resistance to that and her capacity to endure him kept bombarding me, because in her efforts to survive, I learned how to survive.

I volunteered for the navy and served in the Second World War. That did a lot to shape what I was learning about the universe. The biggest debate we had was over why black people were in the war. We resolved that question by concluding that what black people suffered from all the inequalities we faced in America was not as severe as what Hitler had in store for the entire world. We found a reason for self-survival, for loyalty, for patriotism: to fight against the worse evil. Many brave black men and women who made that commitment to our nation died on the battle-fields of Europe and the Pacific. When I got out, I didn't know where to go or what to do. Back home I had to confront the fact that, although we had a lot to celebrate in our victory abroad, there was a lot we couldn't celebrate in America: we didn't have the right to vote, we didn't have the right to do a lot of things. I had a choice, to blend in with the status quo or to rebel against it—not in pursuit of power but of justice.

The one good thing about segregation for a kid bouncing around Harlem was that in our midst lived our most prophetic leaders: W. E. B. Du Bois, Paul Robeson, Marian Anderson, and others. I was really poor, and these icons lived two blocks away. They had to live in Harlem too, so we saw them every day; we heard their voices every day.

I had a job as a janitor's assistant, and one day I did repairs in a building and got as a tip two tickets to the theater. I'd never been to the theater, and I didn't know what the theater was about. What I really wanted was five dollars, but out of curiosity I went. The lights went down, the curtain opened, and when I saw black bodies on a stage artic-ulating poetry written by black writers, and I saw the director was black, I was seeing blackness at work in a productive, joyous, instructive way. I said, that's the environment I want to be in. I had the option of that or street gangs, and I opted to go into the theater.

I found relationships there inspiring. One day we did a play by an Irish playwright by the name of Seán O'Casey, whom I subsequently came to meet. The play was called *Juno and the Paycock*; it was about the Irish rebellion against British conquest and occupation. The play spoke admiringly of the courage of the Irish against the British. I became enamored of Ireland and the history of what the rebels did. After that play, Paul Robeson came to visit us. We were a small group—Ossie Davis, Ruby Dee, Sidney Poitier, and others—and Robeson said to us that a work of art is a noble pursuit because artists are the gatekeepers of truth. Wow. Artists are the gatekeepers of truth. We are civilization's moral compass. Without us history knows not where it goes. We document it; we articulate it; we stimulate it. That moved me; some understanding of that idea was already stirring in me. I got very much involved in theater, and then Robeson introduced me to many of the black elite of that time: the poet Langston Hughes; A. Philip Randolph, the great labor leader; Dr. W. E. B. DuBois, who was probably our greatest intellectual. I turned toward the Left because there was no relief for our political situation from any other direction.

The Left gave me a framework within which to express my artistic work, because there was so much progressive thinking in the arts at that time. All the great writers were on the left, Steinbeck and other novelists, and playwrights whose plays I did and whom I got to meet. This was my education, in the arts and in political philosophy. It was lot to learn, and I decided at that point that I needed to go to school. There was a place called the New School for Social Research in Manhattan, and because I had hardly any formal education, I had to con them into letting me in. It was incredible there, because there was Bea Arthur, this talented young actress; and Marlon Brando, who became one of my closest friends; and Tony Curtis; and others. I looked around the room and I knew one thing for sure: none of us was going to make it.

I was able to pursue these studies because I was getting support on the GI Bill, since I was a veteran, but when the subsidy ended I was broke. I was just a broke black kid hoping to make a living in the theater. My mother was despondent; she wanted me to be a doctor or a lawyer or some other profession that made sense, and I wanted to be in the theater. I couldn't explain it, but I had to do it. It was by some accident and good fortune that I began to have success as a singer, but I was still a pure rebel: *Here's what I like, here's what I will do.* The people in that environment seemed to be so filled with imagination; the plays I read seemed to say all the things I wanted to hear. I saw the opportunity to meet and get to know people who seemed to have a mission, which was to resist injustice. It's as simple as that.

At that point I had met Eleanor Roosevelt, and she had taken an interest in me. I admired her greatly. When she was working at the United Nations on the Universal Declaration of Human Rights she always brought in young Africans, Asians, and Latinos as guests of the American delegation to the UN, and I met a lot of these people before they became heads of state. When I was in Kenya I met Jomo Kenyatta and other Africans who ultimately became heads of state. I loved that experience.

I also met people like Pete Seeger and Woody Guthrie and Leadbelly, and soon my repertoire included all the progressive artists of the folk era. I became one of the instruments of the Left; I had a platform for my cause; now I was a rebel with a cause and a constituency, and I was beginning to understand the power of that and how I could use that power. I was a popular artist with fans in Africa and around the world; people heard my songs and my words; and I gained a global constituency of young rebels from everywhere.

I wasn't an entertainer who was also an activist; I was an activist who was also an entertainer. I was always taking the positions I took without fear, and I was making a career for myself too.

One day I'm sitting at home and I get a call from a guy who was an activist with the Democratic Party. He said, "I've been asked to call you because a young man is running for president who some of us are going to endorse, and we would like to get you involved." At that point I knew Eleanor Roosevelt, but I wasn't engaged in electoral politics in America and didn't know many people who were, so I was surprised when this guy said, "I'd like you to meet John Kennedy." I asked him why John Kennedy wanted to meet me. What had happened was that one of the most visible black people in the world was a young man named Jackie Robinson, an incredible ballplayer who had a spine and stood up. The activist said that Jackie Robinson had bolted from the Democratic ranks and the party was stunned by this; apparently there had been some slight that Jackie deeply resented. He had said, "I'll never deal with Democrats again—they're racists too." Now the Democrats, seeking to fill a gap, were looking at an array of black personalities, and because I was just on the rise then as a singer, the Democratic Party had said: *Let's get him to fill this space and give us a balance before we lose the black vote.*

John Kennedy called me, and we met, and he wanted to know if I would endorse him. I said once I get to know more about the platform and what he was doing I would give him an answer. After my second meeting with John, I campaigned for him and went with him to Harlem and to a lot of other places. In fact we did a film together. We met again in an apartment in Harlem, and he started to ask me questions and I listened to him, and I asked him what he thought about lynching and what he thought about other issues, and he was very articulate. They used that film in the campaign. They showed it in the South, but the Democrats in the South went crazy when they showed the scene of me talking with John. It had great appeal to the black community, but the white community was not about to accept a black man and a white man chatting in an apartment in Harlem. It was a challenge to the laws of segregation.

I went to the inauguration, I sang, I became involved with the Peace Corps. It was your uncle Sargent Shriver, and a small group that became the founding body of the Peace Corps. It sort of took over my life, and that's when I met your father.

As I was working with people from all over the globe, I found that the one thing that energized everyone was the sense of universal opportunity that was associated with the Kennedys. Everywhere I went there seemed to be these high expectations of what the Kennedys could achieve. In the campaign for John, the South had required tricky manipulations. Everything he said in favor of civil rights elicited a great cry of resistance from powerful segregationist southern Democrats. Anyone who spoke out against segregation was called a Communist: Martin Luther King was a Communist, everything we did for the cause was Communist inspired, Communist agitation. Eleanor Roosevelt, a Communist? I looked at all the lists of enemies of the state, and I wondered, *If these are the enemies of the state, then who are the protectors of the state?*

I was a bit of a problem because I was not a Communist and I didn't believe in communism, but I had relationships with people who had been identified as Communists, whether it was as party members or as supporters of the Communist ideology. The Democrats didn't know how to classify me, and I said, "Why don't you just look at what I do and not be too concerned about what people say about my beliefs. Nobody really knows exactly what they are." That includes me, incidentally. I survived McCarthyism because Dr. King gave us a platform to articulate in movement terms what we believed about society and politics.

One of the few people who listened with an open mind to the ideas we expressed that were associated with the Left was your father. So did Sargent Shriver, who was heading the Peace Corps. I was going to a lot of universities to recruit students to join the Peace Corps. I found that often I was caught between what I felt I knew about the Kennedy administration and what a lot of people on the left felt about what was not being achieved by John Kennedy. People who are hungry for freedom do not always embrace those who treat them as a constituency they can manipulate for their own interests. We had had an especially tough time during McCarthyism. We had to defend ourselves constantly against that enemy, and it wasn't over. There was suspicion, and there were the tactics from the right of accusing the civil rights movement of being Communist inspired and controlled. The wounds from that period were by no means healed at the beginning of the Kennedy administration. A lot of us viewed Robert Kennedy at that time in light of his being a servant of McCarthy's committee, which was so damaging to so many friends and colleagues. He had also been part of the committee that investigated the Teamsters union leader Jimmy Hoffa, which a lot of people on the left saw as an antilabor crusade. He had been very tough in Jack Kennedy's campaign. So there was an enormous amount of skepticism when he became Attorney General. That was the context in which Martin Luther King told me to find Robert Kennedy's moral center and win him to our cause.

KK: *I understand that was the way you were looking at it. What I think is that your perception of my father at that time was misplaced.*

HB: The perception that he was right wing.

KK: *The misperception of my father that he was right wing and dogmatically anti-Communist and insensitive to liberation movements. In fact, he was always on the side of the underdog—in part because he was the seventh child. He hated communism because he thought it was repressive, and he hated Roy Cohn because he thought Cohn was repressive. He went after Dave Beck and Jimmy Hoffa because he was pro-union and they were stealing from the rank and file. I know there was a lot of misunderstanding about my father back then, and some of it persists today. It's true that he wasn't particularly involved in the civil rights movement at the start, but he wasn't some Steve Bannon. He didn't come to civil rights without some sensitivity.*

The great thing about my grandfather was that he encouraged his kids to travel around the world and meet with leaders and find out what was going on. That's the reason why in 1956, when Africa's sons were on the march to throw off colonialism, the only United States senator who stood with Algeria against the French was John F. Kennedy. He believed our greatest strength as a country was going to be in having allies who were democrats, even if they weren't pro-American.

Most people mistakenly associate McCarthy with the House Un-American Activities Committee, and the investigations and harassment of people in Hollywood, labor unions, university professors, the Rosenbergs' trial, blacklisting teachers, and the "red scare." But McCarthy had nothing to do with that—I imagine he supported it, but he had no role in any of it. Actually McCarthy's committee—the Permanent Subcommittee on Investigations—was a Senate subcommittee with a narrow focus on rooting out Communists who worked for the US government.

Kennedy was on the committee for four months and stepped down because of the excesses of McCarthyism. Eighteen months later, Kennedy joined the Senate subcommittee as chief council to the minority on the Democratic side. There, during the Army-McCarthy hearings, Kennedy exposed the fact that Roy Cohn was so zealous for blood and so incompetent with facts that Cohn accused Annie Lee Moss, an unfortunate black teletype operator, of being a Communist, based on her association with Robert Hall. It quickly became apparent through my father's intervention that Cohn's Hall was white, while Moss's Hall was black.

Shortly afterward, Cohn stepped down from the committee in disgrace, and later took up a lucrative position as the lawyer for Fred Trump and mentor to his son, Donald Trump.

Martin Luther King was right to ask you to find his moral center, but it wasn't very difficult to find; you didn't need a pick and shovel.

HB: It wasn't until the last years of your father's life that he began to articulate his view of global humanity. His speeches from that period are some of the best ever given in the history of this country. But that side of him—those admirable principles and values—was not evident in his early life, when he was discovering himself, discovering his power, and in contact with McCarthyism. The latter was a huge problem for us. McCarthy was ruthless to the black community. As a matter of fact, not enough has been said about the impact McCarthy had on black life. A lot of people lost work and lost opportunity. Some suicides took place. It was a desperate period.

KK: *Exactly, and I think the popular public understanding of my father has been short of the truth. When he became attorney general, he didn't have strong connections to the leadership in the black community. As attorney general, he started building those relationships with civil rights activists, but even then all his activities were not known very widely, or at all, by some African Americans who were famous but not fully engaged in the movement. That's what led to the confrontation that*

*was reported at my grandparents' apartment in New York in 1963, which
you witnessed.*

*By the time that happened, he had sent troops into Mississippi and
arranged the release of Martin Luther King from the Birmingham jail. He
had sent troops to Montgomery and helped save the lives of the Freedom
Riders. He had established the Prince Edward County Free School in Virginia so black kids would be educated after the county fathers closed down
all the public schools to avoid forced desegregation.*

*So he had done a lot to demonstrate a commitment by the US gov-
ernment to the cause of civil rights, and while the horrific oppression certainly deserved far more activism, the extent of what he had done might
not have been well known to some of the people who were at the meeting
in New York. He asked James Baldwin to call the meeting so he could gain
a more nuanced understanding of the issues.*

HB: I think that's true. The record you talk about was not the most
significant determinant of the attitude toward your father many black
people had. The meeting in New York, however, wasn't an especially
good example of anything, when you look at who was there and what
actually happened. From the start, I never thought that meeting was a
good idea.

When I learned from James Baldwin that he was putting together
a group of people to meet with Bobby Kennedy in New York, I didn't
like the idea at all. Baldwin was not a politically sophisticated person,
and the people he was inviting—people like Lena Horne and Lorraine
Hansberry, and other celebrity types who weren't deeply committed to
activism or Dr. King—were not representative of black leadership or,
and this is important, what other people had been doing in and for the
movement. It wasn't going to help Bobby to talk to these people; they
had nothing to offer him about what the movement wanted or what
it was doing. Anyway, the meeting happened. In the meeting, everyone was very polite, but after maybe an hour or so, a young man by the

name of Jerome Smith, who was a CORE volunteer who had been on the Freedom Rides and was severely beaten, jumped into a discussion about Vietnam. He said, "I don't want any more of this polite shit. What am I here for? You're talking about Vietnam and we're gonna be lying if we say we're gonna be going off to Vietnam." The popular phrase at the time was, "Why should we kill people in Asia, when we don't have any rights here in America?" Bobby was trying not so much to defend what the government was doing in Vietnam as to explain it, and he was getting very upset, because all of a sudden, the whole meeting had become fractured. People zeroed in on the real meaning of a gathering about the civil rights movement, and in that conversation, Bobby said, "Well, you don't understand what we're doing." The response to that was: "We understand what you're doing; what you don't understand is what you're not doing. The world is most appreciative of some of the things that you do, but there are much more basic things you haven't touched on at all." Bobby got more and more upset, and he was particularly upset because he didn't feel that those of us who knew him were defending him from the attacks that others there were making on him. Nothing positive was accomplished. Much to my surprise, the very next day, the *New York Times* had a story about the disruption that had taken place between Bobby Kennedy and the others, and all of a sudden we had to deal with a public interpretation of what had gone on, and that's when Bobby went through his most severe moment of feeling that we were not defending what he knew would be the Kennedy legacy. We said we didn't care too much about a legacy; that wasn't our concern as members of the black community. We said we didn't know how to defend him against the white community, the Ku Klux Klan, and everybody else who wanted to destroy his life politically, because we had a fight with those same elements at an entirely different level. It wasn't just about who the president was or even about what any individual might do with that power when he got it.

Your dad and I began to talk more regularly after that and share our points of view. He came to understand that there wasn't a carte blanche patriotism we could be expected to express regardless of what effect domestic events were having on the black community. We needed much more than we were getting in terms of both recognition and actions. This was especially true in a context where Dr. King was being labeled a Communist by those who opposed civil rights. Over the years I did come to know the deeper character of your father. I felt completely comfortable with him when he was campaigning around the country in 1968, and then he was taken from us.

We have the luxury of hindsight, so let's take advantage of it. One would imagine that with the Civil War and the emancipation of the black population from chains, we would somehow by now have established an understanding that we must all strive to safeguard the institutions designed to ensure that racial oppression should never rise again. We fought slavery and replaced it with Jim Crow; now we confront resegregation, racially drawn election districts, laws designed to keep black people away from the polls, police violence against black communities—a new generation of discrimination, segregation, and hatred.

I have never been as sought after as I am at this moment. I'm no longer in the theater or movies, I don't have any new records, yet I just came from the University of Oklahoma in the heart of a red state, and three thousand students—this is not an exaggeration—came to see me. Maybe 30 or 40 percent were black and Hispanic. The rest of the crowd was white. Why did they all come out? They're not going to hear a great version of "Banana Boat," so what were they expecting? What I discovered is that there is a deep, deep need for the nation to articulate more than it has revealed.

I'm amazed that it's been fifty years since Martin's assassination, fifty years since your father's death. No one in the constituency I talked to so passionately came to Oklahoma. We'll be in Arizona on Wednesday. Then Seattle. Nobody talks about the civil rights now. As a matter of fact, some of them say they don't quite remember what that was.

All these people who came to Oklahoma were filled with goodwill; they wanted to know; they wanted to be involved; they wanted to hear. They realized that somewhere, somehow, something had been lost. What we had achieved in the civil rights movement, up to and including today, has been lost over the past fifty years. It's not in the curriculum; it's not in school; it's not on the pulpits; it's not on the radio stations. They report it every now and then when there's an incident, but there's no ongoing tradition that articulates what that period in our history achieved, so every time a new generation arrives, we have to go through the whole thing all over again. I have to tell you, I'm really goddamn bored going back to Revolution 101.

There's no machine that carries our history forward, because we don't own the tools of propaganda. We don't control the media. We're now just trying to find—not just the black community, but everybody is trying to find—an honorable educational system that will begin to be far more inclusive than what we have now. Nothing works when there's no activism; it can't always require an emergency; there has to be ongoing dialogue and action. I said to an audience, "When last at your dinner table have you ever mentioned in the course of conversation the name Nelson Mandela?" There's a silence. "Where's your sense of responsibility for letting the next generations know about our history?" While we're looking for the enemy, you must look to that part of the enemy that's within us. White folks listen because you're in their face, but you're not in their face any longer. You're in their face for another job title; you're in their face for some person who wants to be the next congressperson, who does not necessarily come with the platform that's all the goodness of humanity. A lot of these guys that are running for office are not deeply devoted to ending poverty. As a black elected official, that's what their mission should be: to change the economic paradigm and to find new dynamics.

While we're at it, let's talk about the church. I am staunchly opposed to the way in which religion has affected the black community. All you ministers, when last on Sunday have you talked about the plight of black youth? Why aren't you doing more about the prison system? Why aren't you devoting at least ten minutes of your sermon every Sunday on the issues of criminal justice? What can we do to change that, or do you just continue to talk about our hero Jesus, and that's it? You guys are guilty of failure to teach. And let's understand: I believe in God. That's not because of anything the church told me! I believe in Him because He is my moral guide through this morass of human difficulty. But the church is as responsible for what we don't do as for what we do. I say to the ministers: Why aren't you raising your voices? Why aren't you using your sermons and speeches to educate the young people today? They know nothing! They know some of the historic imagery, but they don't know the context. They have no analysis of what happened and what it meant. Without that they can't possibly have a powerful, active vision for the future.

KK: *It's a disservice to the students and to our country. I've had this experience, to go into a middle school on Martin Luther King Day and on the walls there are the cut-out colored construction paper letters that spell out "I Have a Dream," and the kids have put up their contributions: "I have a dream . . . of having a pony." The context is truly missing.*

HB: The context is missing. So why do three thousand people come to hear me in Oklahoma, black and white and Hispanic people? Why is there such a great interest in hearing me speak? If we take away the show business part of it, there's no answer—it doesn't make sense—but I think I've figured it out. There's a need to know the history, the struggle, the legacy, and just by virtue of being ninety—it's not a virtue, actually—I'm one of the last authentic parts of a movement that once took place that kids do not know about. They don't know the price we paid for what they have. Most black people don't vote.

People were murdered in the name of getting that right. We have to be vigilant today to make sure the Supreme Court or the president or the Congress doesn't take away what we've gained. The engine of change we created needs fuel. We need to be part of an ongoing legacy of which people are informed, so that we can produce leaders who use the knowledge that comes from knowing history. I'm trying to do as much as I can to fill that void, because you know, ninety years of life teaches you something. You don't have another ninety.

TONY BENNETT

The New York City–born son of a grocer and a seamstress, Anthony Dominick Benedetto, said Frank Sinatra, is "the best singer in the business." He survived the Battle of the Bulge, the British rock-and-roll invasion of America, and the Great Depression, and he is the oldest musician to have a #1 album on Billboard's charts. When he left his heart in San Francisco, millions of fans gave him theirs. He is a national treasure, a troubadour of the Great American Songbook, and has recently performed with Lady Gaga. He is also a terrific painter.

Growing up there was always a stack of 5–6 LPs on the record player, and one or two were Tony Bennett's. Tony campaigned for Daddy in 1968, but I reconnected with him in the wake of the Newtown massacre, when we were both lobbying for gun control on Capitol Hill. Tony won the RFK Ripple of Hope Award in 2014.

Kerry Kennedy: *Tony, you've had such an extraordinary life, and you're ninety years old now and still performing, but a lot of the people who love your singing don't know about your social activism.*

    Tony Bennett: I've always believed in certain things, and when I heard your father speak of his belief in those things, I felt like he and I

———————————— ∞ ————————————

"The world demands the qualities of youth. Not a time of life, but a state of mind, a temper of the will, a quality of the imagination, a predominance of courage over timidity, an appetite for adventure over the life of ease."

—ROBERT F. KENNEDY

———————————— ∞ ————————————

were in it together; like we were supporting each other. I had so much hope for him and what he could do for this country, especially after the tragedies the family and the country had experienced earlier in the decade. So when he was campaigning, I listened to him. I said, "We're finally going to get the right president. America's going to be all right with him." When he was assassinated, it was the most tragic—I've never gotten over it. To this day, I—It's hard to describe it. I just felt it was the end of the America I had hoped for. I had a lot of hope then. I was hopeful about everything then. When he died, I said, "We've all gone crazy."

KK: *It was a terrible time for everybody.*

TB: I was 100 percent behind him and couldn't wait for him to become president, because I was certain he would straighten the whole thing out. He stood for all the right things.

My personal feeling then and to this day is that there's too much violence in America. You can just walk in a store and say, "I want to buy a gun," and they just give it to you. It doesn't make sense. There should be control of guns. Your father stood up for that. I've seen a speech he gave in Oregon just a few weeks before he was shot. He talked about how we had to stop the easy access to guns.

KK: *His aides told him not to raise the issue because there were so many hunters in the audience, and he was heckled when he spoke about the need for gun control, five years after Uncle Jack was killed. Then, in 2015, the very same town, Roseburg, Oregon, suffered from a mass shooting in which 16 people were shot, and eight died. There have been so many mass shootings in our country since then, it's hard to keep track of them all.*

TB: I've seen so much violence in my life. I grew up in New York City, in Queens. I'm Italian, but we had every nationality there. It was a great American city, a real melting pot.

My father was sick for a long time, and then he died when I was ten years old. My mom was unbelievable. She had to raise three children and she worked so hard. I'll never forget one dramatic moment when she actually went to Grand Central and confronted a bunch of businessmen who were on a stage there for some kind of ceremony. She went right up to the stage and said, "Who's going to feed my children?"

That stayed with me my whole life. She was so good, you know. She had to work hard her whole life to make sure her children had what they needed.

She was a seamstress. She worked day and night, and she never settled for anything. The most important thing to her was the quality of her work. We were completely poor, but she'd take a dress she was working on and throw it over her shoulders and say, "Don't have me work on a bad dress." I didn't know it at the time, but that was the greatest lesson I'd ever learn. When I started my recording career, I said, "I'm never going to make a bad record just for money." So I had a fight on my hands. The record company said, "What are you doing? We want you to record this stupid song." I said, "I don't do stupid songs. If a song is intelligent, and if it's well written, then I'll sing it." And they said, "But you're not going to make money that way." I said, "I think I'm going to make a lot of money, because the records will be timeless. They'll never be old-fashioned, they'll never be forgotten."

My father was a beautiful man. He'd take me out on a sunny summer Saturday, and he'd tell me, "Look at how beautiful life is." He'd take me to Astoria Park, where I could look across the river at Manhattan and dream of being famous in New York City one day.

My older brother was a great singer. He was on the radio, and everybody loved him, but he didn't want to do it. I said to him, "We need you to make it. We're so poor." He just didn't want to, so I said, "I'm going to sing." My father used to love to sing in Italy. He was my inspiration. So to this day, I'm still singing.

I went into the army when I was a teenager. It was toward the end of World War II. It was tough in the army. There was a lot of ignorance. People were different—from different parts of the country. If you're a Northerner and they're from the South . . . they don't like the Northerners, you know.

If you're Italian, you're different. Anybody's who's not Italian doesn't like Italians. It was like that. They were against the Jews. There was a lot of prejudice going on. It was tough in the army, and that wasn't even the war.

Near the end of the war I was in the Battle of the Bulge. I was in the infantry, but I never killed anybody. I wouldn't dare. I couldn't. My upbringing didn't allow it. I would never kill anybody. I was trained in boot camp, so I would kind of put up with it, but I was never going to kill somebody.

I got a lot of heat for that philosophy. I would be asked, "What are you doing here?" I said, "Well I was drafted, so I'm here, but I'm against war." I'm still against war. I think it's a terrible situation internationally, but I'm just against war.

We won the battle, and then we walked into a concentration camp. We freed Jews in Germany. We freed them. That was unbelievable. It's crazy, you know—someone's criticized for their religion. I'm not a religious person, but I know what's right. Hating people for their religion, or just for being a certain nationality, that's wrong. That's why we were fighting. We wanted to make sure everybody was treated like human beings. We freed them from that camp, and it felt very good to do that.

It's a different world now. I believed so much in what your dad was talking about, all the things he was saying about treating everybody right, and I believed he was going to be the best president that we ever had. Everything he said he was going to do, I said, "We're finally going to get somebody in there who would get us to where America is supposed to be." I couldn't believe it when he was assassinated, and I never quite got over it, even to this day. I lost hope. It's not the same for me.

KK: *You marched in Selma with Martin Luther King . . .*

TB: Right, it all came about—there was a march in Selma, and there was a lot of violence, and some people died. So they were going to have a second march but they had to cancel it because they were worried about more violence. Then I got a call. It was from Harry Belafonte, and he asked me to come to Selma. I'd never had a call from anyone who was so famous—and he was my age—and I said, "I just don't want to fight." I had those experiences in the war, and I'd seen how terrible it was, and I didn't want to pick up any kind of a weapon ever again. He explained to me about nonviolence and how they were conducting the demonstrations, and he talked about what they were doing to black people in the South. I knew what that was like; I had seen those things in my own life, so I said, "I'll go."

One night during the march, Martin Luther King asked myself and the other artists to perform for all the marchers. There was no place to perform, so someone had a connection to a funeral home so they brought in a bunch of empty caskets. They placed them on the ground for a stage, and we just improvised the whole thing. We just entertained whoever wanted to listen. I sang "Just in Time." It was quite an experience, you know, but then I had to leave. I couldn't go on the whole march because I had an engagement in Las Vegas.

The woman who drove me to the airport was from Detroit, her name was Viola Liuzzo. She had seen the first Selma march on television, when they beat so many people—known as Bloody Sunday. She had told her husband she wanted to go to Selma and help. She had quite a few children back in Detroit—five, I think. She was assassinated by four Klansmen driving back from Montgomery to Selma right after she took me to the airport, for doing that, for driving me and other people back and forth at the Selma march. I couldn't believe it.

She was a wonderful woman. And they killed her. The ignorance of that is unbelievable. Regretfully we still have hatred and violence in this world and I hope that one day we will realize that it has to stop.

I've always been a pacifist, my whole life. What I've seen, in the war and in the South for civil rights, has only made me stronger in my beliefs about this. You know, they asked me to sing the national anthem on many occasions but I prefer "America the Beautiful." It celebrates the natural beauty and promise of this great country.

KK: *So you've never sung "The Star-Spangled Banner"?*

TB: I like to sing "America the Beautiful" or "God Bless America."

KK: *You know, my father said if he became president, he'd make "This Land Is Your Land" our national anthem.*

TB: That's a good song too!

I'm an international artist. I play everywhere. Every country is great, but our country has every nationality, every religion; there's no country like it in the world. It's wonderful. It's a great country. We have all philosophies of the world right here in America. So if this country doesn't get together, the world's not going to get together. Every nationality is here. So it's really the best country, and I'm not just waving a flag here. We represent the chance of eliminating bigotry, even though we haven't done it yet. Some people don't get that, and maybe they never will, but your father got it, and he stood for that.

When I perform for an audience, it's like a command performance for me. My attitude is they're all kings and queens in the audience. They're above me, the audience. I don't look down on them. I look up to them. I respect the public. There are too many people who disrespect the public. They don't get it.

When I'm performing, the audience sees that I respect them. I know how to sing, but that's not enough; that's only part of what people respond to. They sense that I love them and they love me back. And all of a sudden they're cheering me, you know, and it's because they see I'm not a prejudiced person. The music tells them that, and they can feel the love through the respect I have for every individual.

"Decency is the heart of this whole campaign. Poverty is indecent. Illiteracy is indecent. The death, the maiming of brave young men in the swamps of Vietnam, that is also indecent. And it is indecent for a man to work with his back and his hands in the valleys of California without ever having hope of sending his son on to college. This is also indecent."

—Robert F. Kennedy

Senator Robert Kennedy visits hungry children in the Mississippi delta, spring of 1967 (photographer unknown)

---⊶∞⊷---

"What we do need and what 1968 must
bring is a better liberalism and a better
conservatism. We need a liberalism and
its wish to do good—yet that recognizes
the limits to rhetoric and American power
abroad; that knows the answers to all
problems is not spending money, and we
need a conservatism in its wish to preserve
the enduring values of the American society,
that yet recognizes the urgent need to bring
opportunity to all citizens, that is willing to
take action to meet the needs of the people."

—ROBERT F. KENNEDY

---⊶∞⊷---

JOE BIDEN

⌒∞⌒

Joe Biden served as the forty-seventh vice president of the United States, from 2009 to 2017. In 1972, when won his first senatorial bid, Biden was the sixth-youngest person in history to be elected to the U.S. Senate, where he served from 1973 to 2009. Biden served as chair of the Senate Foreign Relations Committee and the Senate Judiciary Committee and is credited with reforms related to drug policy, crime prevention, civil liberties, and the creation of both the Violent Crime Control and Law Enforcement Act and the Violence against Women Act.

As vice president, Biden oversaw infrastructure spending in the wake of the 2008 financial crisis, Iraq policy until the withdrawal of US troops in 2011, tax relief, women's rights, marriage equality, the expansion of cancer research, and much more. He received the Medal of Freedom from President Obama in 2017.

Vice President Biden currently serves as the Benjamin Franklin Presidential Practice Professor at the University of Pennsylvania.

One of the first people to call Joe Biden when his wife and child died in a tragic car accident in December 1972, was my grandmother, Rose

Kennedy. Uncle Teddy was one of the first people to come to the hospital. Our families became close friends and political allies. Vice President Biden accepted the Robert F. Kennedy Ripple of Hope Award in 2016.

REMARKS FROM JOE BIDEN'S ACCEPTANCE OF
THE RFK RIPPLE OF HOPE AWARD

Ethel, when you called me to inform me that I would receive this honor, I told you then what I'll tell you now. Trying not to be emotional about it. Look, I've only had—and this is the God's truth, anybody, including Teddy Kennedy, who became my mentor and one of my best friends in the Senate, can tell you—I only had one political hero in my whole life. And that's not hyperbole. It was Robert Kennedy. And when I received the call, I thought, "This cannot be really happening."

I was a senior in law school. I was sitting in Hancock Airport in Syracuse, New York, where I was waiting for a flight to come in from my state of Delaware. And I heard on the radio—I heard on the radio that Dr. King had been shot and killed. As a high school sophomore in Delaware, I got engaged in the civil rights movement. My state was segregated by law. We had been a slave state. We were a border state, and even though if you listen to Barack Obama, everybody thinks I'm the kid from Scranton who crawled out of a coal mine with a lunch bucket, I hadn't lived in Scranton since I was in third grade. And it makes the people of Delaware mad as hell.

But I sat there and as I listened, waiting for the plane to land—I was in the parking lot, I remember it vividly—and then I heard a familiar voice that I had listened to so many times. And I later learned it was a man standing on top of a truck in Indianapolis saying, "We have to make an effort to understand, to go beyond these rather difficult times." He talked about his favorite poet. "Even in our sleep, pain which cannot forget falls drop by drop upon the heart until, in our own despair against our will comes wisdom through the awful grace of God."

I didn't know then what he meant by "the awful grace of God." That was April 4, 1968. My only political hero was speaking about the man that set the standard for civil rights. It got so many in our generation involved. Then on June 6, I strode across the stage in Archibald Stadium to receive my diploma from Syracuse University Law School, where Robert Kennedy had spoken only a month or so earlier, and we learned that same night that he had been assassinated.

My city of Wilmington, Delaware, was the only city since reconstruction to be occupied by the National Guard for seven months, with drawn bayonets standing on every corner, because a significant portion of it had been burned to the ground after Dr. King died. We didn't have Robert Kennedy standing in Rodney Square, as he had stood in Indianapolis.

I left the stadium that June day to go home to Delaware, to start a prestigious job in the state's oldest law firm. But after only a matter of months, to the dismay of my family and friends, I left. Day after day, walking back and forth to the courthouse, I walked past the guardsmen who were standing on every corner in my city. After winning a case in federal court in which I was just sitting in the second chair for a senior partner, he said he wanted to take me to lunch at the Wilmington Club—it was a fancy club that didn't allow Catholics like me to join in those days or African Americans. The only time I consciously remember telling a lie. I looked at him and said, "My dad is coming in and I'm going to have lunch with him."

And I walked catty-corner across Rodney Square, to the basement on the corner of the opposite side, and I asked for a job in the public defender's office. I remember the guy at the time looking at me saying, "You're kidding. Don't you work for the Prickett firm?" And I said, "Yeah, I do. But I don't feel right." All I could think about was—not explicitly, but implicitly—What would Robert Kennedy do? What would he have done?

Ethel, Jill and I are honored to be with you tonight and with your family. And history will show that Ethel, you, too, are a tidal wave of hope in our time. When you and Kerry told me about this award, I called my whole family to tell them. I had Bobby Kennedy's office when I was in the Senate. I had the desk that he had sat in and carved his name. Robert Kennedy was literally my hero. I never got to meet him. But I was inspired by his passion and by his courage—a courage to walk into the middle of a riot and stand on top of a vehicle and preach peace; the courage to go to South Africa with all the intimidation the Afrikaner government surrounding his visit implied; the courage that you demonstrated as well, Ethel.

Nine years after Robert Kennedy visited South Africa, I was a young United States senator, and I stepped off the same plane in Johannesburg. Part of a congressional delegation, I was the only Caucasian American on the trip. Because I was a senator, protocol dictated that I get off the plane first. And two, actually three Afrikaner soldiers, muscular in short pants, literally came on the plane holding carbines and said, "We'll escort you off."

When I descended the steps of the plane, there was a red carpet that went about sixty feet and then formed a tee. I was the first one off the plane and they were escorting me. When I got to the T I turned to the right. It wasn't until I'd gotten another twenty yards that I realized that the rest of the delegation, including Andy Young and a lot of other people, were heading in the other direction. And I stopped and said, "I'm with them." They said, "No, you're not. You can't go through the same door they're going in. And they can't go in the door you're going in."

And that's when I remembered. I remembered—and I really mean this—I remembered when Robert Kennedy had spoken in South Africa nine years earlier. He said, "Moral courage is a rarer commodity than bravery on the battlefield or great intelligence, yet is the one, essential, vital quality for those who seek to change a world which yields most painfully to change."

I didn't know quite what to do. And I stopped and said, "I'm going with them." They said, "You can't" and I said, "Then you'll have to arrest me." And I walked back and they had this powwow and they decided that they wouldn't let any of us go through any door together except through the baggage claim area. And they went up and they cleared a restaurant midmeal. They cleared everybody out and declared this a neutral space.

And I thought about his trip, and nothing had changed, by the way. Apartheid was still raging; we were engaged in trying to set up boycotts. But everything about your husband, Ethel, echoed guiding principles that I was taught at my grandfather Finnegan's kitchen table. This is real. The two most significant principles were first, everyone in the world is entitled to be treated with dignity and respect; and, the worst sin of all that one could commit was the abuse of power, whether it was physical, economic, or psychological.

To be standing here tonight receiving the Robert F. Kennedy Ripple of Hope Award means more to me than any of you will ever know. It's the single greatest honor of my life. And given the current mood of the country . . .

I'd like to speak about how Robert Kennedy inspired my career, because it's what Kerry asked me to do. To share my thoughts for just a few moments on how to overcome these deep divisions in our politics in our society today.

I remind people, '68 was really a bad year. And America didn't break. Johnson announced he wasn't running for president, Bobby Kennedy got involved, the putative nominee gets murdered in the kitchen. Not long after that, students are gunned down at Kent State. As bad as it was, the center still held. It's as bad now.

But I'm hopeful. I remember when I got to the Senate as a twenty-nine-year-old kid. There was more fundamental division on issues than there is today. On civil rights, unfinished business. On the war in Vietnam, which divided families and divided the nation like nothing else I've ever experienced. The nation beginning the women's movement and all the bitterness it generated. The environmental movement was viewed by those of us who shared those views as though we were kooks.

Robert Kennedy went to South Africa and spoke to proapartheid as well as antiapartheid advocates. He dined with government officials who defended the indefensible and students who risked their lives to fight against that bitter system. In his words, with the purpose not simply to criticize but to engage in dialogue. To see if together, we could elevate reason above prejudice and myth. He did the same the next year in the middle of a battle for civil rights in Greenville, Mississippi; in Bed-Stuy in New York; the year after, in the fight for economic rights for Kentucky coal miners. He went to see for himself how segregation and poverty were ripping our country—poverty greater than today. Children starving with distended stomachs, teenagers with no education—not inadequate, but no education—adults with no jobs, communities with no hope. Individual conversations in huge crowds across rough mountains, rural schoolhouses, inner cities. He was, for those who were there, someone who listened. He listened.

He listened. Even if they didn't vote for him, even if they didn't like him, he listened. And he felt their pain. And he knew it. At that inflection point in our history, because of Robert Kennedy, I, along with so many of my generation, felt it so completely within our power to be able to bend history just a little bit. Just a little bit.

That generation, the sixties, remember what the call was? You trust no one over thirty and drop out. No, remember. Remember, as bad as you think it is today, remember. I ran for the Senate as a twenty-nine-year-old kid and got elected. I wasn't old enough to be sworn in on the day I got elected. Literally, not old enough to be sworn in. I'm the first United States senator I ever knew.

Know why I have hope? I got elected on November 7. December 18, my wife and three children were Christmas shopping. A tractor trailer broadsided and killed my wife and killed my daughter. You know who the first person to show up at the hospital room was? Teddy Kennedy.

Teddy Kennedy. One of the first calls I got was from Rose Kennedy. And the Kennedys did something they always do. They understood, they embraced, they listened. And for nearly forty-four years, as a US senator and a vice president, that's what I've tried to do. I tried to listen. And damn, it's hard sometimes. It's hard.

But that's what Robert Kennedy did. He didn't hesitate to speak out, but he listened. Believing that even at moments like now, when this country seems so divided, we can still find common hopes and aspirations. There need not be this false choice that's being debated now on my side of the political ledger between social justice and economic opportunity. They go hand in hand; they're not different.

And all those neighborhoods—I campaigned for eighty-four events for Hillary this last time out. And I speak at labor union halls, those white guys who are being so maligned right now. And I talk about equal pay for women and they cheer because they know that their economic circumstance was diminished because their wives are not being paid fairly. I talk about violence against women and they cheer because they knew it was wrong. But not a whole lot of people are listening to their plight because they've been kind of thrown on the slagheap.

Did you know the highest suicide rate is men between the ages of forty and fifty-five? My dad used to say, "Joey, your paycheck is about a lot more. A job is about a lot more than your paycheck. It's about dignity and respect." They think they lost it. We don't listen enough.

As Pope Francis said, "We have an obligation to one another to leave no one behind." That we can come from different places but still remain strongest when we act as one America—rich, poor, middle class, black, white, Hispanic, gay, straight, bi, transgender, immigrant, native born. One America, where we live by that most fundamental American notions that all men and women are created equal. We have to take a hard look at the hard truths about our country now and our economy, why so many people feel left out. We have to stop being blinded by anger. We have to start to listen to each other, see each other again.

When one Maasai tribe member meets another, they reach their hand out to each other and say, "I see you." I see you. I don't think we're seeing each other very well. I've been around long enough not to be naive. I know it's going to be really hard, but I'm still optimistic. I know what is possible.

My mother had an expression. She said, "Bravery lives in every heart, and one day it will be summoned." Well, it's being summoned now. Just as Bobby Kennedy summoned it all the time.

Bobby liked Greek poets. I like Irish poets.

My favorite modern Irish poet was Seamus Heaney. He wrote a poem called "The Cure at Troy." And it reminds me of Bobby Kennedy. He said, "History says / Don't hope on this side of the grave, / but then once in a lifetime / that longed-for tidal wave / of justice can rise up / and hope and history rhyme." I don't know, Ethel, it could be presumptuous of me to say. From a kid's perspective at the time, I believe that's what your husband believed. For as long as we are alive, we have an obligation to strive. As my mother would say, "You're not dead till you've seen the face of God."

Just strive to make hope and history rhyme.

If we ever needed the spirit of a single American leader—and there've been some good ones—at this moment in our history, we need those characteristics that were almost unique to Bobby Kennedy. He had more passion than anybody of his generation. He had more patience than was reasonable for anyone to endure. And he listened. He listened. Because I think he believed we have the capacity, or at least we have the obligation, to strive, to make hope and history rhyme.

So I mean it when I say this is the greatest honor I've ever received in my political life. I thank you for it, Ethel. May God bless the memory of Robert Kennedy. May God bless you all and may God bless our troops. Thank you.

BONO

⤫

*Bono is an Irish singer-songwriter, campaigner, and busi-
ness leader. As the lead singer of Irish rock band U2, he has
received twenty-two Grammy awards and been inducted into
the Rock and Roll Hall of Fame. He has been awarded the
Legion d'Honneur in France, granted a knighthood by Queen
Elizabeth II and, along with Bill and Melinda Gates, named
TIME magazine person of the year in 2005.*

*Bono is an innovative activist, co-founding The ONE
Campaign and (RED) along with my cousin Bobby Shriver.
These organizations have campaigned against extreme
poverty, focusing on debt cancellation, HIV/AIDS, anti-
corruption legislation, and women's empowerment.*

As well as ONE and (RED), Bono has worked with Bobby and my
aunt Eunice on Special Olympics and collaborated with other family members on various causes. His admiration for Daddy, informed by
his Irish roots, is particularly meaningful.

REMARKS FROM BONO'S ACCEPTANCE OF
THE RFK RIPPLE OF HOPE AWARD

The Kennedy legacy is a living legacy. And it is worth shouting from
the rooftops.

I see it through an Irish lens, I see it through Irish eyes, and it's probably true that when it comes to the Kennedys I can't quite see straight.
Irish people can't. In our house, the Kennedys were on the same shelf
as the pope and Mary, mother of God. The Kennedys! And in my particularly eccentric house, the same shelf as the royal family! Because
my mother was Protestant, my father was Catholic, and her father had
fought in the British Army—it wasn't popular in the north side of Dublin to have that duality. But you see, from my father's point of view, the
Kennedys were Ireland's revenge on the royal family. In fact, they *are*
our royal family. It took America to produce an Irish royal family... and
I will say the irony is not lost on the Windsors. But here's the best bit: As
my dad would say, "The thing is, you, the Kennedys, you weren't handed
your titles. You earned them. You weren't anointed; you were elected."
And to his great amusement, elected by a majority of Protestants! The
greatest joke of all.

You have no idea what this meant and what it still means to us in
Ireland, those of us whose ancestors missed the boat. You know, we
stuck around, we ate the potatoes. By the 1960s and '70s, when I was
growing up in Dublin, you could almost taste the regret in having stayed
put. Or maybe that was the defeat we were tasting. Or ashes. Either way,
you cannot exaggerate the miserableness or the miserablism of Ireland
at that time—the Troubles, which Teddy Kennedy did more than most
to put an end to; the economy; the brain drain—it was like the famous
dampness of Ireland had finally soaked into our collective spirit, and for
all that Irish resilience and defiance, all our bluff and bravado, our souls
had the chills. And we couldn't shake them.

Enter the Kennedys.

They gave us warmth ... and light ... and pride ... and hope. They
were good looking, they were glamorous, they had money ... and they
had brains. OK, they were "Americans." We knew that. But they never
forgot where they came from. And it's worth remembering that when

JFK came to Dublin in 1963, bringing Eunice and half of the so-called Irish mafia, a Dublin paper called it "A Big Family Picnic." That's how it was described in Ireland. And it was Dubliners climbing lampposts, standing four deep on the streets along the road for hours. And there was a hailstorm that day, and it covered all the fields with white. It was a really mythic kind of mood in the country. The way we looked at it was—and I was only three—but the way I looked at it when I was three was "this is a local boy made good." Well, that's the way our family looked at it and every family. Three generations removed, but it was a local boy done good. That's how the *New York Times* recorded it at the time.

There was a hailstorm. And you know what? The Irish are tough, man. And no Kennedy knew it more and no Kennedy identified with it more than Bobby Kennedy. The toughness. When he was a student at Harvard, he wrote to a friend of his, "Next to John Fitzgerald and JP Kennedy, I'm the toughest Irishman that lives, which makes me the toughest man that lives." The only thing we Irish don't lack is modesty.

But Bobby never went in for that romantic bollocks about Ireland—the nonsense of a sad, simple people with the gift of the gab, rhyming song, bit of drink, little bit of gambling. No. What he felt, I think, and what he reflected, was our fierceness. Fierce loyalty to family, fierce confidence in ourselves, fierce intolerance to injustice.

And I'm no expert but there's a myth about Bobby Kennedy that's always bugged me: the myth says that "Tough Bobby," the family's self-designated SOB, disappeared on that dark November 1963, to be replaced by a new, softer RFK. That he went from the man who sometimes, if we're honest, could inflict some pain, to a man who took on all the world's pain. That's the myth. And like most myths, it reflects certain truths. There's something to be said of this idea of transformation. Even Bobby himself, I've read, said that's what he felt he was undergoing. And no one can go through all the soul-searching and the self-churning Bobby went through after November 1963 and come

---

"*Those with the courage to enter the moral conflict will find themselves with companions on every corner of the globe.*"

—ROBERT F. KENNEDY,
CAPE TOWN, SOUTH AFRICA, 1966

---

out the other end the same person. You understand that you're either crushed by it, or you're enraged by it, made uglier or more empathetic. Clearly, he was the latter.

Nothing speaks to that transformation more than a couple of stories I learned. One from Harry Belafonte, a hero of mine. He told me a story: he said, early in the Kennedy administration, Dr. King had shut down a strategy meeting of civil rights activists because not a single person could come up with a single encouraging thing to say about the hard-nosed attorney general that we call now RFK. And then he talked about when Bobby lay dying—and he had tears, Harry Belafonte, in his eyes—that there was no greater friend to the civil rights movement. That this transformation happened from a tough guy.

And then the second story was from John Lewis, who years later, after Dr. King was killed, Lewis snapped himself out of his grief by saying, "Well, thank God we still have Bobby Kennedy."

But if you ask me—and of course this is way in the distant memory of an Irish boy—but if you ask me, this distinction gets overdrawn. I just don't believe that Bobby in 1963 was transformed from an Irish scrapper to an Irish romantic. I don't buy it. I don't believe he went from being a hardened pragmatist to being a misty-eyed idealist. The truth is he'd always been both and always remained both. And he never saw a contradiction between the two. That's why I wanted to talk about him tonight.

To quote the man himself, "We must," he said, "deal with the world as it is. . . . We must get things done. But idealism, high aspirations, and deep convictions are not incompatible with the most practical and efficient of programs. There is no basic inconsistency between ideals and realistic possibilities. There is no separation between the deepest desires of heart and of mind and of the rational application of human effort to solve human problems."

Was Kennedy a liberal? Yes. A hippie? Never. Never. None of the Kennedys, as far as I know, went in for the flowers-in-the-hair thing. The

Kennedys from my world are punk rock. They wear marching boots, not Birkenstocks. And you know, there's a boot there. And I felt it, actually, on occasion. And I think from Bobby Shriver it was a (RED) Converse sneaker.

The reason I'm talking about this, and I think about it a lot, this phony distinction between pragmatism and idealism. It's really central to what we do in ONE and Red. People who call themselves pragmatists tend to think idealism is a joke. They think idealists have got their heads in the clouds or, worse, up their arse. Meanwhile, idealists think of pragmatism as an expletive. A dirty word. Like *compromise* or *surrender*. Activists like storming the barricades, not cutting deals. It sullies the reputation, like when rock stars hang out with politicians. Ask my band. It kills the street cred, whatever that was. And the band get very cross.

But there's one thing that says to me that this is all nonsense, this divide. And that one thing is Robert Kennedy. Because Bobby—not to mention Teddy and Eunice and the rest of the family, Kerry—managed to do both credibly, successfully. They stormed the barricades *and* they cut the deal in the back room. The deal that saves lives, that advances the cause, that scores a big win for equality and justice.

What, after all, was Bobby Kennedy's trademark, seen in photo after photo? Was it the windswept hair? No, that was Jack. Was it the powerful, confident smile? No, that was Teddy. The trademark, Bobby's trademark, was the rolled-up sleeves. A man at work. Just a hint of muscle. Dreaming of the world as it isn't, yes. But dealing with the world as it is. The most important things getting done. And that is why Bobby Kennedy looms large in my life.

At my home in Dublin, on my desk in my writing room, there is a picture of Bobby. I see it every day. And here in New York, in our apartment, another picture. Our friends imagine it's just another holy picture for a grandiose Irishman obsessed with America. Grandiose, yes. But they are wrong about the motive.

To me, Bobby Kennedy represents the reason, the duality, the modus, the code of conduct, that I aspire to in the fight for justice and for truth and for human rights. His words tell us why or why not. But his actions show us how. That is why, for a lot of us here tonight, that picture of Bobby is a family portrait.

---∞---

"The future is not a gift. It is an achievement."

—Robert F. Kennedy

---∞---

BILL CLINTON

❦

Bill Clinton served as the forty-second president of the United States. After leaving office in 2001, he created the William J. Clinton Foundation, which operates programs around the world aimed at having a significant impact on a wide range of issues, including economic development, climate change, health and wellness, and the rights of girls and women. The foundation builds partnerships among businesses, governments, NGOs, and individuals to work faster, better, and leaner; to find solutions that last; and to transform lives and communities from what they are today to what they can be tomorrow.

I met Bill Clinton in 1987, when we were seated next to one another on a flight from Little Rock to Washington, D.C. I campaigned across the country during both his presidential and reelection bids. He hosted the launch of the play based on my book, *Speak Truth to Power*, at the Kennedy Center for the Performing Arts in 2000, and he has been a constant source of support for our work at RFK Human Rights.

Kerry Kennedy: *Mr. President, you just got off a plane, as usual. . . .*

Bill Clinton: I was home in Arkansas for four days at our annual health conference. I'll tell you about some of the really interesting things we've been doing.

We have this childhood obesity project that we started years ago, and now we've been in thirty-some-thousand schools with twenty million kids; originally it was about working with the staff on exercise programs, nutrition, and those basic things, but we realized we needed to expand our reach, so we started working in the communities. We've got seven or eight communities now where we bring in all the health care people, including public health, and they help us identify other community problems we can work on.

We have a special program for schools and after-school time, and we've reduced the calories going to these kids from drinks, both soft drinks and processed fruit juices, which have a lot of sugar. We did that with no taxes and no regulations. We got all the major producers together and said, "Do you realize that a lot of these kids, when they're in their midthirties, are going to be sitting in wheelchairs with amputated legs from type 2 diabetes if you don't do this? We know you don't intend to be hurting people, but these kids can't take this much sugar, especially this corn fructose, so you need to find a different way to make money." We got an agreement with the companies that advanced the public health which benefits everybody, including the people who need to make money from selling sodas and juices. They put in fruit-flavored waters; they got rid of all full-size fruit juices and soft drinks; and now we have two independent surveys that show the agreement cut the kids' calories from drinks in schools by 90 percent.

We're trying to capture outcomes on weight reduction, but so far we only have three independent studies—two in California and one in Arkansas. All those studies showed that if schools worked for three years to both change the diet and up the exercise, there's a marked reduction in obesity. So now I'm trying to figure out how to get some foundation to study other states. I'd like to study one in Appalachia, because West Virginia has been pretty active on this problem, and possibly one in Mississippi to see if we can have the same impact in places where the adult rate of obesity is still very high. We know that in some of the areas we're in, the adult obesity rate isn't very high, so there's a reasonable chance that a lot of these kids are getting positive support in their homes or neighborhoods. That might not be true in the towns and rural areas that are most profoundly affected: the predominantly black areas of the South and the predominantly white areas in Appalachia and the Upper Midwest.

Our public health connection has led to all kinds of other stuff we can do. In a lot of places now we're working on the opioid epidemic. There's a wonderful little company, Adapt, that produces the first-ever nasal spray version of stuff that reverses an overdose. You can literally be clinically dead and be brought back to life if you get this Naloxone. Then you have an hour when there's no danger of a relapse, so there's time to get real medical attention.

The most surprising thing to me is that Jacksonville, Florida, which is the third-largest city in America in terms of land mass, has the second- or third-largest rate of pedestrian deaths in the country.

The city and county governments have merged; it's one entity. So you can come to the end of a residential street in the old city of Jacksonville, and suddenly you're in the county, and the cars, instead of driving twenty-five miles per hour, are going sixty, while people are still walking, running, and biking. So a lot of people have been hit who never realized they'd left the city limits and stepped into a more dangerous situation. We're trying to help them fix that.

So when you start to look at childhood obesity as a public health issue, you get connected to other public health issues. That's just what I was doing before I got here today.

KK: *As a politician, you fought vigorously against George W. Bush's policies, but as a former president you have worked closely with him and his dad. Talk about that.*

BC: Yes. There's a program I'm doing with George W. Bush, his and his dad's and Johnson's and my libraries, where we pick sixty people a year to meet and work together on common objectives who would otherwise never talk to each other. For example, we had two severely wounded Iraq War veterans—both of them had lost a leg—working with a group that included the African American woman who heads the gay rights movement in Little Rock, and we had people who represent just about everything in between. These people never would have spoken, and they wound up loving each other. They were stunned at how much they agreed on things they could accomplish together. This is just my little effort to push back against all this polarization that's going on. It's really been good.

KK: *I was going to ask you to talk about my father, but I think you've already been doing that . . .*

BC: I know. Well, here's something that's more directly about your dad. It's about my friend who was the prime minister of Japan, Keizō Obuchi.

In his last year as attorney general, your father gave an interview to a young Japanese journalist who wound up becoming prime minister of Japan.

I served with seven Japanese prime ministers, and Obuchi was my favorite. I just loved the guy, and we became good friends. Obuchi got interested in politics because your father gave him fifteen minutes.

Obuchi was the first Japanese prime minister to do that sort of mass hand-to-hand campaigning. He said he did it because he saw the pictures of Bobby Kennedy in '68 and because he had noticed that I would stop the car and go out and talk with people. He was very restrained, but he decided "we're going to downtown Tokyo." It was obvious it was all orchestrated, but for Japan it was a spontaneous event. They had all these schoolkids in their uniforms at designated places waving Japanese and American flags, and we got out and shook hands with them. This was so many years after Bobby Kennedy's death, and he was still influencing this prime minister of Japan and it was so touching. And of course it wasn't just about doing informal handshaking in a campaign;

it was about an approach to people that was different from what had been the usual thing in Japan. Obuchi died too young from a stroke. It was very sad. His successor had been a close friend of his, but had nowhere near Obuchi's speaking ability. Everybody was shocked that he gave such an eloquent eulogy. He said, "When we were young we talked about our dreams. I do not know what happens when one leaves earth, and I wonder if my friend still dreams. If he does I hope all his dreams are coming true."

It was very moving. There was a silver tray with white flowers, and first his family and then his government officials and then everyone there put a flower down in a pile that grew and grew—thousands of flowers. It was an unbelievable tribute. All this was because your father gave Obuchi a fifteen-minute meeting. Isn't that amazing?

KK: *That is beautiful. Thank you for that story. I never knew my father was an inspiration to the prime minister of Japan. But my parents always talked about their trip there. My mother, to this day, can sing all the words to the Waseda University fight song. Daddy had a famous encounter with students during that trip—I don't recall if it was in Japan or Indonesia—but they were anti-American. He always wanted to meet with students, and he never shied away from those who didn't share his perspective. He listened thoughtfully and respectfully to a long-winded attack. And he responded quietly and directly, "I appreciate that you've been frank in your assessment. And I am sure you expect the same from me." Then, with a wide grin and sparkling eyes, "And you're gonna get it." The film clip is very funny.*

Daddy had a great sense of humor and absolute disdain for dictators. He went to Indonesia on that same trip, and was forced against his will to sit through an endless formal dance at Sukarno's palace. Afterward, he suggested that the Americans would like to return the favor and perform an American routine. He then asked Susie Wilson, the very charming and always-game wife of the deputy director of the US Information Agency and the very uptight and solemn young US foreign service officer Brandon

Grove to do the twist. Of course he knew full well that, just a few months earlier, doing the twist had been declared a crime under the lewd-and-lascivious-conduct statutes of Indonesia.

I think that combination of seriousness of purpose and playfulness, or recognition of the absurdity of life, are vitally important to effective leadership.

I wonder if you could tell me more about how my father affected you.

BC: First of all, I supported integration in the South, so I followed what your father was doing as attorney general. As a lawyer and a southerner, I was mightily impressed by the record he made and how he achieved it. When he was elected to the senate I was thrilled; I thought he would be great; but it really hit me again when he went to South Africa and when he went to Appalachia and when he went to the Mississippi delta. I loved what he did in New York City with the Bedford-Stuyvesant Restoration Corporation, which is the community development organization your father was a major force in getting started. When Hillary ran for the Senate in New York, I said the best thing about it was that she might win Bobby Kennedy's seat. This year in the campaign, one of the places I made sure to visit when I was campaigning in the city was the Bed-Stuy Corporation. That has done so well, and it's still doing great work today. New York is a totally different place now, and a lot of it is happening in Brooklyn and the Bronx. I think your father would be very happy seeing all these young people from all over the world, living together, and proving that diverse groups make better decisions than homogeneous ones. What I loved most was what he did on the campaign in 1968. He had both the courage and the good sense to realize that you couldn't have change without gathering into our base people who had more traditional values. He tried to figure out a way to give the same speech to people in Indiana and people in Los Angeles. That's been our great challenge ever since, because after he was killed, Nixon was elected, and we saw the beginning of the triumph of conservative populism. It's had more and less kind faces as it's gone on through Reagan and Bush and Newt Gingrich to Trump. The whole essence of it is the idea that we live in an "Us and Them" world in which I'm determined to make sure we win and they lose. That's the core of it, and simultaneously the media has come to depend on that construct as a reliable way to increase audience attention and participation.

It's a really interesting point of recent history: when the politicization of the media got started. I think it started in the early 1970s, and I think it got worse because Robert Kennedy wasn't elected president. I think if he had lived he would have won. I think he would have faced a divided country and a lot of opposition, but at least he understood that the culturally conservative and the culturally liberal should both want a society in which we can all live, work, and prosper. That's why I think he was really the first New Democrat. He thought you had to both care for the poor and expect them to be responsible if given an opportunity, because a job is always better than welfare. If the Democrats just took care of people without nurturing their aspirations, they would get into trouble. The same if the Republicans took advantage of the prejudice of working-class and middle-class people who thought other people were going to get things they didn't deserve and deprived them of help so they'd never have a chance to achieve their aspirations. It's better to take care of people than let them wither on the vine, but that's never going to be enough to empower them. If you don't enable people to grow and achieve, sooner or later we'll have a society in which we don't take care of people at all. Inequality will be massive. We've been fighting this yin-yang battle ever since 1968.

KK: *The political media, both Left and Right, reflects that conservative view by pitting people against each other in a zero-sum battle; there can be no reconciliation.*

BC: They're smart. As the attention span of the electorate gets shorter, everybody wants things to happen quickly. Our brains are hardwired for "Us and Them" and for conflict more than for unity. When President Kennedy was elected, the average news program was an hour long, and there were three networks, enough competition for them to keep each other honest and enough guaranteed market share to hire real journalists and allow them to dig out the facts and provide context for them. Over time, that's changed. Now the average time you hear a president's voice on television is about eight seconds. We're told that's about the average amount of attention people give before they think of something else.

You can't really just blame the media, though; they've got to make a living. The problem is that nobody believes anything about anybody anymore, and "fake news" is the natural spawn of the cynical environment. I think in a way Robert Kennedy understood what was already happening. He understood that if you wanted real change it had to be rooted in bedrock values. He understood that in order for people to feel common ground they had to know you didn't look down on them and that you were pulling for them and you respected them. He understood that you couldn't just tell people what they wanted to hear; you had to give the same speech to everybody.

When I ran for president in 1992, I did an experiment. I gave a speech in Macomb County, which was supposed to be the home of the Reagan Democrats in Michigan, and then I went directly to an AME church in downtown Detroit and gave the exact same message. It went over because I didn't sugarcoat it. I didn't pretend. I said, "Look, I think work is better than welfare and the best social program is a job. On the other hand, if you think people are going to be able just to get up and go to work when they've never had an education, they've never had training, they don't have any child care, they don't have any support system, you're wrong." When I took on the NRA, I did it with respect for gun owners. I said, "Look, nobody is going to take away the gun you have for self-protection, or for sport shooting or hunting, but we need your help here. They're playing on your paranoia to get you to deny the most elementary safety precautions in this country, and you may not know anybody who's dying, but if you went with me you would: those kids growing up on blocks dominated by gang violence, a lot of them getting killed anonymously, getting shot in cross fires, getting shot by young kids who're told they can't get into a gang if they don't kill somebody." I said, "If I were you I'd want to help give those kids their future. I'm just asking for your help." Now, I had the advantage of having grown up in that culture, so it was more credible, but Bobby Kennedy understood that you had to communicate with people who didn't vote for you. They could never think you were pulling against them. What happens if you create a cynical environment for a short-term media advantage is that pretty soon no one can hear you when you talk straight anymore. It's just us or them.

Bobby Kennedy was of a time when in spite of all we'd gone through in the sixties there was still an innate yearning among enough Americans to put together a coalition of people who could be for change while also honoring family, faith, and work, people who could believe child rearing was the most important job of a society but that women should not be denied opportunities available to men.

As you know your dad started off working for two congressional committees; he worked for Senator [John] McClellan, who was a hard-core conservative, and they got after the Teamsters union leaders [Dave] Beck and [Jimmy] Hoffa, and a lot of it needed doing, and it was tough, and your father had to be tough and he learned to be tough. He started from where he was and grew and grew until his last day on earth. That's another thing I respect. I think that it's a great mistake to say, "We're all fixed in stone, we are who we are; you show me a guy who's no good at twenty, and he'll die a miserable, no-good guy at eighty." That's just not always true. If your heart and your mind are open, you grow.

KK: *Daddy grew. And his roles changed, so his responsibilities were different, from the time he served on those committees until he was attorney general and then senator and presidential candidate. Growing means changing, and changing your mind in politics is criticized as flip-flopping. How have you changed your mind?*

BC: I've changed my mind on a lot of things. I was always against bigotry against gay people because I knew gay people when I was a little boy, but I was limited in my understanding. My drama teacher in the sixties was gay, and we knew he had to be in the closet, and we all loved him. The South was a great place for gay people because hypocrisy was so enshrined because of race; as long as you'd be hypocritical, they let you do it, whatever it was. Later I realized my position on gay marriage was silly, and that was mostly because of Chelsea. She made a lot of friends when she went to work at McKinsey, the management consultants, and many of them weren't from America. They'd never celebrated Thanksgiving, so Chelsea invited them to our house. She also had friends who lived across the country and couldn't go home, so we started feeding them too. One time we had like four gay couples there out of twenty-five people; that's a pretty high percentage. I came to love all these people, I was interested in their lives and what they were doing. Finally, Chelsea looked at me, and she said, "You can't be against gay marriage anymore; it just doesn't make any sense. You need to change, so don't be proud, you know you're wrong." And I said, "You're right. It's not about me, it's about them," and she said, "Exactly, Dad." She said, "Almost every prejudice in the world is perpetuated by people who think it threatens their identity, but their identity is not the question; it's the other person's identity."

I went to the NAACP in early 2015, before Hillary announced for president, and I said, "You know, this crime bill I signed did a lot of good and most AME leaders and clergymen endorsed it because the primary problem at the time was black-on-black violence by gangs. That crime bill changed policing in America for the better and we got a twenty-five-year low in the crime rate, a thirty-year low in the murder rate, and a forty-seven-year low in the illegal gun homicide rate. A lot of people lived who would otherwise have died. But we made a mistake on the sentencing thing; even though the federal government has fewer than 10 percent of the people who are in jail at any given time and we weren't the first, it's wrong, and we need to fix it. There are a lot of Republicans who know we overdid it too, so we have to try. A lot of you were with me on that, but we need to change it." The cost was horrendous. President Obama did something really good at the end of his term that a lot of people didn't notice. He issued an executive order that started phasing out prisons run by private contractors. It's terrible that the Trump administration has reversed that order, and maybe people haven't noticed either. We still have to take the profit out of incarceration. I've become pretty comfortable saying I was right about this and wrong about that, and I've changed my opinion to what I think is right now.

All this stuff I've been talking about is completely consistent with the message your father presented in 1968. I think we'd be living in a different country if he had won the election. People said that to be for traditional values of work and family and faith but also to believe the government ought to empower people to make the most out of their own lives meant trying to have it both ways. That combination made no sense in terms of "Us versus Them" politics.

I remember very clearly what I thought about Bobby Kennedy when I was twenty-two years old. I thought, "This guy is no cardboard cutout. This is a complicated, real-life, red-blooded human being who's wrestled with his own demons, wrestled with America's demons, sought forgiveness for his sins, and is trying to make one hell of a difference, and I hope people listen." I thought he was for real; I never had any doubt about it.

It's hard, and it's harder now than it was then, to do what your father was trying to do, but it's the only thing worth doing in American life.

I remember when your dad announced, I was still working for the Senate Foreign Relations Committee. I remember this like it was yesterday. He didn't announce for president sooner, because people would have said it was just a grudge match between him and LBJ, so by not announcing sooner he exposed himself to the same thing people always said about Hillary: "Oh, you're driven by ambition and just slid by

———————————∞———————————

*"I run because it is now unmistakably
clear that we can change these disastrous,
divisive policies only by changing the
men who are now making them."*

—ROBERT F. KENNEDY

———————————∞———————————

because Gene McCarthy did all the dirty work." In fact, Johnson had won the New Hampshire primary, but he got only 42 percent of the vote. Johnson beat McCarthy reasonably well, but it wasn't a majority, and psychologically he had lost, which made him vulnerable. Instead of trying to answer those charges against him every day, that it was McCarthy who had shown the courage to challenge Johnson, Bobby just kept talking about what he was for and who he was trying to help and how he wanted to bring us all together. Instead of wearing a hair shirt for an eight-second cut because he once supported the Vietnam War, he talked about what was happening and what went wrong and what we needed to do now. He knew that every election is about the future and you can't let the narrative freeze-frame you. In a competitive media environment of eight-second sound bites like we have today, everybody wants the freeze-frame; the pressure for that is even greater than it was then. What happens with freeze-frames is you drown out the possibility of the future. People can't really hear that message; it takes more than eight seconds. That makes it hard to know for sure exactly how someone like Bobby would fare in an environment like this, but I know that in his time he made the most of it. He gave us a chance to create a new future, and that's what we all needed. It's what we all need now.

People need to believe they can make tomorrow better than today. Angus Deacon, a Scottish economist, did a study of declining life expectancy among non–college educated whites in America and what the ramifications have been. Basically he found that there's a clear public health answer for this. It's a matter of more drug addiction, more alcoholism, more suicide, more diabetes, and such unintended consequences as various types of cancer, heart disease, and stroke. The real answer is not just health insurance coverage, because African Americans and Latinos were hit harder by the crash even than whites, but a lot of them now have more family support and community support than small-town and rural whites. They still believe they can make it better, and too many white people don't. So Deacon essentially said what I tried to say two or three years ago. Don't let anybody kid you: these people are really dying of a broken heart. You can't mend a broken heart with the politics of resentment.

Back in the sixties, George Wallace, the segregationist governor of Alabama, won Michigan's primary once. The antibusing crowd moved into Boston that one time, and there were riots. These are examples of resentment winning a battle or two, but in the end, you can't deal with all these divisions with the politics of resentment. You might win an election, but then you either have to change course or you can't do anything. The thing that makes this a great country is not that it's always perfect. It's that we have an infinite capacity for evolution and change; we're always moving toward a more perfect union. Steve Bannon's definition of a more perfect union is basically a white male patriarchy. He's said many times that the best America was in the 1950s. All the white guys were tough, we all loved them. Your family won a lot of elections because they had war records, football records, they were macho guys. I think if Robert Kennedy were alive today he would be one of the most forceful advocates for women's rights, but he'd be smart enough to know it was his history that gave him his street cred to do that. The point is, how to respect people's culture, and respect people, and still tell them they have to change.

I'll give you one more example. I put a lot of tobacco farmers out of business when I was president. I went to a tobacco shed in North Carolina to give the announcement: "You did not do anything wrong, but we now know this causes cancer. You don't want your children to have it, and you don't want to keep making money by selling cigarettes to the Chinese, who are giving it to *their* kids. So we're going to do a ten-year transition plan and here are your three options. Each of these gives you a good chance to come out ahead on this deal." I will always be grateful to George W. Bush on this issue, because the transition wasn't finished by the time I left office, and he funded the rest of it.

When President Obama announced the climate-change rules, he was in a hurry, and I understood that, because he very much needed it to get the rules done so he would have some credibility to get a climate change deal in Paris, which we did and it's worth a lot, even with Trump withdrawing. The EPA director, Gina McCarthy, asked me to endorse it, and I read it, then called and said, "The regulations are fine and achievable. But I have a question. Are you going to announce these next week in Washington?" She said yes, and I said, "That's a terrible mistake," and when she asked, "What should I do?" I said instead, the president should go to West Virginia or Kentucky and announce this standing in front of a closed coal mine. That will (a) point out that they haven't lost a single job to climate change yet; coal has been in decline a long time. And (b) it will show respect. And, he should also announce a big plan for the redevelopment of Appalachia into a whole different economy. I believe Appalachia is also a state of mind; it's Southeast Pennsylvania, and it's Southwest Ohio, too. And she said, "Well, you still didn't carry North Carolina when you ran," and I said, "I know, but I did win Kentucky, the other big tobacco state." The challenge is to advocate for sweeping change and still hold people close, tell them they matter. They don't all have to vote for you, they just have to respect you. That minimizes the politics of resentment, and that's what Bobby Kennedy would have done. It somehow became second nature to him. Maybe because he'd been around all those hard guys like the crime-buster McClellan. Maybe it was just because he was paying attention. Maybe it was because he saw it in his family, how intergenerational changes happened from his father to him and his brothers. It could have been for a thousand reasons. Some people pay attention and others don't. Some people absorb things almost viscerally and others don't. All I know is, of all the people I ever supported when I was young, he had the greatest capacity for growth. He had the greatest instinct about how to reassure people and say we have to change here and we need your help, and you're part of it, and your life matters. Don't leave these people behind here in Appalachia and don't

leave them behind in Watts. Don't leave them behind on the Indian reservation just because you never went to one. You either have an inclusive message or you have an "Us and Them" message. "Us and Them" is
much easier in politics and it has often prevailed, but the only thing that
takes you to the next step is to be inclusive. It's something you either
believe in or you don't. You either feel it or you don't, you either live it or
you don't. You have to recognize that sometimes they are just not going
to be buying what you're selling, but you've got to keep selling it, because
eventually they'll buy it or the country will change into something else,
something not as good.

And now with all this fake news, the logical conclusion of political
coverage over many decades, we're fighting for the whole idea of democracy in the twenty-first century. A lot of people think there's so much
conflict that after you've shattered society into so many little pieces, the
only practical outcome will be a kind of gentle authoritarianism that
lets people have a social release through the media. That's what I worry
about, because I think even worse than the *Citizens United* decision was
the voting rights decision. I read an article that said something like 7
percent of African Americans eligible by age to vote and 6 percent of
Latinos eligible by age to vote could not vote in this election because of
the new restrictions adopted in 2016 without their knowing anything
about them. We don't have a way of counting who showed up and tried
and failed to vote; it would be good to have a device to track that. If we
had electronic voting we could have just put another line in. Meanwhile
there's this amorphous sense in America that people will still have personal freedom but they won't have citizen equality freedom.

KK: *Talk about what drew you to Daddy in 1968.*

BC: Bobby Kennedy walked into the biggest storm you could possibly imagine in 1968, with the country coming apart at the seams. He
knew he was going to get zinged by some people who blamed him for
the Vietnam War and zinged by other people who said he wanted to
run away from the Vietnam War. He knew he was going to get zinged

for trying to dance on Gene McCarthy's grave too, but he just kept rising. Probably the speech of his life was the King speech in Indianapolis, when Dr. King was killed, although I love the speech he gave in South Africa, and a lot of others too. The best speech Ted Kennedy ever gave was the speech he gave at your father's funeral. We tend to forget that politicians are human beings. Your father was a real person, with hopes and fears, with wild ambition and gnawing insecurity, who got hurt when people said crappy things about him and worried about what was going to happen to his family. Teddy painted a picture of your father as a three-dimensional human being growing steadily toward goodness. If we allow our public figures to become two-dimensional cardboard cutouts, the story of the greatest experiment in self-governance in history will come to an end. I wish I could make every Democrat and every thoughtful, troubled Republican read the story of Robert Kennedy's life. I would like people to see that you don't have to agree with him on every issue. That's not the point. The point is that he was a real human being. He was, like the Arthurian knight Perceval, who quested for the Grail, a good man, slowly wise.

FOLLOWING PAGES: Robert and Ethel Kennedy at funeral of Martin Luther King Jr. (Harry Benson)

———————— ∞ ————————

"All great questions must be raised by great voices, and the greatest voice is the voice of the people—speaking out—in prose, or painting or poetry or music; speaking out—in homes and halls, streets and farms, courts and cafes—let that voice speak and the stillness you hear will be the gratitude of mankind."

—ROBERT F. KENNEDY

———————— ∞ ————————

GEORGE CLOONEY

❦

George Clooney is an actor, business leader, philanthropist, and activist. He has received two Academy Awards (for Syr-iana and Argo) and three Golden Globes.

He focused worldwide attention on the plight of people of Sudan and South Sudan, and worked for victims of the 2004 Pacific tsunami, the 2010 earthquake in Haiti, the 9/11 terrorist attacks, and for the recognition of the Armenian genocide.

Remarks from George Clooney's acceptance of the RFK Ripple of Hope Award

To be mentioned in the same breath with Robert Kennedy is, at the very least, humbling. He proved over his short life that he was the best of us. He was right when he said that nations, like men, often march to the beat of different drummers. And still the lesson of our time is that all must march toward increasing freedom, toward justice for all.

I'm going to try to give you a quick explanation on how it is that I'm standing here tonight. In 1968, my father took a break from doing the news, and he moved us all to Columbus, Ohio, to do a television show called *The Nick Clooney Show*, which was fortunate for us because his name happened to be Nick Clooney. I was seven years old on June 6,

1968. And I remember that my parents sat my sister and me down to explain to us that the young senator whom we were so excited about was gone, in the same way his brother was gone, and in the same way Dr. King was gone. And he said, "OK, what do you want to do, kids?" We were Catholic so I decided we should do something like we did for Lent.

My father asked me what I thought I could live without. And we were pretty broke at the time. My mom used to make my clothes; there are some photos of that I'd like to have back. Grade school is a great time to have your clothes homemade—I'll never forget the Nehru leisure suit thing she made.

Toy guns were pretty easy to get your hands on. That and candy cigarettes, go figure. I suggested I could do without my collection of toy guns for a few days. So I put them in a bag and the next day when my dad goes on the TV show, he holds up this bag and he tells half of Ohio that his son brought them in and said, "Dad, I never want to play with these ever, ever again."

It was a great moment for everyone, except for me. I was stunned. I mean it was "never again," you know. I was thinking a few days. I was gonna go for the whole forty-day Lent thing, but, I mean, no more cowboys and Indians, no more cops and robbers, nothing? It was gonna be, you know, playing marbles and dodgeball.

The problem is what my father understood, and what I was too young to: that we had this crushing feeling in our country, that everything we loved and cared for, could be taken away violently. And it happened time and time again. And we were all hurt by that.

I was pretty shaken up for all the wrong reasons. So the next day, I go to school and the teacher stands me up and she tells the story to the class, and then she says, "George is a very good boy." And all the kids sort of come over later and they shake my hands. For weeks, old ladies would come up and say, "You're a good boy."

Being Irish Catholic and seven and in second grade, I am now racked with guilt.

I tried confessing to Father Brinker. That didn't pay. I read in the Bible where the saint would put a pebble in her shoe and walk around for penance. So I filled my shoes with gravel and I jumped off the top of my bunk beds. Every day. You'd hear my parents, they'd hear the sound and go, "Oh, it's George doing penance."

I have spent the last forty years trying to make up for getting too much credit for doing something that I should have just done anyway. I was just starting to feel even, and then Ethel called.

And you know Ethel. I told her that I had a lot more to do before I should be standing up here, and she told me to show up or else she was gonna rain Kennedys down on my ass.

I didn't really understand what she meant until I got here tonight.

Yeah. So tonight, with this great honor, and with this wonderful evening, you have now forced me into another forty years of trying to earn this praise that I've been given tonight. I will do my best.

One last thing, and I don't want to take any more of your time, but to say that we have a chance here of finding a peace deal between North and South Sudan. A couple of million people died the last time they went to war. Senator Kerry has taken the lead, but it's being handled directly by Secretary Clinton, by President Obama—they're personally involved. It means negotiating with people that leave a bad taste in your mouth, quite honestly.

We're so close, but it has to be sustained. And that takes political will. And there is an awful lot of will right here in this room. So a phone call, an email, any message of support right now to anyone you know who's involved, anyone in the administration, any way you can do it. We don't need your money, we need your voice right now, more than anything. Because we are so very close. We have a chance.

Thank you, Kerry. Thank you, Ethel. I appreciate it. And I'll be out buying gravel and a new pair of bunk beds and stuff. Thank you very much.

"Everywhere new technology and communications bring men and nations closer together, the concerns of one inevitably becoming the concerns of all. But our new closeness had not yet stripped away the false masks, the illusions of difference which are the root of injustice and hate and war. Earthbound man still clings to the dark and poisoning superstition that his world is bounded by the nearest hill, his universe ended at the river shore, his common humanity enclosed in the tight circle of those who share his views and his town and the color of his skin. And therefore the survival of the human species itself depends on our ability to strip the last remnants of that ancient, cruel belief from the civilization of man."

—ROBERT F. KENNEDY

TIM COOK

◦✖◦

Tim Cook is the CEO of Apple. His personal encounters with racial discrimination during his childhood in Alabama instilled in him a hatred for discrimination in private affairs and in the workplace. His philanthropic endeavors are widespread. He has supported the rights of minorities and the rights of individuals to personal privacy, and he has engaged Apple in those causes, too. He has contributed to politicians of both political parties.

In articles and interviews, Cook has often cited Robert Kennedy as his hero. He serves on the Board of Directors of Robert F. Kennedy Human Rights. We met in his office in Cupertino, California—where there are three photos on the wall—one of Martin Luther King Jr. and two of my father.

Kerry Kennedy: *You have two photos of my father in your office. Talk about that.*

Tim Cook: He inspires me. I love his idealism, with some pragmatism as well. I love the fact that he had a deep humanity about him, and he seemed to be someone who really cared for all people, lifting up those who were marginalized. I also love his focus on the individual and how the individual can make a difference. In his words, "a ripple of hope."

KK: *Yes, he used that phrase in a speech in South Africa, in 1966. Each act against injustice "sends forth a tiny ripple of hope," and many ripples "build a current which can sweep down the mightiest walls of oppression and resistance."*

TC: That's a powerful concept for me, and a huge inspiration.

KK: *Why do you think he's important today?*

TC: In a lot of ways he is timeless: If you go back and listen to or read his speeches, the messages are as key today as they were in the sixties, when he was giving them, and they were key ten years ago, too, and ten years before that. He had a vision about the things that were truly important to focus on: We can do better, and because we can do better, we must act. Act whenever we see injustice. Act whenever we can make a difference. There were other heroes who did incredible things that, if you listen to them today, you can tell that what they were saying was important at that time, but you don't feel that it's a modern message. His messages are modern.

He's someone I wish I had known. I try to learn from him by reading his words and seeing how he conducted himself.

KK: *Besides love, the quality Daddy admired most was courage. He surrounded himself with people of uncommon bravery—the astronaut John Glenn, the football player Roosevelt Grier, the bullfighter El Cordobés, the mountain climber Jim Whittaker. He admired courage in all walks of life. That's a quality you share. You're the first openly gay CEO of a Fortune 500 company, but you took a full year to consider how to make that announcement. What happened in that year?*

TC: It actually probably took longer than that. There were many considerations, like the details of how to say it in a way that would make a difference for people. Because I wasn't doing it for myself. For me, I would've stayed very private, frankly. The reason I wanted to do it was to have an impact, so arguably the *way* to do it becomes very important: what to say, how to say it, where to say it.

KK: *You wrote an op-ed in* Bloomberg.

TC: I chose to do it in a business publication, because that's who I am. I'm not someone who would appear on the cover of *People* magazine. I also wanted to choose the words carefully, which takes some time because I'm not a poet, so the words don't necessarily come as naturally for me as they did for your father. And then, of course, I had to think about the company. I didn't want to do it at a time when it would distract from something, like a product announcement. I wanted to get advice from people about the how and where to do it, and what to expect thereafter, so I could prepare myself. And finally, I wanted to talk to some people in advance, like our board and folks like that.

KK: *Was there pushback?*

TC: No, I found tremendous support. And I didn't even know some of the people I called for advice. Like I reached out to Anderson Cooper.

KK: *He came out in an email to his friend Andrew Sullivan, the writer.*

TC: Yes, I loved the way he chose to do it. But there wasn't a road map for someone in business. There were people in other fields whom I read about who had done it in a thoughtful and deeply considered way, so I wanted to touch base with them. I also didn't want it to be a press event. I wasn't doing it for press or to make a splash—I was doing it to make a difference.

KK: *A lot of people come out to emancipate themselves, but that was not your issue.*

TC: No, I've been comfortable with myself for a very long time, so I wasn't looking to accomplish anything like that.

KK: *So why do you think you're the first? It's just unbelievable to me, because your response is pretty much the universal response to those who have social power coming out: that people are very, very supportive. What do you think is holding back other CEOs?*

TC: I think there's still a stigma.

KK: *But you said everyone was supportive.*

TC: Everyone was supportive—let me be clear on that. My friends were supportive, and the board of Apple was supportive. But at large, the reality today is still that there are groups within which being gay is rare. Sports is an example. Jason Collins was the first professional athlete in a major American team sport to come out, and that was not very long ago. I think business is kind of like that, too. The stereotypical CEO is white, male, married, kids. If there's a dinner, he's there with his wife. That makes it harder for some folks.

But for me, that wasn't the issue. I was getting a lot of outreach from kids who were struggling, who felt cast out. They knew I was gay because they'd read it on some website or something, and I began to realize there's a greater purpose and a greater need to do it. My own view was that if it could affect one person, it was worth doing. And that whatever kind of heat I took would be worth it.

KK: *One of the things that Daddy talked so much about is the idea of moral courage, which he said is rarer than bravery in battle or great intelligence. It's not the courage to stand* with *your colleagues against a common enemy but to stand* up *to your colleagues, friends, and associates and say that what we're doing is wrong, and risk being ostracized for it. You stood up at a shareholders' meeting and challenged an investor who said: "Why are you doing things that don't have a return on investment?"*

TC: He wanted me to publish a report, specific to environmental issues, that showed every expenditure we made and the return on investment that it generated. He asked me to make a commitment to only do things that had a return on investment. And my response was, "I'm not going to do that." We do many things as a company that don't have a clear return on investment: We make our products accessible to the blind—that doesn't have a clear return on investment, but it's the right thing to do, so we do it. He kept pushing, and I said, "Look, if you have a problem with that, your choice is to get out of the stock, because we're not changing that."

As a CEO, you do a lot of things on gut, and you do a lot of things— certainly I do—where you look at the long term. And I believe strongly that many things are financially very smart in the long term that don't appear to be so in the short term. Some environmental initiatives are like that. In the United States, we run Apple on 100 percent renewable energy. That came about from a series of decisions, but if you go back and look at each one of them, you might say, "Oh, that one doesn't look good." But in the aggregate, all of them added up to doing something spectacular.

KK: You're actually making two different points. One is the argument against quarterly capitalism—against judging companies by how much they made in the last three months. They might not see a return on investment for seven years, or ten years, but eventually they're going to see a return. Which is different from saying, "We're going to do things that get no return on investment at all, and that is still important for us as a company."

TC: Yes. Accessibility is an example. There are clearly things that we do to help people with disabilities that, if we measured strictly by sales and profits and the number of users, we'd never do—in the long term or the short term. We do those things because they're just and right. Now, do other people look at Apple and say, "They're doing the right thing, and I want to buy products from companies that do the right thing"? And so is there a financial return when you look at the reputation of a company? I would say that there is. But you don't see that return when you look at it on a micro basis; you see it only when you look long and broad. So I think it's important for companies not to get so tied into every independent action needing a return.

We're doing a huge education program in the United States for which we picked more than one hundred schools that are underprivileged or underserved—schools where 97 percent or more of the kids are on free or reduced lunch—and we're giving them technology and we're training teachers to teach coding to the kids. We're doing this because we're very concerned about public education in general, but we're also looking at it and saying, "We need more women and minorities in coding," and this is an interesting way to see if we can excite people to get them into it when they're very young, so coding becomes sort of a hobby. Our view is that they'll do it more and more and maybe even someday become an Apple employee. But that's all on faith. And if I listened to proposals like the one at the shareholder meeting, there's no way we'd do this.

KK: *How do we influence other CEOs and investors to see companies that way? Because a lot of CEOs say, I'm stuck—I'd love to have a better supply chain policy or environmental impact, but I can't, because it's costly. And a lot of investors say, I'd love to invest only in ways that are consistent with the programmatic aims of my foundation (for the endowment of a nonprofit committed to environmental protection, for instance, they might avoid investments in fossil fuel stocks), but I can't, because my job is to maximize risk-adjusted returns.*

TC: Well, I think we're doing pretty well with returns, right? Actually, your father gave us this idea. We try to be the ripple of hope in several areas. We think that if we act in a responsible way, at least some other companies can look at it and say, "I can do that."

I'm also hugely optimistic about the younger generation. What I see is a group of kids who are much more socially conscious than any generation that I've experienced in my lifetime. As they enter into their prime earning years, those kids will be the consumers, and they're going to demand that companies be responsible. So I think there are a lot of vectors here that are hugely positive. I get outreach all the time from customers saying, "Hey, I saw you doing this, thank you." Now, I also get the ones that are not so positive, so you have to be willing to take the arrows, too.

KK: *Let's talk about that. How do you decide which issues to take on? For instance, you spoke out against President Trump's Muslim ban—his executive order that restricted immigration from seven Muslim-majority countries. Why that issue and not something else?*

TC: The filter that I use is I look at a subject and say, "Does Apple have standing in it?" Not me, but Apple. And I say, "Can we make a difference by doing something?" I strive very hard to stay totally out of politics. We always try to focus on policy and legislation and steer clear of personalities and elections and so forth. In the case of the travel ban, we looked at it and said, "One, this goes to the heart of why our company is successful: Apple wouldn't exist without immigration. Two, we have a number of Muslim employees, and we have a number of employees from one of the seven countries named in the ban and an even broader number of employees who have families in those countries." So we had cases where families were separated. One employee was traveling and couldn't get back into the United States—her spouse was here. We had a case where parents were trying to join an employee for the birth of their first grandchild and couldn't get in. These are very human stories. Some folks get mesmerized with the numbers, but it's the humanity that we care about. We felt that we had standing to go in, and we thought we had a point of view that might help the situation, so we spoke out.

KK: *One of the issues that we work on at RFK Human Rights is protecting privacy and the right of information, and Apple is right in the midst of these concerns. How do you see the conflict between privacy rights and national security?*

TC: We had a situation about a year ago, the San Bernardino case, in which the US government made a request to us that we found shocking: it asked us to create a product that could penetrate secured, locked data.

KK: *The FBI wanted you to break into the phone of one of the alleged terrorists who had killed fourteen people in San Bernardino, California. You responded with an open letter to customers explaining that unlocking the phone would constitute a "breach of privacy" with "chilling" consequences. Can you explain why you were so resistant to this request?*

TC: Yes. There are many things technology should never be created to do, and this is one of them—not only because of the consequences for privacy but also for security. The reality is, you can't have a back door in just one country. If you put a back door in a system, it could be used anywhere in the world.

KK: *You wrote in your letter that, once created, such a back door "could be used over and over again, on any number of devices. In the phys-*

ical world, it would be the equivalent of a master key, capable of opening hundreds of millions of locks—from restaurants to banks to stores and homes."

TC: Yes. You could imagine a government that wants to target a human rights activist having such a master key. You could imagine a hacker who wants to not only steal something from somebody but also perhaps to sell this information. You could imagine someone trying to figure out where someone's kids are so he could kidnap them—it becomes a safety issue. You could imagine someone taking down a power grid in the United States, and people on life support could lose their lives. There are so many examples you could imagine. And in Ukraine, this actually happened: The power grid was taken down. So these concerns are not just theoretical.

So we looked at all the incidents and possibilities. The question was not just *can* we do it but also *should* we do it. The government wanted us to answer only the "can we" question. And if the answer was yes, they wanted us to do it. And it was so disappointing to hear that from the US government, which should be the beacon for human rights around the world.

Now that more than a year has passed, and we've seen all the hacking that has taken place, and WikiLeaks has posted a whole bunch of data stolen from the CIA, it's not just a theory that these tools can be stolen. My guess is that people today would be much more hesitant to make that request than they were a year ago, because much of what we feared has come about.

KK: *It will be interesting to see how the Trump administration approaches this issue.*

TC: Honestly, it doesn't fall along party lines. It's not red-blue. When this occurred, there were libertarian-leaning people who felt strongly that there's no way we should do this. Keep in mind, this request came under a Democratic administration, and yet there were Democrats who said there's no way this should be done, as well as some who said they couldn't understand why Apple wasn't doing this.

KK: *Was it partly a matter of technical literacy?*

TC: Yes. The deeper people understood the technology, the more they feared the tool being created in the first place—and the more likely they were to say it shouldn't be done. To the degree that people *didn't* understand the technology, they were more likely to quickly just say, "Phone, terrorist, why don't you just unlock it?"

KK: *In a speech, you said that challenges should inspire us: "They do not daunt us. They do not deter us. Like Robert Kennedy, we reject pessimism and cynicism. We see no contradiction between a hardheaded realism and an unshakable idealism that says that anything is possible if we just get to work."*

TC: I loved his optimism. In all the stuff I've listened to, he was never cynical, never negative. He spoke about things as they really were but also painted a picture of what they could be. And all too often in the last many years, there just hasn't been enough of that optimism.

KK: *The easiest way for a politician to win is to sow division in a country, but Daddy sought to bring people together. And he brought together black and white, old and young, what today would be red and blue. He had the backing of George Wallace racists and Martin Luther King activists. So in today's divided country, what can be done to bring people together? What is your role personally, and what is the role of Apple, in bringing people together and healing those divisions?*

TC: When I look at the dysfunction in Congress today, what I see is that all too often the incentives lead some politicians to take extreme-Right or -Left positions, and the middle has been hollowed out. In my view, this has occurred largely through gerrymandering. So I guess if I could do anything, I would probably have a computer system redraw the districts, to kind of bring things back to a new normal. I would also probably limit the presidential term to one and extend it to six years, so that presidents are not constantly running for reelection. I'd take all the money out of the system and say that only *people* could contribute to elections—that corporations could not, that institutions could not. Maybe those huge changes would rattle the system so much that there would be a fresh start. Maybe those aren't the right changes, but I am beginning to think that some structural change is needed. The important thing is that we keep our democracy.

So what can we do? I think we need to recommit ourselves to being great citizens—not only of the country but of the states, cities, and communities that we live in—and play an active role and contribute. We should all think about ways to motivate even more people to engage in improving their lot, and the lot of their neighbors and fellow citizens.

As a company, what can we do? We've tried to convince our people to give more and participate more by offering to match their charitable donations. We have a day of service on Martin Luther King's birthday, when people go out and donate their time. And if someone who maybe can't give money contributes their time, we will match that with money. We also provide ways for people to get involved in company initiatives, like fighting climate change.

It's important for companies to think through how they can provide opportunities for their customers and their users, too. In our case, we touch a lot of people, so we will, for example, rope in some developers for an "Apps for Earth" promotion, with proceeds from the apps going to the World Wildlife Fund. On the user side, there's our Product Red partnership: For every Red product that we sell, we donate to the Global Fund for the elimination of AIDS. To raise awareness, we turn our logo red on World AIDS Day, so people walking into the store say, Why is the logo red? Or we turn the stem green for Earth Day, same kind of thing. All of these things add up to create momentum.

KK: *Ripples of hope.*

TC: Exactly. All of us can do something. Your father had that great insight that—I can't remember his exact words—but it was basically that maybe only a few things or people were able to bend history, but he quickly got it back to the individual and what the individual can do, and that it would all add up to making a difference.

KK: *"Few will have the greatness to bend history itself; but each of us can work to change a small portion of events, and in the total of all those acts will be written the history of this generation."*

TC: I feel the same way about companies. All people should have values, and companies are nothing more than a collection of people, so by extension they should have values as well. Obviously companies should do things to help change the world in their own way, and one of the hardest challenges is picking which things to pursue. So we take on a few causes and put a lot behind them. At the same time, we've said to our employees, "Okay, you make the decision, and we'll match." So everyone becomes a sort of mini foundation.

KK: *And that empowers people.*

TC: It empowers people to do their own thing, because everybody has their own passion. I know that your father was somewhat suspicious of business. But he did think that private enterprise was, as he put it, a vast untapped resource for social change. He also said, there is no more promising asset that we have today than the skills, the resources, and the inventiveness of our private sector. He understood that business has a central role to play in helping society solve its greatest problems. And he saw, even in the 1960s, that coming advances in technology held enormous potential to change the world for the better.

—∞—

"There is another kind of violence, slower but just as deadly, destructive as the shot or the bomb in the night. This is the violence of institutions; indifference and inaction and slow decay. This is the violence that afflicts the poor, that poisons relations between men because their skin has different colors. This is a slow destruction of a child by hunger, and schools without books and homes without heat in the winter."

—Robert F. Kennedy

—∞—

MARIAN WRIGHT
EDELMAN

༄

*Marian Wright Edelman was born in South Carolina,
attended Spelman College and Yale Law School, and represented activists during the Mississippi Freedom Summer of
1964. She took Senator Robert Kennedy on a tour of the Mississippi delta in 1967, during which she met, and later married, Kennedy's legislative aide Peter Edelman. With Martin
Luther King Jr. she organized the Poor People's Campaign
of 1968, and in 1973 she founded the Children's Defense
Fund. She received a MacArthur fellowship in 1985 and was
awarded the Presidential Medal of Freedom in 2000.*

I've known Marian Wright Edelman for almost fifty years, and her
work on children in poverty has made her one of my heroes. As a
mother, I often think of something she said to me when I wrote *Speak
Truth to Power*, "I was blessed at a young age to find a cause that was
worth dying for, and that has made every day of my life worth living."
My hope for my daughters is that they, too, will find a purpose that
makes every day of their lives worth living. We met in Marian's office at
the Children's Defense Fund in Washington, D.C.

Kerry Kennedy: *In your memoir,* Lanterns, *you write that you didn't think much of Robert Kennedy before you met him. You had an idea he was tough and arrogant.*

Marian Wright Edelman: What I knew about him was his connection with the FBI's wiretapping of Dr. King and his work for the McCarthy subcommittee. I had never met him, but my image of him was not good. I viewed him quite differently by the time I finally did meet him in 1967, and was very impressed by his speech in Cleveland about the plague of violence after Dr. King's assassination. I thought he was very moving. I met your dad in connection with hunger and antipoverty programs I was involved in in Mississippi.

I had met with President Johnson's people in the White House, and they thought it was so wonderful what we were doing about hunger and poverty, and there was so much interest, but it was the middle of the Vietnam War and these powerful people wouldn't do anything to help. A Senate subcommittee was on our side and wanted us to make noise to get attention and called me to testify about how well the poverty program was working.

KK: *In March 1967 you testified in Washington before the Senate Labor Subcommittee on Poverty, where Daddy was a member, that thousands of black sharecroppers were out of work, and their families were starving, because of a combination of mechanization and the federal subsidy stipulating that cotton fields lie fallow. Two-parent households were ineligible for benefits, and Mississippi had switched from a free surplus food distribution program to a food stamp program, which required $2 to purchase subsidized food. As many families had no income, there was no money to purchase food stamps. This was all part of an effort by Mississippi political leaders to force poor blacks to join the great migration north. So Daddy joined a handful of senators to visit Mississippi and look at the conditions there. At the time you were a twenty-seven-year-old graduate of Yale Law School, working for the NAACP Legal Defense Fund.*

MWE: I came to testify about Head Start, hunger, and the poverty programs, which were very much under attack by Senators [John C.] Stennis and [James] Eastland and other Southern segregationists. The Child Development Group of Mississippi (CDGM)'s Head Start program had created jobs for about three thousand people. It was based on a new vision of what children could do in early childhood. We saw how excited children were about learning. I loved the program; I'd visit our desegregated school districts and hear complaints from teachers that these CDGM kids were always asking questions, wanting another book. It was a very important program, but Mississippi's senators came down heavily against it, forcing a long renewal fight after the Mississippi Freedom Democratic Party (MFDP) challenged the Jim Crow Democratic Party in Atlantic City. It was the first time people experienced what it was like to have an independent voice, and they liked it.

KK: *At the time, the Democratic Party in Mississippi was whites only, and it effectively prevented people of color from voting. So civil rights activists like Ella Baker, Fannie Lou Hamer, and Robert Moses established the MFDP as an alternative to the Democratic Party.*

MWE: When we testified, we were all labeled Communists and subversives. So I asked the senators to come to the state and see for themselves the conditions there, and Senator Joe Clark and your dad agreed along with Republican senators Javits and Murphy. It was a very moving trip for all of us. It got a lot of attention, and put hunger on the national agenda. I had taken lots of people, including congressmen and journalists, to see the need, but none could command the press the way your father could. It was really a huge step forward in bringing visibility to the urgent need that existed and what the poverty programs were doing to address it. Your father was visibly moved by what he saw in the field, and it was terrific for the cause.

Your father went through the houses we took him to visit, and what I loved about him was his ability to say so much through touch. He went into one house and saw the now famous baby who—someone told me recently had survived and is all grown up—but this baby was sitting on the dirt floor with his very depressed mother washing clothes in a tin tub. There were no cameras inside as your father tried hard to get a response from this child, who just didn't respond. When he went outside, there were children standing around in front of the house, and he asked them what they'd had for breakfast and lunch, and they said they hadn't had lunch or breakfast yet. It was noon, and they'd had no breakfast. Your father had a way of gently touching the cheek with the back of his hand that was worth ten thousand words. I will never forget that.

We went to a number of different houses. In one there were three of the dirtiest little girls which just broke me up. The kids were so out of it, dirty and hungry, and you could not help but be moved. Your dad was so tender to them.

The other incident that consolidated my feelings about your father in a profound way was when we were going through a delta city with sirens blaring in this big motorcade speeding through. The kids came out to see the commotion, and a dog ran out in front of the police car and was killed. Your dad was very angry. He stopped the cars and got out to comfort the child whose dog it was and told the drivers not to drive so fast and make all this noise going through small towns. What he did was so very human; it moved me that he stopped to comfort a suffering boy.

Your father said he was shocked because he'd been to West Virginia and places of poverty all over the world, but hadn't seen anything like these children with bloated bellies and dead eyes and dirty clothes, and had no idea conditions like that existed in America.

The next day he ordered Agriculture Secretary Orville Freeman to get some food down there. Freeman said there were no people in America without any income, but your dad responded: "Yes there are; I just saw them." That was the first time the secretary of agriculture was forced to take the hunger issue seriously. Freeman said, "I'll send my staff back and document what you say you saw." Your dad said, "I'll send Peter back to show you the same families we saw." So they did; they came back the next day, and saw them. But Agriculture officials dragged their feet because the Vietnam War was going on and nobody wanted to jeopardize the war's financing for poverty programs.

The struggle dragged on, and I got completely frustrated because there was still so much hunger. Mississippi was trying to starve them out, and force these poor people to join the migration north. So in August I went to Washington to see Peter and I talked to your dad. I told him nothing had changed, Agriculture was dragging its feet, and still hadn't waived the $2 for families to have access to food. When I told your father I was stopping through Atlanta to visit with Dr. King, he told me to tell Dr. King to bring the poor to Washington.

The next day I headed for Atlanta to see Dr. King like I always did on my way back or forth to Mississippi. That was in August of '67. Dr. King at that time was totally depressed. He had given his Riverside Church speech opposing the Vietnam war, and a lot of people including friends turned against him after the antiwar speech. He didn't know where to go next, and, bless his heart, he had the patience of Job, but it was a very difficult time for him. I kept him up to date on our antipoverty and hunger efforts. He had been to Marks, a little city in Quitman County, Mississippi, still one of the poorest places in the country. Dr. King had been there for a funeral and he had seen a teacher carve an apple into six slices and give it to six hungry kids. It was the first time he almost burst into tears publicly; he went running out of the building. That was his experience in Marks from which the Mule Train for the later Poor People's Campaign began.

At any rate, when I went by to see him in his very modest office, I sat right down and told him how frustrated I was that food still wasn't going to Mississippi's hungry children, and told him what your dad had said, which was: "Tell him to bring the poor to Washington." Dr. King just absolutely lit up. He went home and told Coretta, who wrote about it in her book, and Coretta said he smiled for the first time in a long while. And he called his staff together and talked about what he said was going to be the next big step for us all. The Poor People's Campaign started in Marks. And it started with Robert Kennedy's passion and willingness to push. It was important, though it never had the impact we hoped for; it wasn't helped by the deaths of Dr. King and your father, and it wasn't helped much by Richard Nixon.

We just returned to Marks to do a child hunger watch. Although we have a 100 percent federally funded program for summer months, many states and localities don't use it. I don't know what we're going to find, but I think the issue will probably be obesity. We have school lunches and school breakfast during the school year, and then we have a summer food program that's 100 percent federally funded too, but many of the Southern states won't take the money, so there's a 90 percent drop in participation during the summer. Although there's money, there are states that won't take Medicaid money. I keep a Mississippi office, and I get reports about how "the kids come in on Monday mornings and they've gone without breakfast or lunch over the weekends. If the bus driver's late getting them to school, that means they miss breakfast." We also have the kids who have nothing or practically nothing at all to eat on the weekend; these kids figure out what other kids don't like and they stand behind them and wait until they finish and then ask if they can finish the leftovers. It's horrible, these feeding programs mean jobs for bus drivers and cafeteria workers and food for hungry children. That's not 1968. That's 2017.

Your father's legacy is that he brought food to hungry children by giving a public face to the situation in Mississippi and other places in America. His presence and doggedness made it possible to marshal resources to attack the problem. He got the CBS special that showed a mother with a baby dying on TV. For all our struggles in '64, '65, '66, and '67, it was only when he came that the press showed up. He never gave up. He stuck with it. He was moved by it, and he knew what was happening in Mississippi was wrong. He said he had never experienced anything like it, even in Third World countries. His determination and compassion and persistence were really quite extraordinary.

The single most moving moment of the Poor People's Campaign for me was when your father's funeral train arrived in DC and the hearse stopped in front of Resurrection City.

KK: *That was the fifteen acres near the Reflecting Pool occupied by three thousand poor people to demonstrate against hunger and poverty.*

MWE: And they began to sing the "Battle Hymn of the Republic."

People thought it was all over then, but it wasn't. Your father had planted new seeds and things grew and we and others pushed and pushed. There were the McGovern hearings on hunger in the Senate and around the country and the White House conference on hunger. Today there are millions of people on food stamps—the Supplemental Nutrition Assistance Program (SNAP); the Women, Infants, and Children (WIC) program; all school lunches have expanded, and we have school breakfasts and after-school programs; and the whole hunger lobby remains a significant force inspired by the Poor People's Campaign beginning. All the progress we made happened incrementally.

When we returned to Washington in 1969, President Nixon was not going to let us go from agency to agency and had us come to the White House to meet with him and the whole cabinet. We reported that not enough progress had been made. President Nixon's response was that he was bringing peace in Vietnam. That was not what we wanted to hear. Dr. Ralph Abernathy, Dr. King's successor at the Southern Christian Leadership Conference, attacked the president for not being responsive on the hunger issue. Daniel Patrick Moynihan, his domestic policy adviser and later senator from New York, was furious that we were not grateful just to meet. But within a year he had a national conference on hunger and we were beginning to see expansion of the food programs. By the end of the Nixon years, hunger was virtually on the run. Then

President Reagan came in and tried to destroy the entire safety net. But new voices kept the laws on the books, and although we lost billions of dollars, we saved the laws and eventually got much of the money back. And the fight goes on today as the Trump administration seeks to eviscerate the safety net again. He must not and will not succeed.

KK: *I'm interested in what it was like for you, doing all the things you were doing for children, to be a woman at that time fighting against an establishment dominated by men.*

MWE: I had great parents, and they always made it clear that I was as smart as my three older brothers and my older sister. They made no distinctions; they had high expectations of all of us. That attitude was instilled in me. So I do exactly what my parents did: that's all I do. My dad was a great minister, a great preacher, and my mother was the church organist. She was absolutely the best organizer; she took in children after all of us left home. There was always the sense that I could do anything anybody else could do. The great benefit of segregation was that we were all exposed to [black] role models. When they came to town they had no place to stay except in people's homes. I saw Mary McLeod Bethune when I was eight or nine years old. I will never forget when she spoke at Benedict College; I had never seen a woman command a bunch of men in a room the way she did. She talked about "the blacker the berry, the sweeter the juice." I was exposed to so many strong women, starting with my mother, and I always knew I was as smart as my brothers.

There was always misogyny. I went to Spelman College in Atlanta, and that was terrific. I love the notion—I didn't at the time—of an all-black women's college. We had to be in at five thirty, and it was a ladies' tea party school, but there were many strong, smart, women professors, which was terrific, and Howard Zinn, who wrote *The People's History of the United States*, was the chair of the social sciences department. When I went to Yale Law School, I think they had nine women in that class. You would have thought Attila the Hun invaded Yale Law School. I hated law school. I saw all these people who had terrible complaints and had no lawyers, and I wondered what in the world I was doing at Yale.

All my SNCC friends had gone down to the South to organize for voter registration, and I got some money together so I could go down to Mississippi on spring break. I just felt like I was the luckiest person in the world to have been born at the intersection of great leaders and great events. In Greenwood, where the SNCC office was, there had been a shooting that night, and I went to the SNCC office the next morning, and that was the first time they brought dogs out against demonstrators in the South. I had promised my mother I wouldn't get arrested. But I knew I would get through law school and come back to Mississippi.

KK: *You were the first African American woman to pass the bar in Mississippi. Were you the first woman?*

MWE: I've never checked. I know I never saw another woman lawyer down there while I was there. There were four black lawyers, three of whom took civil rights cases, none of whom had gone to formal law school. I remember my first day in federal court with the notorious Judge [William H.] Cox. I walked into the chambers and they were all struck dumb—all the white men sitting around the judge's conference room. I went and I tried to shake every hand around the table, and not a man would shake my hand. It was like being a Martian. Eventually they tried to be friendly, and we worked out relationships. I got away with things as a woman that I probably could not have if I'd been a man. I probably would have gotten killed if I'd been a man.

One thing I learned is: You take no guff. I have my job to do. They learned after a very short period of time: Don't mess with her. I simply didn't tolerate it. They test you, and that doesn't last long with me, OK? The word gets out to leave her alone. I had zero tolerance, and that reputation got around very quickly. Besides, I had to get up in the morning and get people out of jail, and I had briefs to write. I guess because I had these three older brothers with whom I had to compete, I learned how to be a survivor. When I'm focused on something, don't get in the way.

I took a case for *Ebony* magazine because they had been sued by a young white man who claimed he'd been wrongly named as having been at a party at Ole Miss where there were blacks at the table. He was suing the magazine for libel. Another time I went down to Meridian, Mississippi, for a case before Judge Cox. He had a motion for [Neshoba County] Sheriff Lawrence Rainey and Deputy Sheriff Cecil Price, and this was after the murder of the civil rights workers, [Andrew] Goodman, [James] Chaney, and [Michael] Schwerner [in Neshoba County], and he sat those two murderers down at the table. And, I got so enraged, but I also realized that all of us are capable of terrible things. So much hatred came up in me.

KK: *How did you deal with that hatred?*

MWE: You swallow it. We knew what had happened to those boys. I never forgave Judge Cox. I also had to examine myself. It was horrible. You keep fighting.

KK: *You need allies; no one can do it alone.*

MWE: There are no friends in politics, and now we're facing another huge threat. The key is always to hold on to the infrastructure, no matter how radical the opposition. It's always about redefining the role of government, which means they want to take more money from the poor to give more tax breaks to people who don't need it, and to the military. It's an unbelievable time. I just keep saying we have to focus; we have to fight and be strategic. We've been here before. I just don't want my grandchildren fighting the same battles again.

Today it's going to have to be women and grandmothers and young people in the front lines of resistance. I don't know what we're going to do, but we're not going to go backward. You just have to go to the mat. You cannot lose the food safety net. There are twenty-five big issues, and we'll just have to figure out from our point of view. *How far are we prepared to go? Which three things for children do we have to hold on to at any cost?* We can't have hungry children again.

The point is, women's voices matter, children's voices matter. We need to create a new kind of theater. They cannot have this country, and they cannot have our children's future. It's a difficult period, but I hope women will step up to the plate. We've been in very difficult periods before.

I'll never forget the first time they brought police dogs and tried them out on SNCC kids. There were no lawyers, they were all in Jackson; and I tried to get down to the courthouse. I thought they were going to kill me, but there was a *New York Times* reporter there, and I thought, "He will tell the world what happens here." The media changes have made it much more complicated to develop issues to build a movement; there's so much stuff in the air. Movements don't happen overnight, they don't happen by sitting down, and it's not going to happen from the top. You really have to eat and sleep and cry with people; you have to get back to that basic stuff. Things are very scary right now, but they can't have this country.

―――――――――――――∞――――――――――――――

"In its most profound sense conservation means to care about the public good over private gain."

—ROBERT F. KENNEDY

―――――――――――――∞――――――――――――――

AL GORE

꧁∞꧂

From 1993 to 2001, Al Gore served as the forty-fifth vice president of the United States. He was narrowly defeated in the 2000 presidential election by 537 votes in Florida and a Supreme Court decision that ended a recount. He has been for many years an indefatigable advocate for the earth, which is desperately endangered by climate change. Owing in great part to his efforts, nations around the world are phasing out carbon emissions and converting to sustainable energy sources.

I worked with Senator Al Gore on protecting the land rights of a remote indigenous tribe in the South Pacific in the mid 1980s. One of his first acts as vice president in 1993 was to call in the Malawi Ambassador to the U.S., and threaten sanctions if they continued to imprison dissidents, including the RFK Human Rights Award laureate, Chakufwa Chihana. Gore's intervention helped lay the groundwork for elections six months later, for the first time in nearly three decades, ushering out dictator Hastings Banda and establishing democracy. He won the RFK Book Award in 1993 for *Earth in the Balance*, and the RFK Ripple of Hope Award in 2011 for his work on climate change.

Al Gore: When I was a young schoolboy, I had a headmaster who taught us, "We all face the same choice in life, over and over again, between the hard right and the easy wrong." Robert Kennedy showed that choosing the hard right was not only ennobling but also the way to change the world for the better. The things I remember best about him are the courage and eloquence he demonstrated during his presidential campaign. We hear most often about his eloquent speech on the night of Martin Luther King's assassination, but he said so many other things that stirred our conscience and called us to a higher purpose.

In his speech in Cape Town, he spoke of the danger that those who know what needs to be done, when confronting the obstacles and the opposition, will surrender to the feeling that one person can't make a difference and then give up the fight. There are many people who know what needs to be done, but those with the power to act must act.

During the darkest hours of the civil rights movement, Martin Luther King Jr., heard that people were discouraged and felt their efforts were futile. "How long is this going to take?" they asked. "It seems it will never change." He consoled them by saying, "How long? Not long, because no lie can live forever."

The essential obstacle to solving the climate crisis is the promulgation and acceptance of a lie, the lie that it's perfectly all right to continuously dump one hundred ten million tons of heat-trapping global-warming pollution into the thin shell of atmosphere surrounding our planet every twenty-four hours as if that atmosphere is an open sewer. It is not an open sewer. Heat-trapping gases, it turns out, comply with the laws of physics. They trap heat. The temperature is rising. The oceans are evaporating more moisture into the air, and the warmer air is holding more of it, and thus the water cycle of the entire earth is being disrupted. In recent times we've had once-in-a-thousand-years floods in city after city in countries all over this world. We've had twenty million people displaced from their homes in Pakistan, further destabilizing a nuclear-armed country. An area in Australia the size of France and Germany combined has been flooded out. In my home city of Nashville, Tennessee, not too long ago, thousands of my neighbors lost their homes and businesses; they had no flood insurance because it had never before flooded in the areas that were flooded; it was another once-in-a-thousand-years rainfall. In Vermont, when Hurricane Irene did an estimated $12 billion of damage, the governor of Vermont said, "We didn't used to have the climate of Central America. We used to have the climate of Vermont."

The same heat that is causing downpours of rain and snow is parching the soil and sucking the moisture from the land. In Texas, we've recently seen the worst year-round drought in the history of our nation, worse than the dust bowl in the 1930s by far. Wildfires regularly devastate Texas. I don't want to single out any governor of that state—it's a target-rich environment—but along with too many others, a Texas governor said, "This is a conspiracy by the scientific community to make up the science in order to earn more research grants: a lie." It was a lie when the tobacco companies hired actors and dressed them up as doctors and gave them scripts to read into the camera to reassure people that there was no medical consensus about cigarettes. A hundred million people died in the last century from cigarettes.

Of all the climate scientists who are most actively publishing, 97 percent to 98 percent support the consensus on climate change. Standing up as an individual means standing up with those scientists against our government to demand action. It really is a collective action: those who do not believe the lie, us, standing up against those who refuse to accept that it's a lie.

A great Irish boy, William Butler Yeats, once lamented that "the best lack all conviction and the worst are full of passionate intensity." We have seen the truth of that idea and how perilous it can be. Our government, of which we are so proud and which we love so much, has fallen on hard times. In computer terms, our democracy has been hacked. It's no longer operating to serve the public interest. We have to protect the ecological integrity of the earth while we can; the United States of America has to make a lot of changes. We now have—and I choose these words carefully—a government of, by, and for the special interests that provide the massive campaign and lobbying money that lubricates its operations, spins its revolving doors, and controls its policies and decisions. We, the people, have an opportunity to change that. But each of us, as individuals and as citizens, must be willing to follow the example of Robert F. Kennedy and speak truth to power.

The news media is way too silent about the climate crisis; they know that if they anger a meaningful percentage of their audience, their ratings suffer and it costs them money. It's similar to the scene that unfolds at some dinner tables, when a dysfunctional family suffers with an alcoholic father who flies into a rage if the word alcohol is mentioned. The rest of the family keeps quiet and never mentions the elephant in the room. We know this is true: "All that is necessary for evil to triumph is for good men to do nothing." Being willing to infuriate those who advocate destructive patterns of behavior and destructive public policies is essential, and Robert Kennedy never evaded those opportunities.

He knew that no lie can live forever. Every individual who takes action can make a difference.

Politicians are implicated because their continuing reliance on expensive television advertising has required them to spend the majority of every work day begging special interests for money to finance their campaigns. Human nature being what it is, they naturally tend to think more about what will be pleasing to the potential contributors they're going to call tomorrow than about the long-range public interests of their constituents. Their constituents, they've learned, can often be manipulated with well-crafted television advertising and reinforced by propagandistic news outlets like Fox News and Rush Limbaugh, so they feel safe in ignoring their constituents' best interests and joining the alternative reality put forward by a power bloc that has agreed to support one another's interests. Among these interests are always more tax cuts for the wealthy and more cuts in programs for those in need. All this is packaged with exaggerated fears that change will not be our friend and tied up with resentment of the progress that has been made on behalf of women, minorities, gays, and other vulnerable groups.

Kerry Kennedy: *Do you ever feel like Cassandra, repeating the same dire warnings for decades?*

AG: Well, it's taken some time, but I think most people do believe me now. That doesn't mean I stop trying to convince the rest. I've seen enough in my life to know that change follows a distinctive pattern. It's probably been best summarized by the late economist Rudi Dornbush, who wrote, "Things take longer to happen than you think they will. But then they happen much faster than you thought they could."

KK: *Ernest Hemingway's line about bankruptcy also applies to social change—it happens "gradually, and then all at once."*

AG: Nelson Mandela said, during the antiapartheid struggle, "It's always impossible, until it's done." If you look back on the history of the great moral causes of the last two centuries, they all follow that same pattern: the abolition movement; the struggle for women's suffrage and women's rights; the civil rights movement, of which RFK was such an important part; the antiapartheid movement, which he also supported; and more recently the gay rights movement. All the advocates in all those movements had to fortify their hopes against despair. Dr. King famously reassured us that "the moral arc of the universe bends towards justice." I'm fond of a line of poetry from the great American poet Wallace Stevens, who wrote, "After the final no comes a yes / And on that yes the future world depends." In fact, in the climate movement, right now, we're at a tipping point, the point between things taking longer than you think they will and things suddenly changing much faster than you thought they could. All over the world, change is taking place, despite President Trump's withdrawal of the United States from the Paris climate change agreement of 2015. India recently announced that within fifteen years, 100 percent of that country's vehicles will be electric. China's emissions have shown zero growth or decline four years in a row. Both China and India are on track to reach their Paris commitments more than ten years ahead of the deadline they set. India's moving dramatically toward more solar and less coal. Cities throughout the United States are now making commitments to shift to 100 percent clean energy; most recently the sprawling metropolis of Atlanta made that commitment. Solar jobs in the United States are now growing seventeen times faster than job growth generally. The fastest-growing job for the next ten years, according to the Bureau of Labor Statistics, is wind power technician. A sustainability revolution is emerging all over the world, with the scope of the industrial revolution and the speed of the digital revolution, and instead of starting in a corner of England in a world of 1.5 billion people and spreading slowly to Western Europe and North America, this revolution is emerging simultaneously in rich and poor countries alike, in a world of 7.4 billion people, and it's unstoppable. So no, I don't feel like Cassandra at all.

And by the way, that pattern is also very clear in the world of technology. We've seen it before with computer chips and mobile phones and flat-screen TVs, and now we're seeing it with solar panels and windmills and batteries and electric vehicles. It took a long time for a little progress, and now the progress is moving forward at warp speed. In many places in the world, electricity from solar panels is now less than half as expensive as electricity from burning coal and gas! That trend is continuing, by the way.

KK: *There's a great quote of yours: "When we join forces for a purpose that is manifestly good and true, the spiritual energy released can transform us." It's pretty extraordinary what you've done. You must look back with pride.*

AG: Well, pride, I'm told, is a sin, but yes, absolutely, I do feel that it is a privilege and a source of joy to have work that justifies pouring every ounce of energy you have into it, and that task gives you energy back in return.

KK: *Your commitment was unrelenting in the many years when people weren't listening and when the antiscience brigade dominated, but you never stopped rallying those who believe in science, and now you assert that in spite of Trump, the world will continue to move toward protecting the planet. What does it take to stay the course when it's not clear that you're making an impact?*

AG: I could say I simply didn't have the skill to do anything else. The truth is I've given innumerable speeches to groups I knew full well did not want to hear about the climate crisis at all, not to mention how to solve it. It's just second nature for me by now, and it certainly doesn't feel particularly heroic. It's just what I do. I know it's not futile. And yes, it energizes me. It's worth doing.

KK: *How about at the beginning? Was there a time, maybe on a different issue, when you had doubts?*

AG: Well, there've been many times when I knew what I was saying or doing would cost me votes. I remember speaking about gay rights to people in Tennessee during my presidential campaign in 2000. I said that gay and lesbian people should be treated like everybody else. I must confess that like President Obama and many others, I was slow to endorse gay marriage, and I'm embarrassed to look back at times in my life when I held the view that being gay was somehow abnormal. When you learn what is undeniably true and just, you have to speak what you know to be true and just. If that has political consequences, so be it.

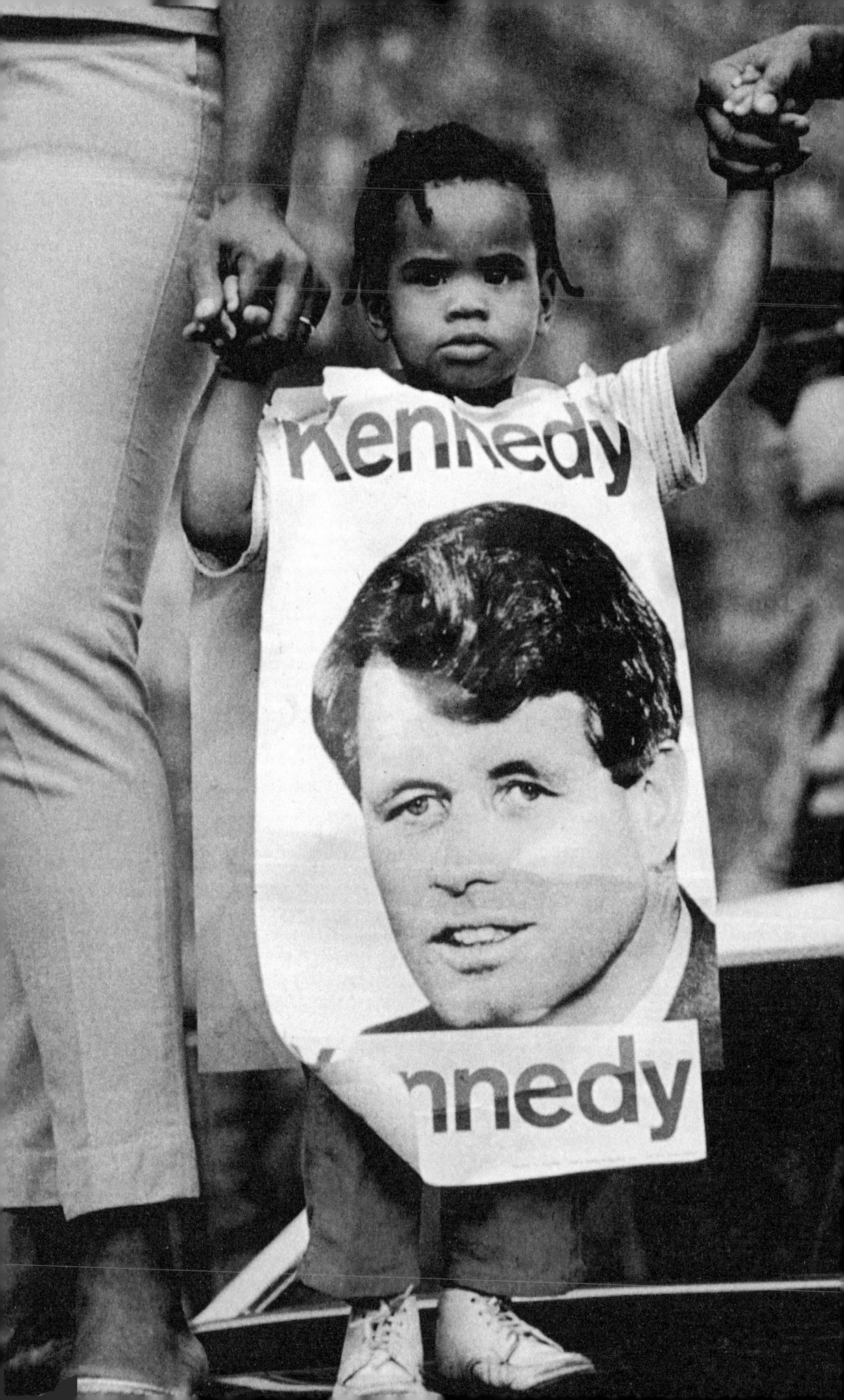
Kennedy
nnedy

"We must recognize the full human equality of all our people before God, before the law, and in the councils of government. We must do this not because it is economically advantageous, although it is; not because the laws of God command it, although they do; not because people in other lands wish it so. We must do it for the single and fundamental reason that it is the right thing to do."

—ROBERT F. KENNEDY

Campaign trail, California, 1968 (Steve Schapiro/ Fahey Klein Gallery)

"All around our nations, Negroes and Puerto Ricans, Mexican Americans and Indians, poor whites in Appalachia and in blighted inner cities, are waking up to what we have. They are demanding their rights as human beings. They are demanding what the rest of us have taken for granted—a measure of control over their lives, over their destinies, a sense of communication with those whom they have elected to represent to government. If we do not yield, if we do not work a virtual revolution in the organization of our social services, the result could be the ripping asunder of the already thin fabric of American life."

—ROBERT F. KENNEDY

LaDONNA HARRIS

⌒∞⌒

LaDonna Vita Tabbytite Harris is the founder of Americans for Indian Opportunity (AIO), which advances, from an indigenous worldview, the cultural, political, and economic rights of indigenous peoples in the United States and around the world. She was a founder of Common Cause, is active in the leadership of numerous other advocacy organizations, and was an honorary cochair of the 2017 Women's March on Washington. Her autobiography, published in 2000, is LaDonna Harris: A Comanche Life.

LaDonna and her husband, Senator Fred Harris, lived down the street from our family in McLean, Virginia. Fred and my father were close allies in the Senate, and LaDonna was one of the leading advocates for Native American rights, which were very important to Daddy both as attorney general and later as senator. We often visited Indian reservations, and our home was filled with extraordinary artwork and craftsmanship from Native Americans. The Harrises often came to our home, and my mother and father took us on walks during the weekend, when we would drop in on our neighbors. LaDonna held a special place in my heart as a child, and I was delighted to reconnect with her after many decades for this interview.

Kerry Kennedy: *LaDonna, let's just go back to that day when you were at our dining table in Virginia in 1965. You were there with your grandmother. Her name was Wiki Tabbytite.*

LaDonna Harris: My husband, Fred, was senator then—he was working closely with your father—and your mother invited us over when she found out my grandmother was coming to Washington. My grandmother had given Lady Bird Johnson a shawl when she was campaigning in Oklahoma City, and Lady Bird said, "When you come to Washington, we'll give you a tour of the White House." It was her first plane ride ever, and she met all the members of the Senate, and your mother invited us to come to your house for tea. All of you were in that little sunroom at Hickory Hill, and you got to ask your questions. My grandmother made you a member of the Comanche tribe and gave you an Indian name. Do you still remember it?

KK: *Yes! Tsah Wakie, it means "One who looks for the best in everything"! I still have the certificate she gave me that day—it's one of my prized possessions. My father had such a special affinity with the Indians, and I picked up on that. When he asked what we wanted to be when we grew up, my siblings all said a lawyer or a vet or a senator and I always said I wanted to be an Indian. Kind of cute, but really it came from a child's understanding of her father's deep respect for and the depth of his bond with so many tribes.*

LH: That's it! Oh, yes, thank you for remembering. It just makes me think of her.

KK: *I could never forget that name. I use it all the time; my kids even know that name.*

LH: Good! Well, she always wore traditional clothes and braided hair, and she told everybody when she got back that she met all of Bobby Kennedy's children, and Ethel—that meant a lot to her, because it was so personal and intimate with your mother at your house. Before she went to your house, the international press wanted to interview her, and they asked her what impressed her the most, and she said, "All these trees."

She didn't say any of the people that she met; she'd had a tour of the White House and everything. She was impressed by the green trees in Northern Virginia too. In Western Oklahoma it's all brown flat plains.

KK: *My father visited Pine Ridge Reservation in South Dakota for the second time during the '68 presidential campaign. On June 5, 1968, he found out he'd won 99 percent of the vote from Pine Ridge. Why was he so popular in Indian country?*

LH: Well, he wasn't just a politician. He showed real concern and real interest. He knew how to talk to people and get them to express themselves on whatever issues that were important to them. Nobody else did that. I call South Dakota and North Dakota our Mississippi—the Indians' Mississippi—the treatment was so blatantly prejudiced there. People up there, how they were treated, it was just two hundred times worse than anything I ever experienced growing up in Oklahoma. They were just so abused, they seemed to be trapped, until he came along. He came in 1963 and gave a beautiful speech to the National Conference of American Indians in South Dakota, and the people responded to him. He made a difference. Those children and young people in Oklahoma, it was the highlight of their youth to meet him. They went on to college, many of them, and they would come up to me years later and say, "Miss Harris, I'm one of your OIO babies, and now I've got a degree, or a master's degree, I'm working on my PhD." OIO is Oklahomans for Indian Opportunity, which was our educational program. Your father touched many lives because he knew how to listen. Your father and my husband, Fred, were trying to protect the poor people in the committee hearings. The Senate was going to change the law to make poor people, including Indians, work for their welfare checks.

KK: *That's not necessarily a bad idea, unless there are literally no jobs at all, which is what they faced in the Dakotas. And government must educate students so graduates are prepared to take those jobs.*

LH: I listened in on that hearing. Your father asked questions in a way that helped the Indians who were testifying make their case. It was poignant. Your father and Fred worked together on a lot of things, along with Senator [Walter] Mondale. They were the youngest members of the Senate, and they all sat together in the back, and they got themselves in lots of trouble sometimes. They stood up against the old guys in the Senate on many issues. It was great!

KK: *LaDonna, what comes through so much in your life story is how you were able both to retain traditional Comanche values and to integrate fully into the dominant colonial society. That had to be a very difficult balance.*

LH: Many times it was. The Southwest Center for Human Relations Studies—they were the intellectuals of Oklahoma—they asked Fred to be on the board and he didn't have the time, but he told them that if they asked me, they'd get two for one, since I'd tell him what I was doing and get his input. When they were talking about African American affairs and labor relations, I asked them, "What about Indians?" They said, "The Bureau of Indian Affairs is taking care of them." I burst into tears. I said, "That's part of the problem." I lacked the confidence to communicate to them what the issue was. Many people have prejudice, and they're not even aware of it. When we were interviewing Indian children trying to figure out how to stop the horrible dropout rate, eighth and ninth graders would say, "Indians can't make straight A's." We would ask why they thought that was true, and they said their teachers told them that. We said, "Well, that girl sitting next to you made straight A's!" They had such low self-esteem.

As a child, I was called *squaw* and *gut eater*. I came crying to my grandmother, and she told me, "They're just pitiful people and they don't understand you. They don't know about Indians. They don't know about our values. Don't be mad; you just have to figure out a way to talk to them." Let me go back to that values thing. One of the things that even Native peoples were saying was that Indian people live in two worlds: their cultural world and the white world. You're leaving your values at home and changing your values when you come off the reservation and go into town. That's not a good thing, because we don't live in two worlds, we live in one world.

So we really worked on that, and we found that encouraging people to celebrate the richness of their own culture was helping them with their identity and making them stronger and more able to contribute. When we reinforced them in their worldview, they became independent individuals. They were Indians who had their own values, living in the larger world, but carrying their values with them.

KK: *Did you still experience a tension between being an advocate for Indian rights and, as a woman, having to advocate for women's rights within the Indian movement?*

LH: I did, but in Comanche culture, it was a more balanced society. There wasn't such a great distinction. Women controlled the home, the cultural and community activities, and we are matrilineal. When a young man married, he came to live with his wife's people, and he would be indoctrinated in the way the wife's family did things. There were certain etiquettes: the mother-in-law shouldn't speak directly to her son-in-law, for example; she should tell her daughter to tell the son-in-law what she wanted him to know, so there would be no possibility of disruption or argument. The culture was designed to alleviate any dysfunction or conflict; we had protocols designed to do that. If a man bragged too much when he came home from war, or said he had done this or that, and that proved not to be so, the woman could give him a war bonnet, and he would have to live up to the war bonnet, which might really endanger his life. A woman could discipline a man publicly if he misbehaved or abused her. Children were never physically punished; I was never physically punished. Parents are supposed to be loving. If some discipline was needed, they could ask the aunty or the uncle to come and verbally correct the children. It was done just with tone of voice. Women's roles were quite equal to the men's: the women were heads of households, while the men were off hunting or raiding. It was a more equitable community, more balanced.

The struggle was never for women's equality in the Native American community, except for where cultural oppression took over. The struggle was to educate the women's movement about women of color. That's where the struggle was.

It was very hard. I was an original convener at the Women's Political Caucus, with Gloria Steinem and Shirley Chisholm. At the start, we noticed that almost everybody was Anglo, so they said, "Can we reach out and get some diversity?" We had sessions with African American women, and they would wind up with each group being almost mad at the other. So they started their own group, and the indigenous women started our own group. I could never figure out what the problems had been with communication. It was insidious; it was so embedded in the American culture that it was difficult to get to the bottom of the disagreements. I felt I had let everybody down. I still don't know how to tell an individual what it is in her behavior that hurts people who are being excluded. I still haven't been able to get that. There's something about it: people have their truth; their point of view is the truth, so somebody else's can't be true. It's white privilege, I guess; that's the term everybody's using nowadays. They don't even see that they're acting that way. They would be appalled if somebody brought it to their attention. It's not something like Jim Crow laws, something obvious; it's more subtle, so you don't see the barriers, you just see that people can't get past them.

The thing about your father was that he knew how to get past things like that. He knew he needed to learn and he wanted to learn. He didn't have an attitude of White privilege toward people of color or any people who were different from himself. You always got the feeling you could share with him, and he would understand what you were saying. My strength, which is from my Comanche culture, is that I would wait to read people. I learned that at a very early age. I think it was kind of a defense mechanism, a way to make sure these people wouldn't be able to hurt my feelings. I would figure out how to work with them. Even in high school, I was the first Indian ever nominated for anything. I give my Comanche grandmother and grandfather credit for it: they taught me how to be fair with people who were not informed about our culture.

If you use a lot of negative energy, they've defeated you, because then they've taken away some of your medicine. I shared many of our Comanche ideas with your dad. I talked to him about how everybody has medicine. That's the philosophy of the Comanche. Everybody has medicine; everybody has value. When people are hurtful, just look at them and think, "Bless your heart, you don't know any better." I don't feel bad about it anymore, though sometimes I still get aggravated. I try to give some of my time to helping people understand Indians. We have a slide show presentation—"Indian 101" workshop, because most Americans don't know much about Native Americans as we are not in the history books. We talk about history, the different cultures and different values, and the whole thing is reinforcing their understanding that our worldview is valuable enough that it should be at the table.

KK: *Mental health is a big issue in Indian Country, where the suicide rates are horrifically high. You've worked to help people with mental health challenges, and you investigated conditions in institutions back in the 1960s. Are you surprised that fifty years later we still don't treat mental health on parity with physical health?*

LH: While living in Washington, there was a need for a Native American to serve on Carter's Commission on the Mental Health of Children. I was the only person without any education in the field; everybody else had two or three degrees and they were professors of psychology or psychiatry. I went to that meeting—and this is the example of not recognizing their own issues. They would come up with something, these great learned people, and they would say such and such, and I would say, "Well, I don't think that would apply to children of color. I know for sure it wouldn't apply to Indian children." They were very condescending; they said, "That's all right, LaDonna," and they just went on. I liked them individually, and I decided to invite them to the house for summer supper. In the meantime, my Comanche relatives from

Oklahoma were in town, because we were starting Americans for Indian Opportunity, so I invited them to come out too. We'd all had cocktails, and Bill, who worked with me and was Comanche, walked up to one of those PhD doctors, and who was wearing a bolo tie. Bill grabbed that bolo and said, "Just be glad it's wooden. If it was turquoise I'd have to whip your ass." At my little dinner party! But nobody heard me when I tried to explain the issue to them. One of my other guests was an African American professor of psychiatry, from Harvard, and they talked to him. He could speak their language, so he didn't sound like the angry black man, but to have this angry Indian attack this guy with a bolo tie, that was just beyond their perception. At the next meeting we had—they had called a special meeting—they said, "We're going to create a committee on the mental health of minority children," and they did that. They said I planned it that way, and I said, "No, I didn't. But I'm glad you're doing this!" On that committee we had two black psychiatrists; a Hispanic; another Indian activist, Ada Deer; a Japanese man who was in a concentration camp as a child; and me. It was a really neat group. The black psychiatrist from Harvard was there too, Price Cobbs, who, with William Grier, coauthored the book *Black Rage*. Our approach was, we looked at the patient, we looked at the abused person. Our conclusion: white racism was the number one mental health problem for children. The Commission wouldn't accept our report. They rejected the report from all these great, learned people; they wouldn't incorporate it. It's somewhere in the basement of the National Institute of Mental Health. It never got published.

What I tell people now is, Let's quit looking at the victims, and let's look at the perpetrators. Let's say, "What is wrong on that side of it?" It's so difficult to talk about white privilege—I don't even love the term—but how do we talk about it so people can look at themselves and see what they're doing? So much of it is from childhood experiences. I know I had to clean up my language coming from Oklahoma, because we had funny little tacky things we said, that were names—"Little Sharpshooter" and things—that were racist by nature. The children and I used to have games at the house, and if people said anything racist or antifeminist, they'd have marks against them and we'd get to make fun of them. They caught me—I wasn't as bad as they were, but we all have it. First you have to recognize how people get that way. We all had little goofy, ugly, racist names for certain kinds of things. We learned not to say those things. And also sexist things, we got sexist terminology out of our vocabulary too. When we talk about race, we tend to look at the victims: "Isn't that a shame what's happening to them?" What you need to think about is what a person in a racist society has to think up in their minds to adequately exist in that society. The browning of America is occurring with our Hispanic population, and ours, and all the people of color are having children, and the other population is going down. I think that's what we're seeing in the West; they're afraid the people of color are going to take over. That's why they were so mean and ugly to Obama. I think they felt he was instrumental in the browning of America, on his own. If you look at our population now, there's nobody really preparing us for it. We look at it as a racist society, which it is. What we need to do is figure out other ways of talking to each other. We need to understand how people deceive themselves. We need to see how that affects people of color who suffer from racism. That's the behavior that makes children of color suffer from mental health issues. Racism can mess up your mind, whether you're a racist or a victim of racism.

I always knew I didn't have the answers. I went to my grandmother, and I said I was having a problem, and she said to me in Comanche, but I'm translating, "I don't know what to tell you because what you're going through is so different from what I went through." She went to an Indian boarding school; she was actually born in a Tipi. She told me, "You're going to have to figure it out yourself. Use your Comanche ways to figure it out. You don't have to have all the answers; the people you're working with will help you solve your issues." We organized Oklahomans for Indian Opportunity; we lowered the dropout rate from 75 percent to 35 percent in the Indian community; we started some businesses; we started Americans for Indian Opportunity; and it was those Indian values that helped me succeed in those things. Those values are still strong; we always go to the community for help, to work out the issues we have. We have an ambassadors program; it's a leadership program. We looked up the word *leadership* in the dictionary and it said "somebody who has authority over someone." We knew that didn't match our values in the Indian community, so we call them ambassadors from their tribe.

Everybody has medicine; some people's medicine is nurturing. Your mom and dad both nurtured you, to have a drive to do good in the community. That comes from recognizing that everybody has value. I think your dad had that medicine—to nurture and to recognize that everybody has value. And he was always a fighter for justice for the poor and minorities.

KK: *LaDonna, talk about violence perpetrated by non-Indians against women.*

LH: We can never stop fighting. In 1978, they took away our jurisdiction. We have sophisticated tribal court systems, but we no longer have jurisdiction over criminal acts committed on the reservation by non-Indians. When people got arrested, if they weren't a member of the tribe, we had no control over them, and there are nowhere near enough federal prosecutors to handle the rapes and other violent crimes. Amnesty International did a study on how many rape cases were perpetrated by non-Indian people coming onto the reservation, and there were a huge number, because serial rapists knew they could get away with it. The Violence Against Women Act was up for reauthorization in 2013, and we fought for and got back the power to prosecute non-Indians who perpetrate violent crimes against Native women on tribal land. It was a great victory, and the women's movement came together and helped us do that—Amnesty International and the women's movement in Washington.

KK: *As I recall, one-third of all rapes of Indian women on the reservation were committed by off-reservation white men. I don't know if I mentioned this to you, but I was the chair of the Amnesty International leadership council at that time. We launched that report at the National Museum of the American Indian in New York City. There was a woman there who said: "My great-grandmother was raped. My grandmother was raped. My mother was raped. I was raped. My daughter was raped. My daughter just gave birth to my granddaughter, and I don't want her to be raped."*

LH: It's particularly bad in South and North Dakota. When I was traveling around, teaching at colleges, I experienced it. You felt like you were in danger all the time. You had to be on alert. There were places in Nebraska and also in New Mexico that were just as notorious. The women voters' organization studied that for a while and found that more of our people were arrested and had longer jail sentences. The Indians in South Dakota were 7 percent of the total population and 16 percent of the prison population. Now they're into the sex trade in North Dakota—that's so scary. It's the oil boom up there. It's destroying the communities affected by it. We can never stop fighting, and we will never stop fighting.

"When your children and grandchildren
take their place in America—going to high
school and college and taking good jobs at
good pay—when you look at them you will
say, 'I did this. I was there at the point of
difficulty and danger.' And though you may
be old and bent from years of labor, no man
will stand taller than you when you say,
'I marched with Cesar.' You stand for
justice, and I am proud to stand with
you. Viva la Causa."

—ROBERT F. KENNEDY

DOLORES HUERTA

In 1962, when farmworkers in California earned minimal pay, had horrible working conditions, and were abused by the growers who employed them, Dolores Huerta left her job organizing for the Catholic Service Organization to join Cesar Chavez in cofounding the nation's first successful farmworkers' union. While working for the United Farm Workers (UFW), Huerta was physically attacked by growers and law enforcement officials and was denied justice by the legal system—a common occurrence for strikers—but through her hard work and persistence, she impelled the passage of many laws that protect farmworkers. She continues this fight today through the Dolores Huerta Foundation, which supports community organizing in low-income communities.

Dolores and I have worked together advocating for farmworkers' rights across the country. She joined me in Albany lobbying for rights to a day off per week, overtime, and worker's comp. Dolores and I met for this interview in my apartment. My daughter, Mariah, who just completed her thesis on Cesar Chavez and Robert Kennedy, joined the conversation.

Dolores Huerta: The first time we met Senator Kennedy was when he arrived in Delano for the Senate hearing in March 1966. There were a lot of spectators in the stands, and people had set up a passageway with flags along it, and the senator was going to walk between the flags. What happened was that when he got there, nobody paid any attention to the flags; they all just crowded around him so enthusiastically that I thought, "Oh my god, we're going to crush him." The people just zoomed in and surrounded him. That walk of honor between the flags didn't work out at all.

We were having a strike at that time, and the Kern County sheriff had arrested some of our peaceful pickets after scabs threatened them. During the hearing, your father asked the sheriff why he had arrested our people, and the sheriff said it was because the scabs had said, "If you don't get them out of here, we're going to cut their hearts out." The sheriff said, "Rather than let them get cut, we removed the cause." Senator Kennedy said, "How can you go arrest somebody if they haven't violated the law?" The sheriff said, "They were ready to violate the law." Senator Kennedy said, "Could I suggest that during the luncheon period the sheriff and the district attorney read the Constitution of the United States?" That hearing became pretty famous, but the main thing was that Senator Kennedy was committed to our cause after that.

The morning after the hearing, Senator Kennedy was still in Delano—we were going to start a farmworkers' march to Sacramento—and the police all got in front of the marchers, to try to keep them from marching. Your father called the chief of police and said something to him like, "Are you going to try to stop them from marching?" There's film of this that shows police dressed in black and white; that was the Delano Police Department. You see them walking away, and that was because your father had told them they couldn't stop the march: they had to get out of the way.

From that time on, your father did a lot to help us. There was no twenty-four-hour medical facility in Delano. They had maybe one or two doctors there, who were very much against the union. To give you an example, there was a farmworker who had hurt his arm, and he went to this doctor, and the doctor gave him some kind of a lotion to put on his arm. We took the worker to Bakersfield to get an Xray, and he had a broken arm. The lotion wasn't going to help that. So we decided we had to start a clinic, a volunteer clinic, and we found doctors who would come on a certain schedule to a house we had rented where the clinic was in one room. I think it was the Garment Workers' Union that was helping to fund this. Your father came to California and did a couple of fund-raisers for us to raise more money for the clinic.

Kerry Kennedy: *I visited the headquarters a few months ago and I was touched to learn that the UFW named the plan after my father—RFK Health. Today it covers tens of thousands of farmworkers.*

DH: Yes, exactly. But the funding is now under attack by the Republicans. . . . In the winter of 1968, January or February, we had all these farmworkers who rode on a school bus from Delano to New York City to picket at the Hunts Point Market. It was icy and cold, and some of the workers who were picketing slipped and fell on the ice, and then they were all arrested. So I called the senator's office and I told him—there was a Latina woman who worked for him for many years, Angie Cabrera—and I said to her, "You know they arrested the farmworkers. Could you send somebody to help them?" They sent an attorney right down there to get the farmworkers out of jail.

It was because of all the things he had done for us that I went to the senator's office to see if he could come out to Delano when Cesar ended his fast in 1968. Your father said he would, of course, and that's when the whole thing happened with people cheering and saying they wanted him to run for president. He did announce he was running just a few days later.

When Cesar did that fast, it was kind of the first time that anyone had done something like that. Now people fast all the time. I remember I was here in New York when Cesar told us he was going to fast. He fasted for seven or eight days, and I remember how I felt sick for him that he wasn't eating. We had a press conference in New York because we wanted people to know who Cesar was and what he was doing and why; we said, "Our union president, Cesar Chavez, is on a fast." These New York labor guys got mad. "What kind of a president would do that? What kind of a kook is that?" It was something novel at that time.

Through everything, Robert Kennedy's support was very important for us. He was sincere, and even though he didn't speak Spanish, he just connected with people. He was genuine; he wasn't uppity. You could tell that he cared.

His support was also important because it put us on an actual stage. When a senator from New York came to speak to farmworkers in Delano and support our union, it was a turning point for us. It definitely put the farmworkers on the map. Before that, people didn't know who Cesar was; they didn't know what we were doing; they didn't know about the struggle.

Robert Kennedy related to working people; he related to poor people; and he was always about solutions. You can think about Bedford-Stuyvesant, too, the Bedford Stuyvesant Restoration Corporation, and the work he was doing there in that neighborhood where poor people and black people lived and still live. Think about when he went to Appalachia. He always connected with the poorest people. Think about the farmworkers. He was about solutions, and people admire him so much for that. He could make that connection with people and work to help them solve problems. This is my philosophy too. People are capable of solving all kinds of problems; sometimes they just need to be taught how. Your father didn't really get a lot of mileage out of going to Bedford-Stuyvesant or going to the farmworkers; he didn't get any great political gain. He just went to the places where people had the most need and where his presence and his support would not only put a spotlight on them but also give people some dignity. A lot of times poor people don't have dignity. Working people don't have dignity. Your father paid attention to their troubles, and he helped them where they needed help. He dignified them.

KK: *Daddy wanted to be there when Cesar ended the fast. He spoke to thousands of farmworkers who had come to the mass, and he modeled his tribute to Cesar on a speech from one of Shakespeare's* Henry V: *"When your children and grandchildren take their place in America—going to high school and college and taking good jobs at good pay—when you look at them you will say, 'I did this. I was there at the point of difficulty and danger.' And though you may be old and bent from years of labor, no man will stand taller than you when you say, 'I marched with Cesar.'" And my father added, "You stand for justice, and I am proud to stand with you. Viva la Causa."*

DH: Yes, that was wonderful, but things are still not good for poor people and working people today. The inequality of wealth and income is extreme today compared with fifty years ago. Back in the sixties, what a CEO made was forty times more than what a worker made. Today it's like five hundred times more than a worker. We have this huge income spread between working people and CEOs, and it affects most people very badly. The working people are struggling; people have to work two jobs, and mortgages are so high—people are getting gentrified out of their homes in San Francisco, Oakland, and plenty of other places. Ordinary people are just not respected.

Politicians today are not respected either, and this hurts our democracy because the politicians today are beholden to corporate interests and to special interests. It's worse now than it was fifty years ago. Your father was someone who wasn't afraid to take on the status quo and the people in power. He wasn't afraid to challenge them. It would be better if our politicians weren't afraid to stand up against the special interest system to defend the rights of disenfranchised people. Your father did that.

I guess *courage* is the big word there. I remember when John Kennedy was president, and the steelworkers went on strike, and he said to the steel companies, "I want to see your books because you're saying you can't give these steelworkers a raise," and that ended the strike. It would be interesting to have a president who's on the side of the workers instead of on the corporations' side, especially right now.

When you think of Senator Kennedy, you know he was for justice. He was for fairness. He was for equality. People talk about this today: "The country is so divided." Well, the country was divided then, too.

A lot of the establishment was for the war in Vietnam, but your father came out against the war, and some people thought it was a betrayal of the whole defense industry and the Cold War. In '68 we met with Gene McCarthy, who was against the war, and we met with Humphrey too, and we asked them to support the boycott we were in at that time, and both of them refused to support the farmworkers.

Once Cesar was asked, "What's going to happen to the union once you're gone?" and his answer was, "If I would have thought that the union would not survive without me, I never would have started one in the first place." When he died so suddenly and unexpectedly, I had to remember those words. Through both the foundation and the organization, we were able to get some important laws passed for farmworkers, especially the right to organize. That is in place now in California, but still not yet in New York.

In California, regardless of who becomes president of the union, we have the procedures and mechanisms so farmworkers can get a collective bargaining contract. It's there, and knowing that made it less of a catastrophe for the organization when Cesar passed away. Cesar and I had a lot in common in our ways of thinking. When we first started the organization, one of the things we really wanted to do was follow Gandhi's model. Maybe it was too idealistic, but we always have tried to stay at the level of the workers themselves. That's why we didn't have salaries in the union, which became a big issue later on when there was a lot of money coming in from dues, and our plan was to get as much money as we could so we could expand to other states. Our plan was to try to have a national organization, and we were so successful in those first years that we thought it was a possibility. We had contracts in Texas, in Colorado, in parts of New Mexico, because California's agriculture businesses had workers in these other states, so the union was able to follow them. We had over three thousand workers under contract in Florida, too, with collective bargaining agreements, pensions, and medical plans. A lot of people who worked for the union saw that money coming in and didn't want to continue on poverty wages; they wanted better lives for their families. So that changed after Cesar was gone, which you can justify, but it did take away from the movement feeling of the organization.

You need faith. When I first went to Delano, I was going through a divorce, and I already had seven children at that time. I wondered if getting involved with trying to create a new union would be the right thing or the wrong thing for my children. I remember taking a hot bath and sitting in the tub for about an hour, thinking about what I was going to do. I prayed. I asked for a sign. One of my daughters was making her confirmation, and I didn't have the money to buy her shoes. She just had these little white tennis shoes and they had holes in them. When we went to the mass, I was dreading to see my daughter come down the aisle with these tennis shoes with holes in them. The parish was in the farmworker area, and just before my daughter got to me, there were little farm girls coming down the aisle wearing tennis shoes with holes in them. I said, "That's my answer." I knew from that sign that working with the union was the right thing to do.

Still, in all the work I've done as an organizer, one of the hardest things has been the knowledge that your struggle for your cause is going to affect your kids.

A lot of people criticized me at the beginning for leaving my teaching job to go to Delano. We were three bilingual teachers in the school district so we always had a lot of work and a comfortable salary. To leave that to become an organizer, not knowing where my salary would be coming from, got me a lot of criticism. My friends said, "Your children are going to become drug addicts; you're crazy to be doing this." People ostracized me when I went to Delano; they thought I was making a foolish decision. It wasn't until the farmworkers got a lot of publicity after Robert Kennedy came that people decided it was wonderful what we were doing. Before that, the people Cesar grew up with in Delano admired him because he did such great stuff when he was with Community Service Organization, but when we started the union they all turned against him. That was because we were going against the growers, and people had friends who were growers. It was an agricultural community. Some people had relatives working with the growers. Also it was during the Vietnam War, and we were antiwar, so people in our community were not always in favor of all the things we supported.

Another thing was that when we were organizing, Cesar's wife, Helen, was in the fields picking grapes. She had eight kids, and people made fun of her because her work was supporting the family while Cesar was organizing. The workers' wages when we first started were like seventy to ninety cents an hour. Our food was basically what the farmworkers got. We had cornmeal and oatmeal and lard and beans and rice and flour. We were only paying ourselves, Cesar and me, like $30 a week, and sometimes not even that much; we had enough to pay the rent, but it was tough. When the strike broke out and we got donations, that kind of saved us.

KK: *Dolores, your commitment to the farmworkers has never wavered. A few years ago you joined me in Albany trying to get legislation passed here [in New York], and there was so much fear about change among those state senators, but you kept reassuring them that their farms would be just fine and they didn't need to depend on exploited labor. You were inspiring.*

You've always been willing to take on an issue even when your family or friends or community didn't agree with you, but it still must have been difficult to come out as pro-choice when you've worked for so long with Catholic farmworkers who are not pro-choice. You used to travel the country making pro-life speeches with Phillis Schlafly, who is credited with single-handedly stopping the Equal Rights Amendment. How did you come to change your ideas about abortion?

DH: You always have to accept that change is constant. You couldn't really stop it if you wanted to. I've known Gloria Steinem for quite some time, and we've argued about a whole range of issues, including abortion. We used to have conversations about this all the time. I'm Catholic, I have a big family, and I always thought abortion was a mortal sin. In all our discussions, we evolved to talking about it in terms of "choice," which I think is a good word, especially for women who are uncomfortable with the issue of abortion. Gloria would invite me to go with her on her speaking engagements, and I would go and speak about the boycott, and I would listen to what Gloria would say to women in her audiences. Later I met Eleanor Smeal, the founder of Feminist Majority, and I listened to her, and I came to understand that women can never be truly free unless they can decide about their own bodies. I see that clearly now. I had a transformation on the issue. The other important thing for me is that we really have to fight for early childhood education, for the sake of the children and also so that women can participate in civic life. That has to be seen as a right we all have, so that women don't feel they have no choice except to be the homemaker and the sole caretaker for the children. We have to free women so we can save the world. I quote Coretta Scott King all the time; she said, "We will never have peace in the world until women take power."

People criticized us for forming the union and for not caring for our children the right way. They will criticize me for my transformation. People are always going to criticize you no matter what, and you have to just keep on ignoring that.

---⚬---

"It is from the numberless diverse acts of courage and belief that human history is shaped."

—Robert F. Kennedy

---⚬---

Robert Kennedy greeted by a local leader in Colombia (Steve Schapiro/ Fahey Klein Gallery)

---∞---

*"Compassion and love and peace.
That's what this country should stand
for, and that's what I intend to do
if I am elected president."*

—Robert F. Kennedy

---∞---

VAN JONES

⚬◇◦

CNN host Van Jones is a social justice innovator who has launched several successful change-making enterprises, including the Ella Baker Center for Human Rights and ColorOfChange.org. A former special adviser to the Obama White House, he rose to national prominence promoting eco-friendly, "green jobs" for low-income communities. Today, his Dream Corps organization leads four major initiatives: #YesWeCode, working to help 100,000 young women and men from underrepresented backgrounds find success in the tech sector; #cut50, working to make communities safer while reducing the number of people in prisons and jails; #LoveArmy, creating alternatives to hate-based political movements; and Green For All, to advance environmental solutions for families and workers living close to sources of pollution.

He is the author of three New York Times *bestsellers:* The Green Collar Economy, Rebuild the Dream, *and* Beyond The Messy Truth. *A Yale-educated attorney, Van's guiding slogan is: close prison doors and open doors of opportunity.*

I met Van in 1998, when I was a judge for the Reebok Human Rights Award and Van was the recipient. His acceptance at the ceremony was one of the best speeches I had ever heard. I went to visit the program he ran at the Ella Baker Center in San Francisco, and was deeply impressed by his cutting-edge efforts combating police brutality. That led to his work on juvenile justice reform and creating green jobs for formerly incarcerated youth. Van served on the board of directors of RFK Human Rights.

Van Jones: You know, I have a great relationship with Newt Gingrich—we work together on opioids and criminal justice—and I fight Koch Industries on all their environmental policies, which are terrible, but I work with them on their criminal justice policies, which are pretty enlightened. It's become increasingly difficult to be a strong progressive who has strategic partnerships and friendships that cross the aisle. It's a real struggle.

Your dad would understand that, and he'd have ideas about what to do. The thing is, he's been the North Star for me politically, even more so than Dr. King. Dr. King is a hard person to pattern yourself after. You can be inspired by Dr. King's words, but you can't model your speaking style on his, because nobody can talk that way.

When I was in law school, I'd fly in from New Haven to Memphis, and my dad would pick me up at the airport and drive us for an hour and a half, all the way home to Jackson, Tennessee. On one of those car rides, I said to him, "The year I was born, 1968: It must have been an awful year. Here you are, you're in your early twenties, your wife's pregnant with twins, and in your own hometown, Memphis, Dr. King is killed, and you're in Memphis when it happens. It must have been shattering."

My dad said, "Well, yes and no."

You can imagine my shock. He was an African American southerner, strong on civil rights, and he said, "Yes and no." We go on about for another mile or two, and I say, "Well, Daddy, why'd you say, 'Yes and no'?"

He says, "We were very hurt and very angry when Dr. King was killed, but we still had Bobby Kennedy. So there was hurt, but there was still hope. Once they killed Bobby Kennedy, everybody gave up."

Now, that's probably the first and last time I heard my father say anything positive about any white person. He was born in 1944. He grew up in wretched poverty under the most aggressive segregation. He joined the military—when everybody was running *out* of the military, my dad ran in, trying to escape from poverty. He gets out of poverty, puts himself through college, puts his little brother through college, puts his cousin through college, marries the college president's daughter— my mother—and they put me and my sister through college. In the mid-'80s, the NAACP had to sue our county to let my dad become a principal—our middle school principal. So my dad felt that white people were tough on him, and in the privacy of our home, he was tough on white people. But his respect for Bobby Kennedy was absolute.

Kerry Kennedy: *Why do you think that was? Did he ever say?*

VJ: Well, I could almost recite what he said on that car ride because it was such a shocking thing to hear. I mean, I had always loved Bobby Kennedy! I had a little corkboard in my bedroom when I was a child, and on the left side of it I wrote "K.S."—Kennedy section. And I'd get my little *Weekly Reader*, and with my little round-blade scissors—you know, so little kids can't stab each other—I'd cut out anything about the Kennedys and tack it on the board with thumbtacks. By the time I got to third or fourth grade, I had so many articles about the Kennedys.

I even gave my *Star Wars* action figures different personas: Luke Skywalker was JFK, Han Solo was RFK, and Lando Calrissian was MLK.

I wasn't the biggest kid. I weighed 89 pounds in ninth grade, and probably half my body weight was my glasses, I was a bully magnet. I escaped the bullies by riding my bike into the woods and reading comic books about my favorite heroes: the Kennedy brothers, Martin Luther King, and the X-Men. I dreamed of someday becoming a champion of the downtrodden. So *I* liked Bobby Kennedy. I just didn't really know where my father was coming from. So I said, "Well, Daddy, why do you feel that way?"

He took a minute before he answered. He said, "You know, Jack Kennedy can give a speech. Man, he can take you to the moon and back. You can just hear his intelligence and his education, and people love to hear him talk. But when Bobby Kennedy talked, you felt he was talking just to you—personally. There was nobody else in the world. He wanted you to understand something."

My dad said, "We don't have any confidence in that *poor* white man because we've been working next to him for long enough to know he's never going to give us a break. But we thought, maybe that *rich* white man, who has enough self-confidence to hear our cause . . . When he left, everybody just gave up."

Well, that stayed with me. I'm twenty-two, first year of law school, trying to figure out what to do and how to do it, and that conversation made me go back to Bobby Kennedy. At that time, you had to work very hard to get a Bobby Kennedy speech. You didn't have the internet. But at Yale I was able to find some of his interviews and speeches, and it freed me. The Bobby Kennedy I found was a revelation—I saw how you could be a man in public life with a sharp mind and a big heart. In full public view, his heart's broken. And he's not even trying to hide it. I mean, you can hear it in his voice—the grief for his brother, the concern for poor kids. I never saw any tears, but you could tell they were being shed. He was completely real, nothing theatrical about him. You could feel him working his way through his relationship to his words and to the crowd and to the country. So I just found, sharing a basic shyness with him, that an overriding sense of public purpose is what gets you past that sadness.

What I took from your dad was the intimacy of his style of speaking. And a lot of my speaking style is directly derivative of the permission I felt from Bobby Kennedy to be emotionally authentic and never to lower the intellectual bar. He showed me that smart-with-heart path. That's why he's been my North Star.

KK: *I recently watched one of my father's last interviews. It was in May 1968, with David Frost, and my father's just struggling the whole time. Nothing is smooth or rehearsed, nothing that comes out of his mouth had been written down beforehand. It is absolutely authentic. He was taking the questions seriously and answering from his heart, and he expected people who heard to understand how seriously he was facing issues that weren't simple. You just never see anything like that in professional politics these days.*

VJ: I recently gave a speech at the South by Southwest Festival, and I said, "It used to be completely acceptable for a Democrat to go to Harlem, sit with the farmworkers, or talk to Native Americans, and then go right to Appalachia and sit with those families, too. But where's Bobby Kennedy? Where did that go?"

Now you have the underdogs pitted against each other, which is always the way, but we've almost accepted that it's supposed to be that way. You have this opioid crisis, this big crisis of addiction that's hitting mostly white folks in small-town America. I would imagine it would almost never occur to a white pastor in West Virginia dealing with an addiction crisis in his congregation that, hey, there are African American ministers in South Central Los Angeles who've been dealing with an addiction crisis for a couple of decades now. Let me call my Christian brother in faith and get some counsel. That would never arise in the moral imagination of struggling white folks in the Rust Belt or in Appalachia. At the same time, you have that African American pastor in South Central, and I imagine it never occurs to her to say, oh, my goodness, there's an addiction crisis that's broken out in West Virginia. Let me call my brothers and sisters in faith over there and see if we might be of service. Might there be a sermon I can share? Might there be a program that I started that I can help you replicate? That's how thoroughly divided we are.

The politicians today don't try to break out of it. They capitalize on it. They extend it. That wasn't Bobby Kennedy. He had a vision of America where everybody had a place of honor and dignity and every individual was expected to be a decent person and do a good job. Now that's almost gone. It's all about blaming the other guy. If you try to point out that maybe your side isn't 100 percent perfect, get ready to be a piñata.

KK: *Have you had that experience?*

VJ: I had it a few weeks ago.

KK: *Can you tell me about it?*

VJ: Well, I pointed out the obvious fact that Donald Trump is an atrocious person, and an atrocious president, but [in his February 2017 address to a joint session of Congress], he gave a presidential speech and he did what presidents do: He didn't go off talking about his polling numbers. He didn't attack the media. He put Americans up in the balcony—for his own political purposes, like every president—and he used their stories well. And in that moment, he, for the first time, looked like a president. I didn't say, "He looked like a *good* president." But with that speech, wow, I was moved emotionally by some of the stories he was sharing, especially of the widow of the Navy SEAL.

KK: *Carryn Owens, the woman whose husband, Ryan, was killed in the [January 2017] bombing raid in Yemen.*

VJ: You would have thought I had joined the Trump administration. Two weeks later, liberals were still kicking my butt because I'd said something kind about somebody on the other side. I got scolded for "normalizing" Trump. I just think that if somebody does ninety-nine things bad and one thing good, you should say, "The guy did ninety-nine things bad and one thing good." That's required if you're going to be a decent person, if you're going to be a fair person. But that's now perilous because we have to stay polarized, because it's now hip to be polarized.

If you're the kind of leader Bobby Kennedy was, your idea of the country is that everybody counts, everybody matters, and everybody has a place of dignity and honor—even your opponents. You don't see that viewpoint today. The liberal stand has become "If you don't listen to NPR, if you don't use all the right lingo, if you're just not like us, you suck. You are heathens. We are the civilizing force, and we're bewildered that everyone won't accept our faith." It's obnoxious, and it creates openings for our opponents to say, "All these PC people look down on us." We've got to say: "Listen, you're a coal miner. Maybe I oppose your view on race, your view on gender, your view on a lot of things, but just as you are, you deserve—"

KK: *Health care.*

VJ: "Health care. Just as you are, you deserve your pension not to be stolen by the coal company. Just as you are, vote against me for the rest of your life—I want you to have a *long* life, though. I don't want you to die of black lung and stop voting against me because you died. I want to keep you alive voting against me because just as you are, you're worthy. *You bring things to this country that we need: your faith, your commitment to family, your work ethic. These are things that we all value greatly, and* I want you to be even more awesome and include in your circle of love and concern black people and Muslims and other people who are also worthy." That's not the same as: "You're a bigot and you're uneducated and you're a toothless, mouth-breathing embarrassment. Now vote for me because my policies are good for you." Nobody is going to do that.

KK: *It's about respect.*

VJ: What was so clear about Bobby Kennedy was that he had deep respect for our traditions, for both the intellectual foundations and the moral purpose of the country. That's not to say he was not a tough politician. He was tough as nails, pragmatic, and ruthless. But that's politics.

For me, the standard is to be able to go into the middle of complete chaos, urban uprisings, with moral clarity for both sides. That's Bobby Kennedy. Now, who would you trust to do that today? I don't see anybody.

For whatever reason, during the 2016 campaign I wound up getting a lot of attention as a commentator, and a big chunk of the CNN audience took to me. So CNN gave me a show we called *The Messy Truth.*

I talked to a lot of Trump supporters in their homes, knee-to-knee at the kitchen table, or at the local diner. And I'm discovering that they don't feel inside the way they appear to us. To us, they seem like this rising force of menace and malice and resentment, and they just don't feel that way at all. They feel besieged and misunderstood and under attack from various centers of power, and I've been trying to challenge progressives to take their pain seriously—and not just their economic pain, frankly. Their cultural anxieties are to be taken seriously as well. Change is hard. We're shoving a lot of change down the throats of a lot of people in the Western democracies—demographic change, cultural change, change around sexuality and gender, new genders being introduced—and change is hard. Some people are gagging on it. We shouldn't slow down. All of these changes are overdue, some of them by thousands of years when it comes to gender. But you have to have some empathy for people when they're going through stages of grief and shock and fear and resentment. Just at the level of understanding the thing. We have to listen to them and try to understand how they experience what's happening to them.

KK: *Do you think that leads to better policy change, to better public policy?*

VJ: Don't care, don't care, don't care. We spend too much time trying to figure that out and too little time trying to figure each other out. Let's try to understand each other first. In a dictatorship, you have to agree. In a democracy, we don't have to agree. So let's say we're going to disagree on policy for a while. And I have no idea what the right policy outcomes are or how to get there politically. I don't know what to do. But I know who to be. We have to be better, we have to try to understand, and that's what we have given up on. We're talking *about* each other but not talking *to* each other.

People say to me: Van, you're giving these guys passes for being racist. No, I'm not. I've been fighting against racism my whole life. I will fight against it in the morning and the evening. I also think there's value in talking to people to try to understand where they're coming from—rather than trying to conquer them or convert people. Yet even just doing that challenges my base. The liberal base doesn't want that. They want you to wear the boxing gloves morning, noon, and night, and to be actively policing every single person around you for any wayward syllable or semicolon or pronoun. And if you aren't doing that, you're facilitating the rise of another Hitler because you're normalizing all this horrific stuff.

I remember when liberalism allowed for nuance, contradiction, surprise, confession. Now we're becoming Trump. Leaders have a tremendous impact on cultures, and his race to the bottom is pulling *us* to the bottom. Trump has no sympathy for anybody but himself. Well, now we have no sympathy for anybody but ourselves. He won't listen to anything past two syllables; well, we won't either. He reduces his entire brain down to 140 characters; well, you're going to have to write 140 characters, and if you leave one character off, I'm going to kick your ass. This is all horrible, so I'm challenging it.

I was in Chicago—Black History Month, big black church on the Southside, everybody comes to hear Van Jones, "Mr. Whitelash," he's going to come and stick it to Donald Trump and stick up for Black Lives Matter. But I didn't say one thing about any black cause. I talked about coal miners in West Virginia losing their pensions, and I got two standing ovations—because we've drawn our circle too small, and people know it. Our job is not to love humans to make them better. Our job is to love humans to make sure *we* don't become worse people over the course of a difficult decade, which we're now in. And it doesn't matter if they vote for us or like us back. That's not the point. The issue is: Can we use the situation that we're in to become better and not bitter? That's the moral challenge for the Left.

We had an election in which our worst nightmares came true. Now we don't have the normal means and mechanisms of power to protect ourselves. The Supreme Court, Congress, the state legislatures, and the

White House are all controlled by our opponents. So the only question becomes not "what you do?"—because anything you do is going to be futile for at least two years, until the next election—but: Who are you going to be? Are you going to be trying to beat polarization with polarization? Just oppose everything? But you found it morally objectionable when the Tea Party did that. So now you're going to become what you opposed? Well, it's a valid choice, but we have to understand it's not the only choice. The other choices are more difficult.

KK: *Speaking of moments of struggle: You were working for President Obama as an adviser on green jobs, and you were ousted because of a smear campaign against you based on what we now call fake news. The claim was that you had signed a petition saying 9/11 might have been an inside job, when in fact you had never signed anything like that. When we were kids, my father used to have us memorize poems and recite them on Sunday nights, and one of his favorites was "If," by Rudyard Kipling. I'll never forget: "If you can bear to hear the truth you've spoken / Twisted by knaves to make a trap for fools . . ." That's what happened to you. It must have been a terrible experience.*

VJ: It was devastating. I think I was clinically depressed for a year. That was a very hard thing to come back from. I wasn't sure that I would be able to come back from it. Not just politically—screw that—but emotionally, as a human being. I had such a sharp rise—relative obscurity in Oakland and suddenly I have a White House job, and six months later, out the back door. I'm not quite sure how I made it through all that. I had a lot of support—good family, good counseling. I lost my faith, and I lost my way, but I also remember feeling this little egg within myself, this egg of goodness and purpose. I remember feeling that I just had to wrap myself around that egg and fall until I hit the bottom, letting these demons that want to kick me just kick me, but try to protect that precious, loving quality in myself and hope for another opportunity. I tell you, at the time, I thought, "What great opportunities are there ever going to be beyond working at the Obama White House?" That's a big cookie to have taken off your plate. You may never find another way to serve that impactfully.

It's not just the fall. When you're on the rise, you're the focal point of your own effort. When you're on the fall, you're the focal point of your enemy's efforts. But then, once you're down and done, everything moves on and then you're the focus of nothing. And that's as painful as anything else. You're not even worth kicking. That dog is dead.

In those times, I looked at my heroes, and that brought some comfort. Look at Bobby Kennedy, who was also in the White House and who had to leave in a much worse way because he lost his brother. And you see him trying to find his way back to purpose, back to "How can I be of some use?" And you see him on that Senate campaign in '66, sometimes wearing his brother's jacket, looking pretty small in it. I thought about how difficult that must have been. The country is in complete turmoil, in desperate need of leadership. He's got huge responsibilities for his whole family, which is also grieving and in shock. His country needs him, his family needs him, but you see him still broken, trying to do his job. That was an incredibly useful example for me.

KK: *What did you learn from it?*

VJ: I learned a lot of bad things, sobering things, about people. When you're in the White House, your phone rings all the time. It literally just sits there and vibrates. When you leave the White House, you can go two days and nobody calls you for anything. And you suddenly realize, "Oh, I thought people liked me because I'm like such a clever guy." But it's actually your position. It's how high your stock is in the public eye. So that was sobering, but it brought me closer to my faith. It brought me closer to God. There are some things that you can only learn in pain—that you can only learn when all the distractions and titillations of public success are not available. So I learned how to pray. I learned how to fight on through the valleys when it's difficult.

I learned how important it is to be there for people when they're down. You know, Prince, the rock star, reached out. He gave me a lot of encouragement. So when I see somebody get tripped up in the media cycle, I try to reach out because it matters a lot to them in that moment. There are Native Americans out there getting sprayed with water hoses because they don't want their kids drinking poison water, and nobody comes to help. Or they come to help for ten minutes, and then the camera moves on and nobody comes back. Or the coal miners . . . Or the Muslim mom whose kids are going out the front door with their hijabs on, she doesn't know if they're going to get hurt. I understand how lonely the struggle can be. I think that if you bear your own cross the right way, you can come out the other side with a little bit more wisdom. Your dad loved that poem about wisdom: "Comes wisdom to us by the awful grace of God." That's true: It's awful. But I've learned: Your successes give you your confidence, but your setbacks give you your character.

I rely for my inspiration on so much that your father said, but the truth is that for me it's really about who he was being when he was saying that stuff. You were talking about how he was kind of groping for the truth, that he was exposed doing that in interviews. To me, that's a sign of high integrity. Because even if you had the answer yesterday, it doesn't mean it's the right answer today. It doesn't mean you haven't learned something or seen something that might make you reconsider. I think that's a beautiful quality.

When I say your dad is my North Star, I'm very serious about it. I don't prepare when I go on television—at all. If it goes well, it goes well. If it goes badly, it is a horrific experience, I'll tell you that. I've had both. But all too often, I sit there and my colleagues have already written out their "talking points." They have a checklist of talking points they're going to bang through, and they don't give a damn if Mars just fell from the sky. They're going to say what they came on the air to say. And they have an audience of whatever their little tribe is, and as long as those people give them a pat on the head for having said this one great thing, they're fine. I don't do that. I sit there and I try to listen to what people are actually saying. If I can give anybody credit for having said something interesting or surprising, I'm going to give it to them—Left or Right, it doesn't matter—and then see what truth I can find from that moment. I learned more from watching your dad do that than from any of the great lines on statues and in books. So I don't have a favorite Bobby Kennedy thing to say, I have a favorite Bobby Kennedy way to be. And I'm chasing that.

"Few are willing to brave the disapproval of their fellows, the censure of their colleagues, the wrath of their society. Moral courage is a rarer commodity than bravery in battle or great intelligence, yet it is the one essential, vital quality for those who seek to change a world which yields most painfully to change."

—Robert F. Kennedy

JOHN LEWIS

❧

John Lewis was born in Pike County, Alabama, the son of sharecroppers, and attended segregated public schools. Inspired by the activism surrounding the Montgomery bus boycott and the words of the Reverend Martin Luther King Jr., he joined the civil rights movement. He organized sit-in demonstrations at segregated lunch counters in Nashville, Tennessee; was a Freedom Rider; and was beaten and arrested.

From 1963 to 1966, he was the chairman of the Student Nonviolent Coordinating Committee (SNCC), which he helped form. At the age of twenty-three, he was an architect of and a keynote speaker at the March on Washington in August 1963.

In 1964, he coordinated SNCC's efforts to organize voter-registration drives and community-action programs during the Mississippi Freedom Summer. The following year, he led over six hundred peaceful, orderly protesters across the Edmund Pettus Bridge in Selma, Alabama, on a march to Montgomery for voting rights. News broadcasts and photographs of brutal attacks on the marchers by Alabama state troopers exposed the cruel reality of the segregated South and hastened the passage of the US Voting Rights Act of 1965.

Lewis has been awarded over fifty honorary degrees from prestigious colleges and universities throughout the United States, and has received numerous awards from eminent national and international institutions, including America's highest civilian honor, the Presidential Medal of Freedom. Serving as a US representative from Georgia's Fifth Congressional District since 1986, he is known as "the conscience of the Congress."

Each March, Congressman Lewis leads a delegation to visit civil rights sites in Alabama, organized by The Faith and Politics Institute. I've joined several delegations, and Congressman Lewis joined twenty-three RFK family members for the fiftieth anniversary of my father's visit to South Africa in 2016.

Kerry Kennedy: *John, I'm talking to people about my father and why people value his example today. You're one of the few people in the book who actually knew him, so I wanted to talk to you about that.*

John Lewis: I didn't know him in 1961, but he helped me out of a jam. I'll tell you how that happened.

The Congress for Racial Equality created something called the Freedom Rides, and I applied to be one of the Freedom Riders. Thirteen of us were selected, seven African Americans and six whites. At our orientation in Washington, DC, we went over the way of peace, the way of love, and the way of nonviolence. We were going to violate laws against integration, and it would be dangerous. Some of us wrote letters, like wills, just in case something really bad happened to us.

On the morning of May 4, some of us boarded a Greyhound bus and others boarded a Trailways bus, and we headed south. In Rock Hill, South Carolina, my seatmate and I attempted to get into a whites-only waiting room. A group of men attacked us—they were Klansmen—and left us in a pool of blood. The police came and asked if we wanted to press charges, but we said no.

The buses continued through Georgia. Between Atlanta and Birmingham, in a little town called Anninston, Alabama, there was an attempt to burn people on the Greyhound bus. The bus was fire-bombed. The people on the Trailways bus were beaten in downtown Birmingham. CORE suspended the rides; they felt they were too dangerous. The US attorney general, Robert Kennedy, suggested there should be a cooling-off period. James Farmer, the head of CORE, said, "You know, Mr. Attorney General, if we cool off any more we'll be in a deep freeze." I went back to Nashville, where we organized another group to start off where the first group had left off. Ten of us left Nashville on Wednesday, May 17.

Our bus reached the outskirts of Birmingham. Bull Connor, the police commissioner, had heard we were coming. He stopped us and said, "Let me see your tickets." Our tickets showed our next stop was Montgomery. Connor ordered the Greyhound driver to drive the bus into the downtown Greyhound station and ordered all of the Freedom Riders to stay on the bus. Two hours later he brought police officials to put cardboard and newspaper on the window so reporters and news media couldn't see what was happening.

They put us in protective custody, and we stayed in jail until Friday morning. At four a.m. they drove us to the Alabama-Tennessee state line and dumped us out of the car. We didn't know what was going to happen; a black family took us in. We made a call to Nashville and they sent a car to take us there, but we said we wanted to drive back to Birmingham and continue on by bus to Montgomery. Every time the loudspeaker in Birmingham would announce a bus going from Birmingham to Montgomery, the bus driver would refuse to drive the bus.

One time we tried to go on the bus, and the bus driver said: "I only got one life to live, and I'm not gonna give it to CORE or the NAACP."

Robert Kennedy was very interested in us getting out of Birmingham. He thought it was too dangerous for us to stay there, and at one point he got so desperate he said, "Well, let me speak to Mr. Greyhound." He thought that there would be black bus drivers willing to drive the bus. Eventually they made an arrangement with the Greyhound company for the bus to leave at eight thirty on Saturday morning, May 20. There would be a plane flying over the bus, and every fifteen miles there would be a patrol car. Every now and then on the ride you'd look out the window and see a patrol car or the plane.

When we arrived in downtown Montgomery, an angry mob appeared out of nowhere and started beating members of the press. If you had cameras or pad and pencil in those days you were danger. We saw reporters and photographers just lying on the street bleeding. Then they turned on us. Several of us were hurt; some were hospitalized. It was very violent. I thought I was going to die. I was beaten unconscious.

KK: *The next evening, The Freedom Riders and 1500 others, along with Dr. Martin Luther King Jr. gathered at the First Baptist Church. A white supremacist mob 3000 strong gathered outside, and threw bricks, Molotov cocktails and stink bombs. Tear gas filled the church.*

JL: Your father and President Kennedy called out the Alabama National Guard. If it wasn't for your father, Kerry, I don't know if I would be sitting here today.

In the end, the Freedom Rides helped bring about desegregation of public transportation all through the South, but it was a long struggle.

Now I'll take you a little further along, to 1963. We had a campaign going on in Cambridge, Maryland. It was headed by a young woman by the name of Gloria Richardson, who was a great leader most people don't remember today. We had sit-ins at movie theaters, bowling alleys, and restaurants, and we were focused on economic rights; we wanted better wages and jobs. This had been going for several years and, in 1963, we had a big riot there, in June. There was martial law and they sent in the National Guard. In July, Robert Kennedy called us to come to Wash-

ington, and we went to the attorney general's office. He invited the head
of the National Guard to come—the governor of Maryland had already
sent four hundred National Guardsmen into Cambridge to halt the dis-
order and violence—and several local people came from the community, and Gloria Richardson and me. At that time I was chairman of
SNCC, the Student Nonviolent Coordinating Committee.

Robert Kennedy wanted an update on everything that was going
on in Cambridge. He was very interested in that fight, so we told him
everything that was happening. He kept saying to us that we could solve
the problem in Cambridge by giving the people a chance to negotiate, to
work it out, because people were afraid there was going to be more serious violence in that part of the eastern shore of Maryland.

At one point during a break in the meetings, he called me aside and
said, "John, now I understand. The young people, the students have educated me. You have changed me." That was something that amazed me.
Your father was a quick learner—he understood the issues, he identified
with the people and their needs. He was a fair referee, but he also went
with his passion and his heart.

Gloria Richardson and the others agreed to what they called the
"Treaty of Cambridge." Gloria wasn't too happy about it; she didn't
trust that the local officials would hold up their side of the agreement
on everything, and they didn't. Some parts of the agreement we made
held, and eventually it led to school desegregation and also to desegregation of the buses and the library and the hospital in Cambridge. But the
demonstrations and conflicts continued until the civil rights bills were
passed in '64, '65, and '66.

When Robert Kennedy started the whole effort in Brooklyn, the
Bedford-Stuyvesant Restoration Corporation, he came by once to meet
with the folks at the Field Foundation in Manhattan, which supported
a lot of activism for the voting rights bill and other civil rights efforts. I
was working there when he came over, and I met him, but it was really
in 1968 that I got to know him better.

During the '68 campaign, I was working in Indianapolis.

When your father first announced—it was on a Saturday, March 16, I believe—I sent a telegram to him that said, "I want to help. What can I do?" He asked someone to contact me, and the message was that he wanted me to go to Indiana to work in voter registration and to help organize the community. I went there, and I was working with Earl Graves, who was on his staff, and several other people, doing voter registration and setting up meetings. On the night of April 4, we had organized this rally in a transition neighborhood of Indianapolis. There were debates about whether Bobby should come and speak, and I was one of the people who said he must come and speak to the audience. We had heard that Dr. King had been shot, but we didn't know his condition. We didn't know he had died. So it was Robert Kennedy who announced his death to the audience. He said: "We have news that Dr. King has been assassinated." He gave an unbelievable speech.

We all just cried. I have not been back to that spot since, but I made a commitment just a few days ago to go back for the fifiteth anniversary.

That evening of April 4, we went to Bobby's room—I don't remember the name of the hotel, it was an old hotel—and we all cried some more, and we made arrangements to go to Atlanta to help make preparations for the funeral. I think Bobby canceled all of his speaking engagements—except, I believe, for one in Cleveland.

KK: *Yes, he talked about "the mindless menace of violence" and how it was cowardice and had never righted any wrong. Then he said, "There is another kind of violence, slower but just as deadly, destructive as the shot or the bomb in the night. This is the violence of institutions; indifference and inaction and slow decay. This is the violence that afflicts the poor, that poisons relations between men because their skin has different colors. This is a slow destruction of a child by hunger, and schools without books and homes without heat in the winter." That was considered a radical thing to say.*

JL: When he came to Atlanta, we met at the Regency Hotel, a group of us. It was about three o'clock in the morning, and your father and mother said they wanted to say a prayer for Dr. King. It was my responsibility to lead them through the education part of Ebenezer Baptist Church, and we went downstairs and viewed Dr. King's body. The next morning the family members attended the service, and Bobby walked the whole route from that church through the streets of Atlanta. I've said this in the past: He was the only white politician in America who could have walked with that crowd. There were other white politicians at the service, but they didn't march. Hundreds of thousands of people walked from Ebenezer Church to the Morehouse campus, where there was another service.

I was with him next in Oregon, and to this day I think about it. The students at Portland State asked me to present Robert Kennedy, and I introduced him. It was an honor to be able to present him to that crowd. I've gone back there once since, to speak at Oregon State.

After that, I went on to California. I teamed up with Cesar Chavez, and it was just amazing. The two of us—we went into these wealthy neighborhoods, speaking to mostly wealthy white families for the contest between Hubert Humphrey, Eugene McCarthy, and Bobby. We also organized black and Latino communities in LA County and thereabouts, but the neighborhoods we worked in—it was this Latino guy and this black guy, knocking door to door, saying to white people, "You've got to vote for Robert Kennedy."

KK: *How did they receive you?*

JL: They received us well—very well.

KK: *Did they know who you were?*

JL: Oh, yes. Yes.

KK: *I can't imagine having the two of you come to my door. People must have been shocked and thrilled.*

JL: In the motorcade and around LA County, there were thousands of people. You knew, you felt it in the air—he was going to win. You knew it was going to be a victory. People by the hundreds and thousands gathered along the streets and waved and cheered for Bobby. The people loved him. It was the Olympic champion Rafer Johnson and the football star Rosey Grier in the car with him, and people were grabbing all over the place. They wanted to touch him.

That night, at the Ambassador Hotel, I did not go down. I went to the suite. I was in the suite, and your aunt was in the suite—Pat Kennedy; Jack Newfield of the *Village Voice*; Teddy White, who wrote histories of presidential elections; Charles Evers, Medgar Evers's brother, other people—and Bobby was joking with me. He said, "John, you let me down. More Mexican Americans turned out to vote than Negroes," or something like that. He was teasing me. He said, "I'm going down to make my victory statement, and I'll be returning."

Everyone turned away from the TV screen after Bobby finished his victory speech, and everyone was talking and laughing, waiting for him to come back upstairs. A woman cried out, "Oh, my God," and I looked at the black-and-white screen of the TV, and the commentator was saying Bobby had just been shot. I dropped to the floor and I couldn't stop crying. Over and over again I kept saying, "Why? Why? Why?"

I just wanted to get out of there. I went downstairs and walked through the ballroom, where people were still sitting amid the red and blue streamers; I was in shock, I was crying. I walked back to my hotel. It was three a.m. when I fell asleep. The next morning I packed my bags and got a flight back home to Atlanta. I think I cried all the way, literally. It was one of the saddest times of my life. We were flying over the mountains. It was June. We were flying over the hills and the mountains, and you could still see snow, even though it was June.

Later the next day, June 6, someone from the campaign, a friend or family, called and invited me to come to New York and stand in an honor guard. In the evening, I stood with the Reverend Ralph Abernathy, who succeeded Dr. King at the Southern Christian Leadership

Conference, and he asked me to ride the train from New York to Washington, and several members of the family and other people who were part of the campaign also asked me. Along the way we saw people all over just waving and crying, and I remember seeing your brother Joe, who was walking up and down in the train, greeting people and thanking them for being there. Somehow, I didn't want that train to stop. I wanted it to just keep on going, but I knew we had to get to Arlington Cemetery.

When the train came into Washington, the Poor People's Campaign was going on there. The train stopped in front of what they called Resurrection City, and they sang "The Battle Hymn of the Republic." It was very uplifting and moving. It was a salute to Bobby Kennedy and to his memory. People knew they had lost a fighter, a warrior for their cause. People were convinced that if he had lived, they would have been better off. Everyone believed he would have been elected president. I think they knew something was dying in America and something was dying in all of us. I truly believe that's what was happening.

I think about Robert Kennedy often—and about Dr. King and President Kennedy too. If it hadn't been for Bobby, I wouldn't be involved in American politics. At difficult times, I've often asked myself, "What would Robert Kennedy do?" I've felt, on many occasions, when I was trying to decide whether to run for office or do anything: "Someone, sometime, someplace, has to pick up where he left off." I know he inspired an entire generation. So many of the young people who read about him, who listened to his speeches—those people have gone on to do things in his spirit.

He was an inspiring human being. He inspired us to stand up and to speak out, to be courageous. He had noble aspirations. He wanted not just to make America better but to make the world better. He really believed we could all do that. You know, he went to Mississippi, to the delta, to the Southwest, where people were suffering. He felt the pain and the hurt. Many of us today, as politicians and elected officials, we don't go to many of these places. We can all learn from him. We all have dreams, and he wanted to make the dreams real. It wasn't just about racial justice for him. It was about economic justice.

That is so important to recognize for us now, because in our country, that's really the number one issue. There's such a division between rich and poor, the people who are struggling and feel locked out of everything. Robert Kennedy's message to us today is to help those who need help the most, the most vulnerable segment of our society: the poor, the downtrodden, the desperate mothers, the out-of-work fathers, the hungry children. I see it in the eyes, and in the faces, of people who've been put down because they're immigrants, especially the Latino population. Bobby identified with Cesar Chavez. He loved the man! And when Cesar broke that fast, Bobby was there with him.

Your father was just a wonderful man, a loving human being. When he died, our country, and our world, lost a determined dreamer, a man of hope, a man of possibilities. I'm sorry . . .

When I think of where the country could have been . . . where the world community could have been . . .

I truly believe something died in all of us. I know something died in me. And that's why I look at his picture in my office, and I look at the bust at my home in Atlanta . . .

I'm sorry. It's so emotional.

That's why you have to keep going, moving on, and trying to inspire more young people to stand up, to get up.

KK: *John, you are right, something in our country died. We lost Jack, we lost Dr. King, we lost my father, and we lost Malcolm X. People were stunned; it seemed that all hope was being gunned down. I feel that the American heart was broken, or a large piece of it. It was broken again and again in those years. People said, "No. I just don't believe in it anymore." I don't want to have that hope and then see it shattered again.*

JL: People didn't want their hearts broken again. A lot of people felt that way. "Why should I have faith?" You have these people who you love, and then something steals that love away, shatters that dream, and . . . What do you do?

KK: *I think it hardened our country.*

JL: You pick it up, you keep going. You have to find a way.

That night, you know, when your father spoke after Martin was killed, when other cities were burning, Indianapolis was so peaceful. A lot of people really think the words that Bobby spoke, that speech—it saved that city. Maybe other places too . . .

---✦---

"Democracy is no easy form of government.
Few nations have been able to sustain it.
For it requires that we take the chances of
freedom; that the liberating play of reason
be brought to bear on events filled
with passion; that dissent be allowed to
make its appeal for acceptance; that men
chance error in their search for truth."

—ROBERT F. KENNEDY

---✦---

Campaign volunteers, 1968, Rondondo Beach, California

---∽---

"A true democracy, to survive, to prosper,
must have a strong, dedicated, militant labor
movement. Its leaders must be devoted to their
members, to an ideal. In my judgment a labor
movement is the backbone of democracy."

—ROBERT F. KENNEDY

---∽---

STEFAN LÖFVEN

❧

Stefan Löfven has been the prime minister of Sweden since 2014. He was previously a welder, a trade union representative, the chairman of the union IF Metall, and he is the leader of the Swedish Social Democratic Party.

His father left before he was born, and his mother, unable to raise him but unwilling to give him up, placed him in foster care when he was ten months old but would not allow him to be adopted. He was raised in the far reaches of Sweden by a lumberjack and a health care visitor.

When I was in Stockholm in 2013 to launch the RFK Human Rights education program, Speak Truth to Power, Stefan Löfven and I had a wide-ranging discussion about labor rights worldwide and U.S.- Swedish relations. Since then we have kept in contact.

Stefan Löfven: When Robert Kennedy died I was eleven years old. Even if I couldn't fully grasp it then, I remember being sad at the time. Later in life I came to understand the significance of his life and he has been an inspiration to me. I especially appreciate his views on the responsibility of having power, how you use power, and how you develop "good power." I share his belief that politicians should not live off the public, but for the public. Your task, as a political leader is to accomplish things for the people, not for yourself.

Robert Kennedy kept his eyes fixed on the future. I think we can learn from that in our times, as we fight populist movements and extremists around the world. These movements try to attract people with simple messages and by appealing to people's fears. Robert Kennedy described it very well when he said, "There are people in every time and every land who want to stop history in its tracks. They fear the future, mistrust the present, and invoke the security of the comfortable past which, in fact, never existed." He returns several times to this idea: What can we do for the future? We have to do something; we cannot just go along. We have to do something and also remember that the past wasn't that good. It is easy for people to talk about the past because it gives people a feeling of security. But that security is fragile. Instead, we need to focus on how to make things better in the future. In the Social Democratic Party in Sweden we want to address how people can feel more hope. I believe that this can only be done by showing that there is a path forward together. The key message is that we can shape the future collectively, and to show people they're not alone. *We can do this together.* Your father has been an important inspiration for me in this approach.

These are not just domestic issues. We need to solve them at the international level. Take for example a German businessman whom I met. He had moved his businesses from Germany to Hungary to the Czech Republic and finally to North Africa. He told me, "It's getting more expensive every time, because wages are going up. So now I'm thinking of moving to Uzbekistan or Tajikistan." Globalization should not be exploited to become a race to the lowest wages. Rather, we must make sure there are decent working conditions and decent wages for everyone.

Robert Kennedy talked about the world community. He recognized something I also found as a trade unionist: Talking to people around the world, you notice the similarities much more than the differences.

Workers in Latin America or Asia are to a large extent concerned about the same matters as workers in Sweden: they want their children to have a good education; they need a job, they need somewhere to live, they need social protection. They will ask: "What happens if I get sick or lose my job? What will happen to my parents when they grow old? If they get sick, will they get the health care they need?" These concerns are similar all around the world. By this insight, I concluded that we must work to improve things not only in Sweden, but also internationally.

Workers everywhere feel disconnected today; some even distrust democracy. When people are unemployed for a long time, or when real wages haven't increased for many years, people start feeling left behind, and start to lose hope and fear falling further and further behind. And then, it is easy to become attracted by a simple message: "Here's a solution." In Sweden, the extremists say: "If only all those refugees weren't here, everything would be fine." Our task must be to show the real solution: a government investing in housing, in training, in health care, and in schools for the children. We need to show that if we do this together, we can shape a better future.

Kerry Kennedy: *In the United States, people feel they've been struggling and the immigrants have jumped the line. They were told that if you go to school, work hard in a terrible factory or mine under backbreaking conditions, you'll be able to own a home, give your children a good education; your parents will be taken care of; you'll have a secure retirement; and your children will have a better life than yours. But the factory moved away, the home mortgage is underwater, the schools didn't teach their now unemployable children, their parents didn't save enough for retirement, and, too often, their communities are suffering from opiod addiction. The system they bought into isn't working. The elites get tax breaks and grow richer, they are frustrated and angry, and immigrants make a convenient target. They've decided what they're going to do is put somebody in charge who will blow up the whole system. Voilà, Donald Trump.*

SL: There are many similarities to the debate in Sweden and I think that it is hard to reach out to people who have developed such mistrust. But the solution is to be clear that we share their concerns and that we will tackle the problems. For example, we must take a tougher stance on crime. A good society cannot include gangs that threaten whole parts of cities. We need to build a safe society. As regards immigration and the refugee situation, European regulations and multilateral work must improve. We need to protect the right to seek asylum and more equally share the responsibility of receiving refugees. But we must also make it possible for immigrants to work and have high expectations on them to become a part of their new countries. They should have language training and education so that they can contribute in the labor market and not compete with lower wages and bad working conditions. At the same time, we need to invest in housing, education, and health care for everyone, so that people who already live in the country and have a tough situation don't feel threatened. When we accomplish this, immigration can be an asset to a country.

We've shown that it's possible. Sweden was one of the poorest countries in Europe in the late 1800s and early 1900s. Some 1.2 million people left Sweden, most of them for the United States, because we were so poor. Today we're one of the richest nations on earth. We still have our problems, but we have one of the fairest distributions of wealth, and where there are gaps we're working on closing those gaps. The labor movement in the late 1800s and early 1900s were able to change the direction of the country. We've done it once, we know we can do it again.

To find ways to constantly improve people's lives, that is what politics and trade union work is all about for me. When I started as a welder, I went to my first workplace, and I saw there were no chairs or tables to sit and have your coffee or sandwiches. We sat against a wall on little wooden boxes. I said, "This is 1981. We can't sit here. We have to have chairs and tables." I got the answer that there were no chairs and tables, but I insisted and we got that changed. All of a sudden we were sitting like decent people, like we should. That triggered my engagement in trade union activities.

I think part of my interest in trade union work and politics came from my childhood. My foster parents were workers; they were not very active in the trade union, but my father was involved in getting buildings built where people in the labor movement could hold their meetings, and my mother was active in the women's social democratic movement. We didn't discuss politics much at home, but I learned by what they did and how they did it. I often listened when my best friend's father, who was an active social democrat, had conversations with my father. They were so concrete, and they discussed politics in a very local, practical way: "What can we do to improve that road or that school?" That inspired me and awoke my interest.

There were so many moments in my early days, sitting in a group at the job, or in a meeting, or at a conference, when I was thinking "I'm not going to say anything," but I could never stick to that. When I felt something was important I had to speak up. But I have tried to make sure to always search for the pragmatic solutions.

As a local trade union, we had our differences and disputes with the company. But we saw that if we were pragmatic we could make changes happen. You can't just shout about everything; you have to show that you're interested in reaching a compromise so that everyone benefits.

I discovered over the years that the best way to get people to come along is if you trust them, if you engage them. When we were manufacturing trains and I was the local trade union leader, the company told us, "There's another company competing with us, so we need to improve. We need to be more efficient." We were thirty-five workers manufacturing this train, and I went to everybody, saying, "How can we do this more efficiently?" The workers themselves came up with the ideas. In the end, we could do the job with two-thirds of the workers, and with fewer people on the project we were able to keep the train manufacturing in the company. This was possible because the workers didn't feel threatened. They knew then that there was another part of the company that needed workers. Those who didn't stay on making trains got other jobs." What this taught me is that if workers feel secure they will accept the changes that are necessary and contribute to innovation and development. People need to know that if you are temporarily out of a job there will be help for you to find a new job, you will be able to get the skills and training you need, and you will be able to handle it financially for yourself and your family. Without that security, people will not accept changes and we would never have innovation.

Thinking change—and how we adjust to change—makes me wonder about the change that took place in your father after President Kennedy was killed. Is that something you can help me understand better?

KK: *I'll be happy to try.*

I don't think he changed significantly in who he was or in his values, but he approached things from a different point of view. When Martin Luther King died, Daddy quoted Aeschylus: "Tame the savageness of man and make gentle the life of this world." You could sum up the first phase of his life in the phrase: tame the savageness. He spent a lot of his life standing up to bullies. He did that in high school; he did that in college; he did that in law school. He did it when he was working for the McClellan committee, which was investigating criminal activities in labor-management relations, mainly corruption in unions. He did it when he worked for McCarthy, too, because during that four-month period when he was actually on the job there he spent every day fighting against Roy Cohn and the other people who worked for McCarthy who my father thought were unfairly going after certain people accused of being Communists. When he went after the union leader Jimmy Hoffa, it was on behalf of the rank-and-file union members who were being bullied and robbed by organized crime. During the civil rights movement, of course, he was fighting for activists and all black people against the white supremacists, the segregationists, and the Jim Crow system of the South. That was the attitude, the action plan, of the first part of his life. The other part of his life, the part that seemed predominant after Uncle Jack died and my father left the executive branch, is expressed by "make gentle the life of this world." That second part, which some people saw as a change, had always been part of him, but not so much on the public stage. That meant compassion and love, and also fun, joy, and laughter. He had a different role after Uncle Jack died, when he faced death, violence, poverty, hatred; it was a time not so much about winning a fight or a court case but more about understanding, compassion, and love.

The way my father changed was not the way many people think he did. He didn't change from conservative to liberal or from tough and ruthless to compassionate and socially conscious. Part of it is that when he changed jobs, his perspective changed. He had to be tough as a prosecutor and as a campaign organizer. After his brother died, he went through a long period of mourning, and then he became a US senator, and in that position he was able to act out of his compassion for poor people, for people who were oppressed, for people who were bullied, for people who were persecuted, segregated, disrespected. He did a tremendous amount of work on hunger issues in the United States, on people living in poverty in urban areas, like the Watts neighborhood in Los Angeles, or the black ghetto of Bedford-Stuyvesant in New York City. He aligned himself with the farmworkers who were being organized by Cesar Chavez and Dolores Huerta, and he advocated for the Indians who lived on reservations in desperate poverty.

When my father was liberated from the burden of working on behalf of someone else and from the responsibility of prosecuting criminals who were fighting back with the best legal talent, and from fighting against state and local governments that had been repressing black people for hundreds of years, he took the side of the victims who had suffered at the hands of those he'd been prosecuting. I think it's true too that when President Kennedy was killed, he found a new perspective on life and death. He thought: "I'm just going to say what I want and go where I want and do what I want." This was a frustrating attitude for a lot of his aides, who kept saying, "You can't go into a white neighborhood and start talking about compassion for people who aren't white. That's not going to fly." Or, "You can't work on civil rights and then go try to get farmers to vote for you. They'll hate you." But my father had the same message for everyone, which is, "What's going on with your life? You're a farmer, what are you struggling with? You're somebody we need to help. Let's all work together." He hadn't changed very much, but his role had changed, and when your role changes, the way you act changes, because then you have a different job to do, a different purpose. I think that really is an important part of the answer to how he approached things differently late in his life.

SL: I remember the speech your father gave at the Democratic Convention in 1964—he received a ten- or fifteen-minute standing ovation. He had been through so much over those years. It took time for him, not to get over it, but to handle it.

KK: *It took him a long time. He read Camus and the Ancient Greeks. He thought, he took long walks. Once he became engaged in communities, working on antipoverty issues, he started to feel fully alive. He hated the routine work of the Senate, but when he was out in the field, when he was in the Mississippi delta, when he was in Appalachia, when he was working on bringing jobs and innovation to the inner cities, he felt more in touch with people and more grounded. By the time of the '68 campaign, he had found his true voice.*

A lot of people run for office because they're simply ambitious, or the idea of higher office excites them, or they feel that "this is my career" and they must take the next step. My father didn't approach the presidency like that at all. He felt a responsibility for Vietnam. He felt our country was going in the wrong direction. It had nothing to do with personal ambition or ego or glory. He ran out of a sense of duty, a sense of responsibility, and a sense that he could play a role in righting what was going wrong in our country and in the world. He thought he had to do it.

SL: I recognize that very much. I often refer to one thing your father has said: "We must recognize the full human equality of all of our people before God, before the law, and in the councils of government. We must do this, not because it is economically advantageous, although it is; not because the laws of God command it, although they do; not because people in other lands wish it so. We must do it for the single and fundamental reason that it is the right thing to do." You do the right thing because it *is* the right thing. It takes a lot of confidence to say that politically.

Self-confidence is very important if you want to lead. During my trade union time, we had a difference with a company on the pay rate system—without explaining the details, it meant I had to push the workers to accept an agreement they didn't like. It was a very tough time and I had to face a lot of criticism. But I found out quickly that the best way to do it was to be straightforward and meet with people face-to-face. There is a feeling when you are sure you are doing the right thing, you feel it inside, in your heart, and you stand by that position. This confidence takes time to develop, but you need to have this kind of strength if you want to bring people together and do good things.

For me it has been very important as prime minister to keep on meeting with people face-to-face, especially on the most difficult issues. The best part of my work is really the conversations with people that are not in the spotlight of the political debate, about everyday life, the problems we face, how to solve them and how our society should develop. I try to do that as much as possible.

Your father once said that "or we can make an effort, as Martin Luther King did, to understand and to comprehend, and to replace that violence, that stain of bloodshed that has spread across our land, with an effort to understand with compassion and love."

How we treat each other is the most basic thing. Each of us has a responsibility to try to understand the other person. That is something that is guiding me in my work, and something in which your father has been an inspiration to me.

"Progress is a nice word but change is its motivator. And change has its enemies."

—ROBERT F. KENNEDY

SHIRLEY MacLAINE

◈

Shirley MacLaine is an actor, dancer, and author, and the winner of the Academy Award, the Kennedy Center Honors, and the AFI Life Achievement Award from the American Film Institute. MacLaine is known for her New Age beliefs and has written extensively about her experiences in past lives. She campaigned for Robert Kennedy in 1968 and for George McGovern in 1972.

One of my early memories is of being in the back room of a big event with Shirley MacLaine, I must have been four or five. I was playing with her row stretch rhinestone bracelet, and she took it off and gave it to me. I kept that bracelet for years, and it always made me feel a special closeness to her. She was friends with my parents in those days.

Shirley MacLaine: We were in Los Angeles mostly and I think Vegas, too. We would meet up with the Rat Pack—Peter Lawford, Sammy Davis Jr., Frank Sinatra, Dean Martin, Joey Bishop, backstage after a show or go out to a club. Bobby was intensely relaxed. You would never say he was completely relaxed. Even his fun-loving part was intense. But he was funny, he was very, very quick, bright, and witty. And very aware. I never saw him drink. Usually when we were at parties everybody else was pretty soused, but Bobby wasn't.

KK: *You introduced Daddy at the Sports Arena in downtown Los Angeles in 1968. It was a spectacular lineup with Sonny and Cher, Jerry Lewis, Carol Channing, Joey Bishop, Henry Mancini, Angie Dickinson, Alan King, Andy Williams, Mahalia Jackson, Gene Kelly, the Byrds, and even Maharishi Mahesh Yogi in his yellow Rolls-Royce, along with a warm-up band that sang "This Man Is Your Man" to the tune of "This Land Is Your Land." There were fifteen thousand fans in the arena and hundreds more spilled onto the street.*

SM: The crowds adored him. I was with him and Rosey Grier, who was his bodyguard quite a bit of the time in California.

KK: *Rosey was a giant, and a member of the Los Angeles Rams' "Fearsome Foursome," the most dominant defensive line of their era. But off the field, Rosey was gentle and used to teach needlepoint.*

How did you meet Daddy?

SM: Gosh, it was so long ago, I don't recall. I remember past lives, so you would think I'd have an easier time remembering this one . . . I think I met him with Jack, maybe through John Lewis.

Earlier, John had arranged for me to stay at Unita Blackwell's home in Mississippi.

KK: *Unita was the SNCC [Student Nonviolent Coordinating Committee] voter-registration organizer there, and when her son and three hundred other students were suspended for wearing SNCC buttons, Unita sued the county, the case went to the Supreme Court, and the county was forced to desegregate the schools.* Blackwell v. Issaquena *is a seminal civil rights case and she is a hero of the civil rights movement.*

SM: I met Stokely Carmichael and some of the really explosive black lefties at her home. It looked like the Klan knew there was a white woman in the house and they burned a cross on the front lawn. When that happened, I was just an observer, basically. Unita had been through all that.

KK: *What did you do?*

SM: There wasn't anything you could do about it, actually.

They lit it up and ran away. And it was quite a distance from the house.

Later, in 1973, I invited Unita to come with me on my woman's delegation trip to China.

KK: *Wait, Nixon only opened diplomatic ties with China in 1972. Tourism didn't really start until years later. How did you get visas?*

SM: Yes, I'll tell you who got me in with the Chinese: the shah of Iran.

Can you believe that? The Iranians loved films.

KK: *You are just full of surprises. When you were a kid you played baseball on an all-boys team—and you held the record for most home runs.*

SM: Oh, you know, I was a tomboy and I did all the stuff that the boys did, and I beat up any boy who beat up a smaller boy.

KK: *What was that like, breaking that barrier?*

SM: I didn't see it as a barrier, I saw them as stupid. I don't know how that happened. I've always been very comfortable with the yin and the yang of myself, let's put it that way.

KK: *How would you describe who Robert Kennedy was?*

SM: Basically, someone who terrifies bad people. But also I loved the relationship that he had with his brother, the president. And the way they worked together.

KK: *Why does he matter, fifty years later?*

SM: Good question. Especially asking me that today. Did you see what's going on? What the fuck is going on?

---✧---

*"If we fail to dare, if we do not try, the next
generation will harvest the fruit of our
indifference; a world we did not want—a
world we did not choose—but a world we
could have made better, by caring more for
the results of our labors. And we shall be left
only with the hollow apology of T.S. Eliot:
'That is not what I meant at all. That
is not it, at all.'"*

—ROBERT F. KENNEDY

---✧---

CHRIS MATTHEWS

⌒⊗⌒

*Chris Matthews, born and raised in Philadelphia, served for
two years with the Peace Corps in Africa. Returning home to
the United States, he became a presidential speechwriter, a
top aide to Speaker of the House Thomas P. "Tip," O'Neill Jr.,
a syndicated columnist for the* San Francisco Examiner *and
now hosts MSNBC's* Hardball. *He wrote* Jack Kennedy: Elusive Hero *and* Bobby Kennedy: A Raging Spirit.

We met in Matthews's office in Washington, D.C. After our talk,
Matthews brought me downstairs, and showed me the studio
where one of the Kennedy-Nixon debates took place.

Kerry Kennedy: *What do you think would have been the difference
in this country had my father survived the 1968 campaign?*
Chris Matthews: One way to answer that question is to look at this
country when we were left without him.

I attended the October 1967 March on the Pentagon. The mood of
those protesters of the Vietnam War was hopeful. There were young
couples pushing baby carriages, religious leaders and all kinds of young
people. We believed we were making a difference, that change might be
coming, that we might be able to end the war.

This sense of optimism grew as, first Senator Eugene McCarthy of Minnesota, and then your father entered the contest for president. There was a strong, resilient antiwar message out in the country. The people supporting the war, President Lyndon Johnson and later Vice President Hubert Humphrey, were being challenged. Voters knew they now had an option. Even with the murder of Dr. Martin Luther King, there was still a small measure of hope.

With the loss of Senator Kennedy after the California primary, the mood of this country turned ugly. The most bitter scenes of all came at the Democratic National Convention that August in Chicago.

But think about it. Imagine that instead of the rioting between students and police we saw in that convention city, Robert Kennedy had arrived to champion the antiwar cause. Think of the scene in that convention hall if it was Bobby Kennedy standing at the podium. It could well have been like the 1964 convention when every delegate applauded him seemingly forever. Imagine that instead of the rioting and the tear gas, the Democrats might have left Chicago united and inspired. Instead they left like the walking wounded, headed toward defeat in November.

KK: *How were things different between the time you left the country for Africa and the Peace Corps in the fall of 1968 and when you returned home in early 1971?*

CM: It was the difference between day and night. Before I left, the mood in the country, even in the anti–Vietnam War movement, was hopeful. When I returned home, I felt a real negativity in the air. Drugs had become common. People were cynical and downbeat about where the country was going.

We had Richard Nixon as president. Instead of a war cut short, which Bobby Kennedy proposed, Vietnam continued to rage. Young Americans continued to die.

That's the big thing that would have been different. With Robert Kennedy as president, we would have ended the Vietnam War in early

1969. Instead, it went on for four more years with Americans still doing much of the fighting.

KK: *What led you to make the big effort to write a book about my father?*

CM: One is history. In researching and writing about President Kennedy, I discovered the huge, central role Bobby played in his life and career.

It was Jack who credited his brother with getting him elected to the US senate in 1952. He said Bobby had the best political organization in Massachusetts history. Without that success in '52, it's hard to see how John F. Kennedy could have run for the Democratic vice presidential nomination in 1956 or the presidency in 1960. Becoming a senator was key and it was Bobby who ensured that his older brother did just that.

It's widely recognized that Bobby Kennedy was one of the greatest-ever presidential campaign managers. No one knew that better than the man who won the election. Jack gave Bobby full credit for putting everything together and making it work. His one big mistake was his stubborn resistance to his brother's selection of Lyndon Johnson as his vice presidential running mate. Jack needed Johnson to win Texas and elsewhere in the south. Without those states, there would have been no New Frontier.

KK: *What was that second reason you mentioned for writing the book?*

CM: It's about today. I believe your father personified what we need now in this country.

Think of those people standing in salute of Robert Kennedy when his funeral train rolled down from New York to Washington. All those faces, white, black, many of them poor. Bobby wanted to unite those faces. He wanted to build a coalition of the country's working people.

I often think of one particular family standing along those railroad tracks in June 1968. The father has his arm in a crisp salute. So does his son. All three members of the family, including the wife and mother are dirty from work. Yet they've come out this day to register their respect, more than that, their patriotic affection for Robert Kennedy.

It reminds me of some folk wisdom a country boy from West Virginia once shared. "Do you know why the little man loves his country?" he asked. Then, looking me direct in the eyes, he gave the answer. "Because it's all he's got!"

That's the kind of deep patriotism that was shown to Bobby Kennedy's funeral car as it passed on its way to Arlington Cemetery. People who have nothing loved this man born to wealth. Why? My hunch it's because he so clearly and passionately loved his country just as much as they did. Like them, Bobby was a gut patriot.

I'd like to think it's because of such families that Bobby Kennedy ran for president. He feared that the Vietnam War and the social conflicts at home were bringing real division, real trouble to the country.

Preventing that division and trouble was the goal he set himself: bring the country back together. "If the division continues," he said, "we're going to have nothing but chaos and havoc here in the United States."

A unifier at the top is what we don't have in current national politics. Instead, we have leaders who divide people in order to gain and hold power. Poor and working whites are urged to vote for a candidate because he opposes the aspirations of minorities. They are told that they climb upward when others are shoved downward.

Bobby Kennedy argued the opposite. He would do anything to get across the ideal that we're in this together. In the Indiana presidential primary, he even rode around the city of Gary with the city's first African American mayor on his right, the city's most popular citizen, the former middleweight champion Tony Zale on the other side.

I wanted to write about a political leader who united. It's the reason we need someone like RFK today.

KK: *What could he teach us today?*

CM: You told me a couple times that the key to your father was getting the boot off people's neck. It's to show compassion for people in trouble.

Today, there's a nastiness in our leadership, an attitude of every man for himself. It's hurting the country, robbing America of our soul. Your father believed that America was a great country. He wanted America also to be a good country.

KK: *What was the first clue to my father that you came across?*

CM: When I came back from two years in Africa with the Peace Corps, I wanted to be a legislative assistant to a senator, much the way Ted Sorensen had started out with JFK. The first job I was able to get was working for a Democratic senator from Utah. Wayne Owens, the senator's top aide, had been Rocky Mountain coordinator in the Robert Kennedy presidential campaign.

The best job Wayne could offer me at first was that I'd work in the office during the day, answering mail and doing some basic legislative work. Then, I would moonlight as a Capitol policeman. That's where my salary came from. It was a patronage job.

It was a familiar arrangement back in those days. Harry Reid, the future Senate majority leader, worked on the Capitol Police when he went to law school. Mike Barnicle, political commentator, was also on the force.

Personally, I learned a lot during those few months as a Capitol Policeman. One of the stories I learned was that there was one Democratic senator who made a point to always greet the Capitol Police officer on duty when he passed him in the morning. The others didn't bother; they just walked past like the man wasn't worth their time.

It showed that a figure I had always saw as a liberal, concerned for minorities, people in trouble, had respect for men responsible for enforcing law and order. My other reaction, which cut closer, was that he wasn't some elite liberal who supported the people but didn't have time for individual people out doing their job. In other words, he was the real thing.

Bobby would say that cops, waitresses, firefighters, construction workers were his people. I think losing a reputation for that kind of one-to-one affection with working people is the big reason the Democrats lost states like Pennsylvania, Wisconsin, and Michigan in 2016.

KK: *What more did it tell you that he seemed to go out of his way to greet the police?*

CM: I knew Bobby Kennedy stood up for people in trouble, including minorities. What made him truly impressive is how he stood up for law enforcers as well. He believed that the law and justice should work hand in hand. A good police officer can be a force for good. He or she should be a protector of rights, including those of minorities. He believed that law and order is the only way to protect those rights.

KK: *What led you to entitle your book about my father* A Raging Spirit?

CM: I believe Bobby Kennedy was, from the time he was very young, a deep believer in good and evil. He saw the world as a Catholic. There is right and there is wrong. He spent a good many years of his life, especially on Rackets Committee in the late 1950s and later as attorney general as he put it, "chasing bad guys."

There were the crooked labor leaders like Dave Beck and Jimmy Hoffa, a man Bobby saw as pure evil, who stole brazenly from the Teamsters funds. Later came the Mafia figures themselves, frightening characters, true menaces to society.

That said, I don't think Bobby Kennedy ever pursued a goal half-heartedly, whether it was backing his brother Jack in a political fight or taking after hit men in organized crime.

Bobby also displayed some of his "raging spirit" running his brother's campaigns. Jack wanted to be liked. When it came to getting the job done—winning!—Bobby was willing not to be so likeable. He took the responsibility personally of ridding the campaign of hangers-on, the one willing to tell workers they were not going to get paid, that the Kennedy operation was strictly a volunteer effort.

Let's face it. There were particular roles in the campaign Jack avoided for the obvious reason that doing those jobs made enemies. In such cases, he put his brother to work.

One case was when late in the 1952 Senate race, Jack decided he wanted to keep his campaign separate from the governor's. He did not want the other Democrat's collapsing campaign to bring down his.

Keeping the governor at arm's length was Bobby's job. And it was Bobby who the governor ended up blaming for his loss, not Jack.

That was another part of Bobby Kennedy's "raging spirit." He was ferocious in looking out for his family.

KK: *How do you see my father's role in the New Frontier?*

CM: After writing *Jack Kennedy: Elusive Hero* I knew that the history of that administration could not have happened without your father. Bobby Kennedy was central—I would say indispensable—to his older brother's presidency.

Just two examples: the Cuban Missile Crisis of 1962 and the Civil Rights speech in 1963.

In the first case, Bobby started out as a "hawk," someone who wanted to go into Cuba and blow up the nuclear missile sites the Soviets had built there. Then, as he often did, he reconsidered. He realized the number of Cubans and Russians who would be killed in such an attack. Like his brother, he worried how the Soviets would react. Would they take West Berlin? What would the US do then?

Bobby also played a critical part in the resolution of the crisis. It was he who leaked to the Soviets the idea of removing the US nuclear missiles in Turkey if the Soviets agreed to remove theirs in Cuba. That secret trade ended up saving the world from the risk of a nuclear war.

On civil rights, it was Bobby who pushed his brother to give the historic speech he gave in June of 1963. You can see him doing just that in that excellent documentary by Robert Drew.

KK: *Why do you think people across the political spectrum so respect my father?*

CM: A number of reasons: courage, honesty, passion for the cause. Name another politician who would go into a tough inner-city neighborhood knowing he had to tell the crowd that Dr. Martin Luther King had just been killed. Or another candidate who'd tell tough gun owners in Oregon we have to do something to keep guns from criminals and people with mental problems. Or tell college students that they shouldn't have draft deferments while other young people are being called to fight in a war.

There's something else: nobility. I remember reading what writer Patrick Buchanan, really an archconservative, said about your father's concession speech when he lost the Oregon presidential primary. He said that he could not have been more impressed by Bobby's performance than if he'd won.

KK: *Would Robert Kennedy have won the election in 1968?*

CM: I think it's impossible to say. Certainly, events would have gone greatly different. Had RFK won in New York after winning California, he would have finished the primary season on top in the polls. From there it would have been trench warfare, delegate to delegate. I do believe if he'd beaten Hubert Humphrey for the nomination, he would have beaten Richard Nixon. I think he would have drove him crazy.

Then, again, who knows? Bobby Kennedy himself didn't. He believed he was engaged in an "honorable adventure."

"I can accept the fact that I may not be nominated now," he said in his last days. "If that happens, I'll go back to the Senate and say what I believe, and not try again in '72. Somebody has to speak up for the Negroes, the Indians and the Mexicans, and poor whites. Maybe that's what I do best. The issues are more important than me now."

I think that fatalism of his is one reason for the strong love for him. I can remember conversations over in Swaziland with a fellow volunteer. It is hard to appreciate now the level of hope people placed in your father.

KK: *How do you think President Kennedy's death affected my father?*

CM: People write about the dramatic change in your father after what he could only refer to as "the events of November 1963."

I think the loss of his beloved brother was traumatic. His younger brother Ted worried if he would make it through the loss.

But the fact is Bobby was very much the same person early in life as he was late in life. For one thing, he always had a generous streak for people in trouble.

From childhood, Bobby Kennedy showed a large heart and a generous spirit. Your family friend Lem Billings once said what a "generous little boy" he was.

His high school roommate and lifelong friend Dave Hackett said he always had compassion for those facing problems.

When a Catholic priest on Harvard Square began preaching a doctrine of "no salvation outside the Church," Bobby wrote a letter of complaint to the Cardinal.

Look at the courage he showed inviting diplomat Ralph Bunche, the first African American to win the Nobel Peace Prize, down to speak at UVA law school, then insisting the audience be integrated. On top of that, they had their guest stay overnight even though your mother recalled people throwing things at the house all night.

What changed in Bobby after Jack's death was his shift in purpose. Before he focused on, as he put it, "chasing bad guys." After the shock of Dallas, he focused on the victims. As a member of the Kennedy family hinted to me, he may have decided that villains take care of themselves; they create their own hells on earth. So he decided it was better to focus on life's victims.

I remember telling your mom what I thought was the difference between President Kennedy and your father. "Jack was charm; Bobby was soul." I think she liked hearing that.

———————— ⚬⚬ ————————

"We must deal with the world as it is. . . .
We must get things done. But idealism, high
aspirations, and deep convictions are not
incompatible with the most practical and efficient
of programs. There is no basic inconsistency
between ideals and realistic possibilities. There
is no separation between the deepest desires of
heart and of mind and of the rational application
of human effort to solve human problems."

—ROBERT F. KENNEDY

———————— ⚬⚬ ————————

Robert Kennedy greets crowd on campaign trail, 1968 (Steve Schapiro/ Fahey Klein Gallery)

"The gross national product measures neither our wit nor our courage, neither our wisdom nor our learning, neither our compassion nor our devotion to our country, it measures everything, in short, except that which makes life worthwhile."

—ROBERT F. KENNEDY

GAVIN NEWSOM

◦◦◦

Gavin Newsom was mayor of San Francisco from 2004 to 2011. His decision in 2004 to issue marriage licenses to same-sex couples was a first step on the path to the legalization of same-sex marriage throughout the United States. When he launched a universal health care initiative in San Francisco, it was also a first step. In 2011 he was elected lieutenant governor of California, and since February, 2015, he has been running for governor in the 2018 election. In his campaign, he has advocated for tougher gun laws, the legalization of recreational marijuana, and the adoption of a universal health care program for California.

We met in Newsom's San Francisco office, across the street from his restaurant where they serve wine from his PlumpJack vineyards.

Gavin Newsom: Robert F. Kennedy's speeches are so contemporary that if I gave them today, I'd get a standing ovation. I don't know of anyone who gives speeches like that. They're jaw droppers. I can connect every single one of them to where we are in the world today. That's praise for the vision of the speeches, but not a great testament to how far we've advanced.

    Kerry Kennedy: *It does highlight the lack of progress, but the problems he talked about were the most daunting issues facing our country:*

race, poverty, injustice. He knew progress would be slow. But he also spoke about enduring American values and ideals: that each person can make a difference, that those closest to the problems are most likely to know the solutions, and that we need to treat one another with dignity and respect, be tough with the bullies, and love our country.

GN: Bill Clinton in '92, and in fact, the Democratic Leadership Council, the New Democrats, took much of their program from your father. His ideas were not just prophetic but also influential. We need to pay especially close attention to his ideas today because, as idealistic as we may be, we need to bring our message back to earth.

We need to give it life, to make it actionable. We need your father's hard-headed pragmatism. Oliver Wendell Holmes said that because "life is action and passion, it is required of a man that he should share the passion and action of his time at peril of being judged not to have lived." Robert Kennedy was about passion and action. Holmes added that we would all be judged and ultimately judge ourselves by the extent to which we contribute to the life of our city, state, and nation, and the world we're trying to build. To me, that notion of civics is so important. It's the idea that we have agency, that we're not bystanders in the world, that we can shape the future; there's no guy or gal on a white horse who's going to save the day; we all have a responsibility.

If we want to have responsibility, citizenship, and agency, we have a tool today that people didn't have back in the sixties. We can use technology to advance democracy by making government accessible. Your father talked about how so many minority individuals were demanding their rights as human beings, how they wanted "a measure of control over their own lives, over their own destinies, a sense of communication with those whom they have elected to government."

The technology we have today can be a tool of empowerment and civic engagement; it can enable active, not inert, citizenship. Justice [Louis] Brandeis wrote, "The most important political office is that of the private citizen." Today we have the private citizen with access to the internet.

There's an important connection between your father's empathy and this ideal of citizen participation. Your father was able to see the world from someone else's perspective. He wanted to show other people how to get that same range of perspective. There's a notion of global interdependence that your father was on to before a lot of other people were. To live in that world we need to know how we can be connected to lots of other people in all kinds of different circumstances all around the nation and the world.

KK: *How did you first become aware of Bobby Kennedy?*

GN: There's a picture of my father and your father, literally days before your father lost his life, when my father was running on the same ballot for the state senate. Your father signed it to my mother, Tessa. My mother passed away about fifteen, eighteen years ago. An interviewer once asked me, "If there was a fire in your house, besides your kids, what's the one thing you would grab?" I said it would be that photo. I am not exaggerating when I say Robert Kennedy inspired me to get into politics. That photo means a lot to me.

My parents were divorced, and the picture connected me to both my father and your father. The picture had always been on my mother's wall, so it connected me to her, too. I wondered: "What is it about that picture?" It created an inquiry. Why is he important enough to be on our wall?" I had to start learning about the person in the picture. I dove into that period in history, and I've been more inspired by that period than any other time. There was that idealism. There was the language that transcended the times, something magical. There was a different kind of politics: hardheaded, pragmatic. These things resonated with my own sense of politics, as a businessperson with twenty-three little businesses who is progressive in my desire to change the world. I connect to all of that, and truly it started with a photograph.

KK: *As a politician, you've taken progressive positions on the environment, marriage equality, homelessness, health care, and marijuana, among other controversial issues.*

GN: That photograph and what I did in 2004 on marriage equality are directly connected. Your father talked a lot about the shortness of life; he was very aware that a person's time is limited and our wisdom is limited, too. A person might get just one chance to step up and do the right thing, so he urged us to do the right thing: strike out against injustice, never let anyone explain it away, be authentic, be bold. Even people who hated your father admitted he was authentic. I remember the moment when I made that decision on marriage equality. I remember thinking, "I've made the decision. I'm going to do this tomorrow." There were five more days of discussions after that, but I had already made the decision. The sense of authenticity was exhilarating. My striving for that was inspired by your father.

You know what? It's addictive. Once you've done something truly authentic, you're like, "God I want more," because you don't ever again want to live a life "managing" problems or explaining them away or "failing more efficiently." Fifty years from now, I don't want to see the same problems I'm facing today. As they say in psychology, it's time for pattern interrupt. All the issues are more pronounced now: the income inequality, and wealth disparity, the fear of the other, and the xenophobia and nativism.

I get restless. When I see these difficult problems, I feel like I have to do something. Here's your father again: "The world demands the qualities of youth: not a time of life but a state of mind, a temper of the will, a quality of the imagination, a predominance of courage over timidity." I introduced Governor [Jerry] Brown with that quote three weeks ago at the State of the State. He's turning seventy-eight, and he's a man of action who's done a magnificent job here in California because he's a youthful seventy-eight-year-old who has a predominant love of courage over a love of ease. We're not talking about chronological age; it's about a state of mind. It's an energy that prevents you from resting when there's something wrong; it's a feeling that you have to right that wrong. That comes from the Day of Affirmation speech, of course—your father's greatest speech, in my opinion. Not just the words, but the context. . . . Apartheid South Africa didn't allow black South Africans in to hear your father speak.

KK: *Yes, actually, June 2016 was the fiftieth anniversary of my parents' trip to South Africa. RFK Human Rights organized a delegation with twenty-three members of my family, six members of Congress, including John Lewis, and Polly Sheppard and Felicia Sanders, the two women who survived the church massacre in Charleston. As you remember, the next day, at the arraignment, Polly and Felicia said to the shooter, "I forgive you."*

We followed my parents' steps all throughout South Africa and we ended up at the University of Cape Town, where he gave the Day of Affirmation speech. One thing I didn't know about their trip was that the South African government refused to give my parents a visa for six months. Then, a couple of days before the trip, the regime said no press, so it was only my mother and father and a couple of aides. When they arrived in Pretoria, the South African government pulled their security detail. Five years before, Dag Hammarskjöld, the secretary general of the United Nations, had died in Northern Rhodesia (now Zambia), and many credible people suspected that the South African government had killed him. My parents were bold. When they flew over Robben Island (where Nelson Mandela and other political prisoners were held), they asked the pilot to tip the wings for the prisoners below. After that action, the pilot was stripped of his flying license.

Ian Robenson, the student who had invited Daddy to speak, was banned, and placed under house arrest. When Nelson Mandela came to Boston, he told the story of Daddy visiting Robenson, and suggesting that they talk in the bathroom, where Daddy opened all faucets to make the bugging devices fail. Robenson, surprised, said, "Where did you learn that?" and Daddy, with an easy laugh replied, "I was the attorney general, you know."

GN: The Day of Affirmation speech was gutsy; you didn't have to read between the lines, it was full throttle. Those words are powerful and they're a good reminder. It's not youth; it's the energy and commitment of youth.

KK: *Yes, and he spoke about the four great dangers to all social movements—futility, expediency, timidity, and comfort—all the ways in which we tell ourselves not to try to create change. But creating political change is what your life has been about. You don't really fall into a liberal or conservative camp, so you're sort of a hybrid. My father was that, too. He said: "What we do need and what 1968 must bring is a better liberalism and a better conservatism. We need a liberalism and its wish to do good, yet that recognizes the limits to rhetoric and American power abroad; that knows the answers to all problems is not spending money, and we need a conservatism in its wish to preserve the enduring values of the American society, that yet recognizes the urgent need to bring opportunity to all citizens, that is willing to take action to meet the needs of the people."*

GN: I created a program called Care Not Cash; the idea was to cut cash grants for homeless people and replace them with more shelters and other services. When I announced it, I paraphrased that exact quote. I said, I've supported spending more money in the past five years and poverty is getting worse, not better. I said liberalism needs to be redefined. There was a lot of opposition. I literally had to move out of the house because they spray-painted my house. I ended up having to move to an apartment building where they had security people downstairs. Finally we won at the ballot box. In many ways, this was a demonstration of why I became mayor. I was arguing for taking away money from poor people, the most vulnerable, homeless people, as a solution. I mean, good luck doing that as a liberal. It really is redefining liberalism— at least that's one way to put it. By the way, the program has been a phenomenal success. We radically changed people's lives; thousands of people got housing because of what we did. My worst critics, even to this day, ten, fifteen years later, recognize the merits of it. It was difficult, but the whole effort was based on your father's words. I need the inspiration, believe me. You don't know how difficult it is as a politician to try such a radical move with respect to your ideology, to your label. It's a big thing to find a solution outside the usual lines in which the game of politics is played. In this case, at least, the result was that we helped people.

KK: *Change is inevitable, but it's frightening. People prefer the status quo, even if it's uncomfortable. It's predictable.*

GN: There's nothing more difficult than changing the order of things. There's a huge constituency for the status quo. This is particularly true as it relates to antipoverty programs, particularly as it relates to those that have been beneficiaries of the status quo as it relates to governmental largesse, or private-sector and nonprofit largesse. And they're going to fight like hell to hold on to their piece of the pie or their trophy that they have on the wall, and frankly, that's one of the fundamental great challenges of our time.

Fortunately for me, in a way, I have pretty severe dyslexia, so there's no linearity in my thinking. I was never going to succeed being rote or walking down the old cow path; I've always had to come at things from different angles. I started something many years ago called the "Failure": every month, I reward the biggest screwup with a bonus that's over $1,000 now. At the end of the year we announce our twelve biggest failures at our annual party and we announce the Failure of the Year award. The idea is that we're celebrating initiative. It's also about taking responsibility: don't just sit there, do something, learn from your mistakes. It's about change; it's about disrupting the status quo; it's about that creative buzz that comes when you try something different.

Change is inevitable; we've proven that twice, with Obama and Trump. Progress is not. That's a major distinction, and we've got to face it.

KK: *Daddy said, "Progress is a nice word but change is its motivator and change has its enemies." That's the struggle, right there.*

GN: You have to lean into the world. It's what I used to say to my staff here: Live life out loud. Be fully expressive in life. Everyone has the capacity to flow with the forces of life. Learn from it, don't follow others. Step up and be authentic, and don't be ideological. That's another thing

I love about your father: he was never ideological. Be open to argument, interested in evidence. I don't want to be a bystander in the world. I try to shape the future. Your father said, "We cannot stand idly by and expect our dreams to come true under their own power. The future is not a gift: it is an achievement. Every generation helps make its own future."

The determining factor is your purpose. "Why am I here, why am I doing this, what's the motivation?" It's not just being something, having a big title or reaching a certain status. You have to do something once you get there. That's your father's spirit. You don't have to be something to do something. It's this notion that so many of us wait to be this or be that: "When I'm mayor, when I'm governor, when I'm president, I'll do this." I mean, of course your dad was a senator and had formal authority as attorney general. But people like Sarge Shriver and King himself, and Gandhi, and Cesar Chavez: none of them had formal authority, but they still changed the world. At the end of the day, you don't think of Nelson Mandela as a one-term president and the things he did in that term; you think about his moral authority and what he accomplished in his lifetime. Again, that's your dad; it's his moral authority. He didn't need to be president. He left us a sense of genuine possibility. That's a transcendent legacy, and maybe it's more powerful than what could've been achieved in two terms and a presidential library.

BARACK OBAMA

꿍

*Barack Obama served as the forty-fourth president of the
United States from 2009 to 2017. Born in Hawaii, he studied at Occidental College and Columbia University before
attending Harvard Law School, where he was the first African American to become editor of the Law Review. He served
in the Illinois state legislature and the United States Senate.
He lives in Washington, DC, with his wife, Michelle, and his
daughters, Malia and Sasha.*

After Hurricane Katrina shattered New Orleans, then Senator Barack
Obama presented the RFK Human Rights Award to lower ninth
ward community organizer Stephen Bradberry, and spoke about the
influence Bobby Kennedy had on his life. A few years later, in the White
House, he again presented the award, now to two of Zimbabwe's leading dissidents, women who had been imprisoned over fifty times simply
for demanding basic rights. I interviewed former President Obama at the
Seeds and Chips Expo in Milan, Italy, where he addressed the future of
food and technology. The frenzied hope inspired by Obama's 2008 campaign echoed the spirit of optimism and unity of Daddy's presidential bid.

Barack Obama: When your father passed away I was seven, so I was too
young to experience directly the incredible inspiration he brought to

the country. I could only see it then through my mother and my grand-parents; I think they felt differently about themselves and about America when they heard him speak. It wasn't until I was older and I became a student of history and politics that I understood the role he played in getting an entire generation to reexamine some of its fundamental assumptions about race, poverty, and our responsibilities to our fellow men. The politics I tried to practice drew from the work he did and the example he set. For me personally what was most important was watching the trajectory of his career. Because I think that for young people getting involved in politics sometimes there's the sense that you come in and you're a finished product—you know exactly who you are and what you believe and you just get started on that. My experience has been that in fact you grow as you have more experiences and see new things. As much as any of our great public figures, Bobby Kennedy grew before our eyes—he came in as attorney general and a key adviser to the president, and that was both an institutional role and a familiar role. By the time he was running in 1968, you had a sense of somebody who had really gone inward and examined himself, and asked, "What are the things that are most important to me?" and as a result of that became more willing to risk taking positions that were hard, that challenged the status quo in ways that very few politicians were willing to do. With each step in that process he was more willing to dig deeper and push harder against the inequities that he saw around him; in this he's an extraordinary example of not just how public officials should live but how we should all live.

This progression was an example to me when I first got involved in politics. I was inspired by the civil rights movement, I was inspired by your father's campaign, but I think there's a tendency to operate with a great deal of caution. You're worried about making mistakes. You're worried about making a gaffe or seeming unsophisticated in how you approach a particular issue or problem. As I became more practiced in dealing with some of the biggest issues, I was able to overcome those fears and do a better job of acting on what I believed was right. Later on, by the time I was president, I was willing to talk about issues not from any consideration of how my words would play but out of a real need to speak as truthfully and honestly as possible.

Kerry Kennedy: *Can you point to an example?*

BO: America is divided around the cultural meaning of guns. There's a rural-urban split, there's a regional split. I'm respectful of the traditions around gun ownership, but after Newtown, where twenty children were killed, and when I looked at my hometown of Chicago, where there's so much gun violence, it became very important to me to name this as a source of incredible pain and violence, particularly among our youth. It's always difficult to talk about the intersection of race and criminal justice, in part because no politician wants to look like he or she is soft on crime. We all want to be safe and we all appreciate the incredible pain that victims of crime suffer. Yet if you look at everything from the application of drug laws to the death penalty, the biases in the system are . . . they can't be denied. When I was president, I decided it was important for me to speak out about this, even though I knew it was always going to cause a backlash. Bobby Kennedy, as well as anybody, understood that at some point, if you're going to stay engaged in politics and not simply be complicit in our problems, if you really want to bring about solutions, you have to take a controversial position. I think back to his example whenever I face taking a stand that might be unpopular.

KK: *Robert Kennedy said in 1968 that in forty years we could have an African American president. At that time people thought it was impossible. What's your prediction about forty years from now?*

BO: Well, I think if you just look at the demographics of the country, we will see presidents from all sorts of backgrounds. I think that's inevitable. We will have a woman president—*that* is inevitable.

KK: *I hope it won't be forty—*

BO: Right, I hope it won't take forty years to do it.

―――――――――――――∞―――――――――――――

"We have seen the savage, bloody evidence
that there is today within our borders an 'other
America,' with its people too long denied a
share on our affluence, almost without hope
for improvement, no longer willing to live out a
nightmare distortion of the American dream. This
is the other America which subsists today in the
ghettos of our crowded, modern cities, with a legacy
of deprivation and indifference. . . . I believe that, as
long as there is plenty, poverty is evil. Government
belongs wherever evil needs an adversary and there
are people in distress who cannot help themselves."

—ROBERT F. KENNEDY

―――――――――――――∞―――――――――――――

KK: *Agreed, but that's an easy one. What do you think is unimaginable today that will actually happen in forty years?*

BO: Well, I'll tell you: it's entirely possible that how we think about our racial divisions will have fundamentally changed forty years from now. This is in part because I'm watching a younger generation that isn't as caught up as we've been with the traditional divisions. The culture of our young people is a polyglot culture. The way the younger generation thinks about love and marriage between races is entirely different from when you or I were growing up. And what's also true is that it's not just a black or white issue—you have Latinos and Asians and people from all different cultures. So I think that necessarily that will change for the better. I'm less optimistic if we don't make good choices about divisions of class and economics. The biggest concern I have, a concern your father had years ago, is that our democracy functions well when every person feels he or she has a stake, when everybody feels it's possible to make a difference. The Appalachian communities that Bobby Kennedy visited fifty years ago are still the other America. The inner cities are still the other America. So despite all the technological and social developments between 1967 and 2017, what's been surprisingly constant in our society is the economic stratification, and in many ways it has gotten worse. Our greatest challenge is to have a democracy that is responsive to the people, but for that to happen we need to have an economy that's responsive to the people. At a time when globalization and new technologies are changing our economic conditions every day, this requires vision, and it requires courage and empathy on the part of those of us who've had the luck to benefit from this new economy. We still have to do a lot of work to achieve that.

KK: *My father was devoted to reaching young people, and I know you are too. You've said that in your postpresidency, you want to focus on the next generation. How will you do that?*

BO: When I think about Bobby Kennedy's legacy, what stands out isn't laws or policy. It's inspiration. What he and Dr. King, and other great leaders, were able to inspire in people was action; people followed the example these men set and went out and did something themselves. That's why I always quote your father's Ripples of Hope speech. The impact of any individual is always going to be limited, but if we can inspire, if we can motivate, ten people, a hundred people, a thousand people, ten thousand people, we can make big change. I benefitted in my own campaign from the incredible energy and idealism of young people. In my postpresidency, the focus will be on training, supporting, spotlighting, convening this incredible next generation of young people, encouraging them to be active, giving them the tools they need to be effective citizens—nothing can be more important than this. With this generation we have a chance to build bridges of young leadership across national boundaries, racial boundaries, and religious boundaries. One of the things we did during my presidency was to start a young leaders program in Africa and in Asia. In fact, the first place we did it was in a town hall your father had visited in Soweto. We used that as the launching point for something we called the Young African Leaders Initiative that now has over 200,000 young people between the ages of twenty and thirty-five who not only have received training in how they can enhance the work they're doing in nongovernmental organizations, health organizations, and human rights organizations, but also are now learning from each other, so there's a network. What I'd like to do is to broaden that, make that more systematic, because if we can take an outstanding young activist who's teaching girls in a small village in Tanzania and put her in touch with a terrific teacher in an inner-city school in Chicago, and they are learning from each other how best to achieve their mission, not only will we see better results, but also we're going to create a climate in which government is more responsive. That's because these young people will end up putting pressure on elected officials to do the right things. So I'm very excited about the next generation. They're more sophisticated, they're better informed, they have the world at their fingertips, or at least on their phones, in ways that we didn't have. I think they're more open-minded and comfortable with change. But they're also a little bit more cynical about institutions, and part of what I want to do is make sure they realize how their involvement, their voices, can make a difference in these institutions.

KK: *Daddy often talked about youth as our greatest hope, but he also recognized that disaffection among youth spans economic conditions— so he reached out to kids who were dropping out of school in inner cities and he challenged wealthy students who joined large financial institutions rather than serving their communities. So reviving faith that one can make a difference is vitally important. But also then, as now, one of the challenges we face arises from the gap between those in the next generation who have the resources to fulfill their potential and the kids in Chicago who are afraid of getting shot going to school. It's difficult to bridge that breach.*

BO: That's true, but here's the interesting thing: I was in Chicago for a day two weeks ago. In the morning I met with about twenty at-risk men between eighteen and twenty-five who were part of a program to help them get jobs. Almost all of them were African American; I think one was Latino. Many of them had been in prison; many of them had been shot; many of them had fired shots. Later, in the afternoon, I was at the University of Chicago with some of its top students who were already involved in government or activism. What was striking was that the conversations I had with those two groups weren't very different. The young men in both groups were hopeful about the possibilities for their future. They were all responsive to adults giving them attention and a sense of direction. They were all somewhat cynical about existing institutions. Yes, we have many young people who grow up in the toughest of circumstances, and nobody's paid them any attention. The good news is that they're resilient, and it doesn't take a lot to point them in a positive direction. We haven't been giving them enough support in directing themselves, but if we make even a small investment in mentorship programs and job opportunities, if we expose them to a world beyond the street corner, they will respond. When you talk to the incredibly talented young people at the University of Chicago or at Northwestern, it's true they have more resources, they have more confidence, but they're no more confident about how to direct their energies. I know what I'm talking about here: I was one of those young people. I was the young man who was angry because he didn't have a father around and got into trouble and did drugs. I've also been the hotshot young college student who was trying to figure out how to channel his idealism. Both of those young men needed mentors, guides, teachers to say to them, "You count, your voice matters, and here are some tools you can use to make a difference. Here are organizations you can be part of. Here's a community that recognizes your talents." That's how those young people can thrive, and I think I'm in a good position to help with that. It's what Bobby Kennedy did for millions of Americans, and he also did it for young people in Soweto who became the parents and grandparents of some of the kids I've met.

KK: *You know, Mr. President, that's similar to the work we're doing with the Robert F. Kennedy Human Rights education program. It's called Speak Truth to Power.*

BO: Tell me about it.

KK: *The curriculum ranges from kindergarten through law school, and we've reached millions of students on every continent.*

It focuses on human rights, but it also includes social-emotional learning, community organizing, and ways to create change. It's an empowerment agenda, to transform victims into activists. We provide a book of lesson plans, and we also have hundreds of them online. Our aim is to get students to self-identify as human rights defenders—because when they look in the mirror and they see someone who knows how to make a difference, that is life changing.

BO: That's wonderful.

KK: *We also initiated RFK Young Leaders for urban professionals who are generally between twenty-two and forty-five years old and are interested in social justice. We invite local community organizations to speak to the Young Leaders and ask for volunteers—one month the speaker might talk about mass incarceration, and the next maybe human trafficking. Anyone who wants to attend, comes, and anyone who wants to volunteer has that option. We link capacity with need. And the young leaders have the bonus of meeting others who are interested in making a difference.*

BO: I think that's terrific. The challenge is to pull all the wonderful efforts out there together so that the whole is greater than the sum of its parts. One thing I learned first through organizing and then in politics is that there are many good efforts being made that people just don't know about. They need to know that they're not alone in the fight, that there are others who feel the same way they do and are making the same efforts they want to make. One thing you mentioned that we all need to work hard on is improving how we use the internet more effectively to reach young people. They get so much information from the internet. That can be for good, but we've also seen how much of it is trivial and commercialized and unreliable and how hate groups can also organize using the internet. I'm not sure we're doing a good enough job in projecting our values, Robert Kennedy's values, to kids who spend most of their time on their phones and get most of their information that way. That's something that didn't exist when your father was working on these issues. Over the next several years we need to work with Silicon Valley and social media organizations on how we can spur activism through these digital processes—not to replace the work that's being done on the ground but to motivate and supplement it.

I want us all to work together on that.

―∞―

"*Look, there are no playgrounds. There's no place for these kids to play. They're just like you; they have the same wants and needs.*"

—ROBERT F. KENNEDY

―∞―

SOLEDAD O'BRIEN

∞

Maria de la Soledad Teresa O'Brien is the daughter of an Afro-Cuban mother from Havana. Her father is from Toowoomba, Queensland, Australia, and is three-quarters Irish and one-quarter Scottish. Both were immigrants when they met at Johns Hopkins University in Baltimore, where they could not legally marry in 1958, because "miscegenation" was illegal in Maryland until 1967. They married in Washington, DC, and had six children, all of whom went to Harvard.

Soledad has been a correspondent or anchor on NBC, MSNBC, CNN, Al Jazeera America, and HBO Real Sports. *She is currently the anchor of* Matter of Fact with Soledad O'Brien *on Hearst TV and is also the CEO of Starfish Media Group, a multiplatform media production company she founded in 2013.*

During our conversation, Soledad expressed a depth of understanding about the intersection of race, poverty, and immigration in America which is all too rare.

Soledad O'Brien: I grew up with the complicated realities of race in America, and I've always thought Bobby Kennedy was one of the few politicians who understood those realities. As a privileged white person who had opportunities not to care at all, he made a commitment to dig down into experiences that were not his own and speak bluntly about what he learned. What's always resonated since I started reading about this as a kid is that some people are willing to work for better race relations, and he was one of those. He wasn't afraid to talk bluntly about the problems in America, and about how America has failed some of its citizens. Most politicians don't do that, right? Politicians love to do either the cheery version or even the version in which some Americans are better than other Americans. This idea that they haven't done a good job around race, around how people could come together and understand issues of race—I've always observed that it's uncharacteristic for politicians to get into that. I guess that's a long way of saying Robert Kennedy was a politician who ventured into areas where a lot of other people were afraid to go.

Racial conflicts in America have always been stark and complicated. Not enough has improved since 1968. I'm just wrapping up a documentary shorts project in Detroit where we looked at a lot of the economic and racial-justice issues. The data show that African Americans in Detroit are worse off today than they were in the summer of 1967, when the violence erupted. Obviously, some things have changed, but it's still very tough to have conversations about race and poverty anywhere in America. People are very resistant to that, maybe more overtly today than before. We've moved off trying to figure out the answers to some of those big questions. Fifty, sixty years ago, people were trying to figure out what causes poverty and how to fix it; they were asking, "How do you help people in poverty?" I don't know that there's any ongoing public conversation about how we can deal with poverty and racism in America today. Years ago we had better leadership on that issue, and that certainly includes your father. People just don't want to have those awkward conversations about desegregation. We have more data, but we're not using it for anything positive.

Kerry Kennedy: *When I interviewed Barack Obama for this book, I asked him what he thought would be different forty years from now, and he said, "How we think about our racial divisions will have fundamentally changed. . . . The way the younger generation thinks about love and marriage between races is entirely different from when you or I were growing up. . . . So I think that necessarily that will change for the better."*

SO: I hate to be saying this, but I completely disagree with the former president of the United States. Look at how much the number of mixed-race people has grown over the past forty years. It was a tiny percentage, but now it's one of the fastest-growing demographics. It's quite large, in fact; probably 7 to 9 percent of the population is of mixed race, and you still can't say, "Look at this now; we've solved this entire thing." A lot of young people—my children would be a good example—do think about race very differently, but they still confront racism at some point. In a public school not far from where we live, a bunch of kids were reported chanting at their classmates, "You're going to be deported now." These were eighth graders. A lot of people think it doesn't matter until they're confronted with situations in which it actually does matter, when it has an impact on the opportunities I'm getting or not getting, or when it has an impact on how many people are in leadership in this company I've just joined as an intern. It does matter. So I don't think it's reasonable to predict that the next generation will be all "Kumbaya" around race. I think they're having different experiences, but a lot of the structural racism issues will still exist.

You know, even though I'm the one with a public profile on these issues, I have five brothers and sisters who are all, in individual ways, addressing racism. My sister is an eye surgeon in Harlem. She has long advocated that the eyes are a really good way to determine someone's health. People who are diabetic have all kinds of issues with their eyes, for example. My sister works in communities with people who desperately need basic health care. She's not on television, but she's always been fighting for racial justice in the receipt of health care; she fights the

"Of course there are hazards in debating American policy in the face of a stern and dangerous enemy. But those hazards are the essence of our democracy. Full and informing debate is the basis of our system. We take the chance of freedom because we believe reasoned argument can move us to reasoned action. That is why we have always believed the right to dissent so fundamental to our system."

—ROBERT F. KENNEDY

depredations of poverty in her medical office. My sister Maria many years ago was having a discussion on the question, "What is black?" A professor had said to her that she "wasn't really black." So if you're Afro-Latina, what are you? What does it mean to be black? My sister Cecelia is a lawyer who does a ton of pro bono work, and this is crucial for any movement toward equal opportunity for poor people. Each person addresses this struggle in her own way. My platform is a microphone and a little screen on a few people's televisions. I try to figure out how to tell stories out of my personal experience that I think can resonate for other people.

My personal experience is that the immigrant experience and the race experience are inextricably tied together, even though they often tend to be seen differently. Usually we think of race as interchangeable with ethnicity. That's an issue that's been particularly interesting for me to cover, because there's so much data on it and because you can always tell when you hit a nerve. Today there's ongoing conversation around immigration and immigration reform, which can be distilled from the conversation about race but often intersects with it. I did a story in Lewiston, Maine, where people were talking about immigration, except they were actually talking about race, because Somalis were a key part of the discussion. Immigration and race often come bundled together.

I've always been interested in understanding *why*. Why do people feel free to line up and taunt their eighth-grade classmates about deportation? Why does someone feel so angry when a woman is running for office? Why is there this intersection of anger about immigration, race, and gender? I'm not thinking just of Hillary Clinton, but other women, any woman. Look at how often the comments are violent. Every single day someone is tweeting something that's inappropriate—hostile toward women, hostile toward African Americans, hostile toward Latinos, hostile toward people who are gay. It's just insane. It's such a crazy time, and the question that interests me is: Why? What's going on now? What flames are being fanned? Why?

The truth is that every week the *Washington Post* and the *New York Times* try to answer that question. What is happening? Is it economic anxiety? Is it that the leadership wants to fan the flames? Is it a great way to get media attention? Twenty years ago, if you were a white supremacist, it was hard to get on television. Now, if you're a white supremacist, I could probably get you booked on somebody's show in about ten minutes. This is where we are. We give a platform to people we know are despicable because we know it will drive ratings.

Why does racism drive ratings? I think we'd all agree that when you put people like that on TV, you elevate their platform. You're not in any way, shape, or form hoping that somebody throws tomatoes at them. You're trying to create something over the top and promotable so your show will stand out. People want attention. There was a time when you would frame certain things very carefully. I know because I was around then. I remember when David Duke was running for governor of Louisiana. We had these intense, thoughtful conversations about how you cover someone who spews hate. At the same time, the man is genuinely running for governor in Louisiana, so you need to talk about him and you need to cover him. Those subtle newsroom conversations rarely happen today. If someone is going to be disgusting and over the top and improper, you can just be sure that's going to be good for ratings. We've elevated those people with very little critical assessment of the effect they're having on our discourse. I think the political leadership has decided there's a real upside to having divisive conversations. It's not even dog-whistling anymore. Congressman Steve King of Iowa is a really good example. He says horrific things about African Americans and Latinos, and the response is, "Remember back in the day when Steve King said something and people would actually bother to comment? No one bothers to comment anymore." So, you know, the media has aided and abetted, and the political leadership—well, it wins because this stuff galvanized voters. If you layer on top of that the current widespread economic anxiety—people feeling like they're falling behind—it's very attractive to blame people who are different. It's OK.

KK: *The press is doing terrible things like never before, as you've just described, but the press is also under attack like never before. How does that impact who we are as Americans?*

SO: The press is under attack in a very intentional way because politicians intend to undermine the people who are saying bad things about them. Some of the press is doing some of the finest reporting we've ever seen, and that's wonderful. At the same time, there's a lot of crap around. I remember years ago now when I got a CNN breaking news alert that Britney Spears had cut her hair. At some point you're complicit in people being able to attack you. We're at a really troubled time, not just because people are attacking the media, but because the media itself is struggling to figure out what good journalism is. What is good reporting? What are the stories we should tell? What is the best way to tell those stories? It's a really scary time for the industry, not just because of the hordes of people who are trying to undermine the press, which it clearly serves their interests to do. If you can prove the press is wrong most of the time, it undermines anything negative they might say about you. The press is a broad category, but it's hard to ask people to take you seriously when you undermine your own seriousness too often. I think that's a real challenge. I think it's hard to say, "We stand for *X*" at the same time you're promenading the white supremacist of the day because you know it will build your ratings.

My approach is to do very little political reporting. We do a weekly public affairs show now, and it's really about context, which I like a lot. I really like being able to say, "If we're going to talk about the First Amendment, what does the First Amendment actually say? If we're going to talk about gerrymandering, what does that mean? What's going on with that?" Tit-for-tat political football is not interesting to me. Twenty-four hours of Trump every day is not interesting to me. It's not educating people; it's just over-the-top anxiety provoking for people. Whether you're talking about Fox, or you're talking about MSNBC, or you're talking about CNN, the coverage is just a little over the top for me.

We do some really good documentaries. We try to tell some surprising stories about people's lives, whether it's about veterans or about African Americans or about Latinos or about education. My documentaries are not on just one issue; they're about human beings who exist, whom we don't get to hear a lot from. If you had to pin someone down and force them to watch one of my documentaries, well, that person would get the idea that there are a lot of remarkable stories that deserve more airtime.

When I was growing up, my parents were obsessed with just a few well-known people. They were obsessed with the Kennedys. They were obsessed with the founder of the *Catholic Worker* newspaper, the activist Dorothy Day. They were also intensely interested in Martin Luther King and Rosa Parks. Those were the people they looked to, what those people said, what philosophies of life and action motivated those people. My parents admired them, though I don't think they ever had an opportunity to meet any of them. In the case of your father—and I'm talking about myself now too—I think the fascination has a lot to do with this: He was remarkable in that he was a politician who was willing to grapple with the complicated stories around race when everybody else wanted to dodge the issue completely. When you look back at that time, he and the others were willing to call it as it was. They were willing to say, "These are the issues in America. This is what's not working." It's a different time now. People are not quite so willing to do that, at the risk of not being perceived to be patriotic. Back then, we thought asking a question was patriotic, to say that America has its flaws and our goal is to help make those flaws go away; our goal is to make the nation better. That approach was considered patriotic. Today, it's unpatriotic to acknowledge the problems everyone knows we have. When I look back now and think about it, I believe a lot of people today would say that what your father was saying then was un-American. I think your father and Martin Luther King and Dorothy Day and Rosa Parks are some of the people most invested in America and most interested and committed to America and the American philosophy. But we live in interesting times.

KK: *My father quoted the Chinese curse that said, "May you live in interesting times."*

SO: And James Baldwin's words about desegregation, which I can't quote precisely, are that "this is not the solution, people. It's the first step." That is the honest approach to race that we don't hear enough of: "It's tricky stuff, people. It's not going to be solved tomorrow. We have to navigate through it." I think the politicians who are willing to say that are few and far between today.

---⚬---

"The future does not belong to those who are content with today, apathetic towards common problems and their fellow man alike, timid and fearful in the face of new ideas and bold projects. Rather it will belong to those who can blend passion, reason, and courage in a personal commitment to the ideals and great enterprises of American society. It will belong to those who see that wisdom can only emerge from the clash of contending views, the passionate expression of deep and hostile beliefs."

—ROBERT F. KENNEDY

---⚬---

Robert Kennedy, Saint Patrick's Day Parade, March 17, 1958, NY (Harry Benson)

―――――――――――――――― ∞ ――――――――――――――――

*"I don't think any of us thought of public
service as a sacrifice or as a means strictly
of repaying a beneficent country. We looked
to it as an opportunity for an exciting and
fulfilling way of life. Since public affairs
had dominated so much of our actions and
discussions, public life seemed really an
extension of family life."*

—ROBERT F. KENNEDY

―――――――――――――――― ∞ ――――――――――――――――

MATTEO RENZI

✦

Matteo Renzi is the leader of the Partito Democratico (Democratic Party) of Italy. He was prime minster between February 2014 and December 2016.

As Mayor of Florence, Matteo Renzi invited RFK Human Rights to open our Italian headquarters there, in a thousand year old building used as a cloistered convent and later as a juvenile prison. One of my favorite photos of Daddy dominates Renzi's Rome office. Harry Benson took it at the Saint Patrick's Day parade in New York, on March 17, 1968, the day after Daddy announced he was running for president.

Matteo Renzi: I first remember my mother speaking about Bobby Kennedy when I was in primary school. She told me: "A man who was a minister in John Kennedy's government decided to send the army to ensure that young colored men could study in the university." She was talking about 1963—I was then about ten years old. My mother also told me about the problems in South Africa. She told me about apartheid. We discussed the history of slavery in the United States, and then we came to the story of the Alabama students whom Bob Kennedy helped get into the university.

At the time, there were many scandals involving politicians in Italy, and she said it didn't have to be that way.

We talked about this man, Robert Francis Kennedy, Bobby, RFK, as a point of reference for a generation. So I read a book about him, and he became a point of reference for me, too.

A few years later, as a high school student in 1992, I read a book of his speeches. I remember the speech about the gross national product. It was one of the most famous in Italy. He said, "*Non misura né il nostro spirito né il nostro coraggio, né la nostra saggezza* né la nostra *conoscenza, né la nostra compassione* né la nostra *devozione al nostro paese, misura tutto, in breve, tranne quello che rende* la vita degna d'essere vissuta."

KK: *That's from his speech in Kansas, actually the day after the photo was taken, March 18. He said that the GNP "measures neither our wit nor our courage, neither our wisdom nor our learning, neither our compassion nor our devotion to our country, it measures everything, in short, except that which makes life worthwhile."*

MR: Yes. The first time I stayed up watching an election was November 1992, Clinton-Gore. When I ran for office, first as a university student, then for president of Tuscany, and after for mayor of Florence, I wove RFK quotes into my speeches. One I often used was: "*Alcuni uomini guardano le cose come sono e chiedono: perché? Io sogno cose non ancora esistite e chiedo: perché no?*"

KK: *That's how he ended his stump speeches in 1968: "Some men see things as they are and ask why? I dream things that never were and ask: Why not? "*

MR: "*Perchè no?* "OK, we can change, so why not?" I think it is one of the most powerful messages of the new generation, before the arrival of "Yes, we can." "Why not?" and "Yes, we can" have the same message of hope: Hope stands against hate.

I have always been active with Boy Scouts and Girl Scouts, and I remember a discussion with my Scout groups about Bob Kennedy in 2006 or 2007. I think it was for the 400th anniversary of the city of Florence, and we showed the film *Bobby*, in schools throughout the city.

KK: *Your focus on youth is only natural, because you were, and still are, so young. You were almost the youngest mayor of Florence and the youngest prime minister.*

MR: I became president of the province at twenty-nine and prime minister when I was thirty-nine.

Of course, I have used a quote from your father about youth: "*Questo mondo richiede le qualità dei giovani: non un periodo della vita, ma uno stato mentale, un temperamento della volontà, una qualità dell'immaginazione, una predominanza del coraggio sulla timidezza; dell'appetito per l'avventura sulla vita tranquilla.*"

KK: "*The world demands the qualities of youth. Not a time of life, but a state of mind, a temper of the will, a quality of the imagination, a predominance of courage over timidity, an appetite for adventure over the life of ease.*"

MR: I consider this absolutely true, and I hope it's true for me. The point is that today's political leaders need to change, especially in Italy. For twenty years the public debate was about the age of politicians. I became prime minister in part to disrupt the old generation. So my message is that youth is not simply *carta d'identità*—your ID card, your years—but it's a quality, a state of mind.

KK: *One of the things you're known for is trying, as you said, to disrupt, to create change, not for the sake of disruption, but for the sake of the future and to make the country better. As a political leader, how do you effectively confront the enemies of change?*

MR: This is a very important point, particularly in this moment, when a lot of people are afraid of the future and of change. Technological innovation, for instance, is inevitable, but it means change, and people are scared because those changes can be dangerous. But if you really believe in progress, you know that innovation creates the possibility for a better tomorrow. It's not easy to reconcile faith in the future, in change, in progress, and endure the pain and the suffering of people on the margins, particularly poor people. Your father combined a message of hope for future generations while expressing deep concern for people who were poor, black, elderly, vulnerable. This permitted him to be the only white leader to enter the ghetto during the terrible moments after the death of Martin Luther King and to have the respect of the poor people. This is the challenge for us today. The new generation of people on the left have a great vision for the future. This is good. I respect my past but I love my future. My country is looking toward the future; it is not nostalgic. At the same time, we must help people who are facing difficulties, we cannot forget them. That is the lesson of Robert F. Kennedy, this capacity to have vision, lead change, create progress, but at the same time have empathy and compassion and help for people who are suffering.

KK: *You've embraced the Third Way as progressive social policy matched to fiscal restraint, but some have said that is the vision of government that has predominated in Europe over the last twenty-three years and that it is exactly the current establishment that young people who are antiestablishment are fighting against.*

MR: The Third Way started with Tony Blair's emphasis on education—not liberalism, investment, or the economy. Another piece of it was to be tough on crime while being serious about addressing the causes of crime. So the Third Way means a lot of things. As an economic strategy, it was good for the nineties, for Bill Clinton and Tony Blair. But it is a model for the past, not today. Now we need a different economic strategy, particularly in Europe. I've fought against the austerity policies of the European Commission and European institutions.

KK: *The Third Way is associated, as you say, with Clinton and Tony Blair, and they were the disruptive youth of their generation. You're a different generation.*

MR: Absolutely. And Justin Trudeau in Canada is a different generation, and Emmanuel Macron in France is a different generation. We're not the Third Way. We haven't a name. Perhaps this is the millennial generation of leaders. Of course, Justin is older than me.

Robert Kennedy with his siblings, and parents, Ambassador Joseph Kennedy
and mother Rose, at their home in Palm Beach, Florida. Front row: Edward;
Middle row: Robert (holding rabbit), Joseph, Jean; Back row: Rosemary,
Patricia, Eunice, and Rose (Kennedy family collection, JFK Presidential Library and Museum)

OPPOSITE: *(top to bottom)* Edward, John, and Robert Kennedy, Palm Beach, Florida ABOVE: Robert and Ethel cutting the cake on their wedding day, June 1950 BELOW: In Jerusalem, 1948, as an accredited correspondent of the *Boston Post*, when the British mandate was coming to an end (Kennedy family collection, JFK Presidential Library and Museum)

OPPOSITE: Robert and Ethel's honeymoon, Hawaii, 1950 ABOVE: Robert Kennedy managed John Kennedy's Senate campaign in 1952 BELOW: *(left to right)* Robert, Jacqueline, Ethel, and John at Palm Beach, April 1957 (Douglas Jones)

OPPOSITE: *(left to right)* Robert Kennedy, Joseph, Ethel, Michael, Kerry, Robert Jr., Kathleen, David, and Courtney tobogganing at Hickory Hill (Kennedy family collection, JFK Presidential Library and Museum)
ABOVE: *(left to right)* John Kennedy and Robert Kennedy at Hickory Hill (Kennedy family collection, JFK Presidential Library and Museum)

OPPOSITE: Watching returns on election night, November 1960, Hyannis Port, MA (Photo by Jacques Lowe, © Jacques Lowe Estate) ABOVE: RFK talks with miners before the West Virginia primary in May 1960 (Robert Lerner, *Look* magazine photograph collection, Library of Congress) BELOW: Ethel and Robert Kennedy in Berlin on the balcony of the Schoneberg Town Hall, 1962 (photographer unknown)

ABOVE: RFK with the Ex Com, the group of top advisers summoned by President Kennedy to meet during the thirteen days of the Cuban Missile Crisis in October 1962 (White House photo) BELOW: RFK and JFK strolling together toward the Rose Garden, before JFK made his historic speech in June 1963 calling for a civil rights bill outlawing discrimination in public places. RFK urged the president to speak "in moved terms," as RFK's aide Burke Marshall recalled. (White House photo)

ABOVE: *(Left to right)* Martin Luther King Jr., an unidentified associate, and Robert Kennedy, Department of Justice, Washington, DC (Justice Department photo) BELOW: Joseph P. Kennedy Sr. celebrates his birthday with his family on September 8, 1962. (Kennedy family collection)

ABOVE: Robert Kennedy and Lyndon B. Johnson, October 14, 1964 (Yoichi Okamoto)
BELOW: Robert Kennedy with Chief Albert Lithuli, Nobel Peace Prize laureate, Durban, South Africa, June 1966 (photographer unknown)

ABOVE: United Farm Workers union leader Cesar Chavez shares a moment with Robert F. Kennedy at the end of a twenty-five-day fast in support of a grape growers strike, Delano, California, March 1968. (© 1976 George Ballis/Take Stock/The Image Works) BELOW: Campaigning in Kansas, March 1968 (Harry Benson)

ABOVE: A family photo in front of Hickory Hill. Mummy is holding her tenth baby, Douglas. My youngest sibling, Rory, was still a twinkle in God's eyes. (left to right) Maxwell, Christopher, Kerry, Kathleen, Ethel holding Douglas, Robert, Joseph, Robert Jr., David, Michael (Steve Schapiro/ Fahey Klein Gallery) BELOW: Robert F. Kennedy joins Oglala Sioux chiefs at pow wow, Pine Ridge reservation, South Dakota (photographer unknown)

For Ethel, with warm admiration, Coretta

ABOVE: RFK and Ethel pay their respects to Coretta Scott King after the assassination of Martin Luther King Jr., Atlanta, Georgia, April 1968. (Ethel Kennedy collection) BELOW: Christopher Pretty Boy and RFK, Rosebud Reservation, 1968 (Father Paul Steinmetz, S.J.)

ABOVE: Robert Kennedy greets his supporters at Bolsa Grand High School in Garden Grove, California (Sven Walnum Photograph Collection)
BELOW: *(left to right)* Maxwell, Robert, Christopher and John Glenn at Disneyland, June 1968 (Robert F. Kennedy Collection)

KK: *So much older. He's forty-five, and you are only forty-two . . .*

MR: I joke with Angela Merkel because during G20 she told me, "Justin is younger than you." "No, Angela, I am younger than Justin. Justin is more beautiful than me, but not younger!"

The situation is not easy, but there are a lot of leaders around the world who grew up with a great message from your father, and we are giving that message of change, empathy, and hope to the next generation.

KK: *Will you be prime minister again?*

MR: It is not possible to say. Italy has had sixty-four governments in seventy-one years. Twenty-eight different prime ministers. So governments don't last very long. My government was the fourth-longest out of sixty-four. This is the approach to checks and balances in Italy, but it means there is little stability for the government, and that is a problem. My idea was to create a better model through constitutional reform, but unfortunately, we lost.

The traditional politician in Italy spends his entire life in office, but that's not my intention. If I return to the prime minister's office, I imagine I'll focus great attention on innovation, technology, the environment, cities, and culture. I'd like to help Italy and to change Europe.

KK: *If you don't see yourself as a career politician, what do you want to do long-term?*

MR: When I lost the referendum, I preferred to end my political career. I resigned as the leader of the Partito Democratico, I resigned as prime minister, and I told myself, "Okay, this is the time to start a new life." I was very excited about a great new experience. Unfortunately, I listened to a lot of people, starting with my wife, my team, and my friends, who told me, "It's stupid to stop now, because a lot of people believe in this idea of change." I decided to continue in politics for now, but if I think about my future I see being at a university, studying and writing books. My other dream is winning the Championship of Italy with Fiorentina, our football team.

KK: *I wish Fiorentina all the luck! Now could you tell me about your Democratic Party app?*

MR: Yes, of course. The traditional approach to political organizing in Italy is top down, disseminated through the six thousand *sezioni*, or Democratic Party clubs across the country. They hold meetings, put on events, offer educational opportunities, and so forth. But now we can do much more using technology, so we created an app. The app permits us to communicate a message of hope, of change, of investment in the future. The one man who personifies empathy, grassroots involvement, high values, and a brilliant future is Bob Kennedy. For that reason, the app is called Bob.

KK: *That's beautiful.*

MR: I used the name—I'm so sorry just to take it.

KK: *I imagine he'd be pleased.*

MR: The application is here. Bob PD. The Partito Democratico with the inspiration of Bob Kennedy.

I want to say that I'm really glad to be talking with you about your father and to tell you that Bob Kennedy first, in the narrative of my mother, was a myth. He was a global brand in my mind, not a man. Then I read about his history, and there I learned about his personality, his success, his problems, the difficulties he faced, and the results he was able to achieve. I understood all that very clearly so I showed the students the movie about him. That is why now I want his name to continue to be on the minds of the next generation, as a model of values, empathy, compassion, and vision. For that reason, we call the app Bob. For every mobile phone there can be the PD Bob. This human being, Bob Kennedy, is our model for living for others.

JEFFREY SACHS

᪇

Jeffrey Sachs is the Quetelet Professor of Sustainable Development and professor of health policy and management at Columbia University and a special adviser to UN Secretary-General António Guterres on sustainable development goals. He has also held many other important positions in economic development, global macroeconomics, and the fight against poverty. He is the author of The End of Poverty *(2005),* Common Wealth: Economics for a Crowded Planet *(2008),* The Price of Civilization *(2011), and other influential books.*

Jeff and I sit on the board of Ethics in Action, The Sustainable Development Goals Center for Africa, and SDGUSA. Jeff and his wife Sonia are two of my dearest friends. Few have done more to reduce global poverty than Jeff Sachs. We spoke in his office at Columbia University.

Jeffrey Sachs: Your father was my first political love. I was fourteen in 1968, and I looked up to him during his run for the presidency. I had already thought about and learned about a lot of things, but it was the first presidential campaign where I was really paying attention. In primary school I had known about President Kennedy, and later I was energized against the Vietnam War. It was the beginning of my coming of age, and your father grabbed me and has never let go. I've continued, over fifty years, to refer to his wisdom, his leadership, and his eloquence. He really let everything loose in the 1968 campaign; it was the go-for goodness, something so deep and unusual, by a unique politician. People loved him. Everything came from his heart. It was not normal politics; he was reaching for something very different. That's why it's so important for us to think about him today, about what he did and what he stood for.

Robert Kennedy—and John Kennedy too—practiced the kind of leadership we desperately need. Their guidance can still help us today with the serious problems we face. You can study the Cuban Missile Crisis. That was a time when the two of them saved the world, and much of it had to do with the way they led.

What they did took courage, fortitude, and careful moral reasoning. When President Kennedy's executive committee met, you had all the foreign policy and military specialists gaming the situation, guessing whether the missiles the Russians were putting in Cuba would be ready to launch or not, thinking about how many people might die in a first strike or what would happen if the Unites States retaliated. You had two people, with a couple of others in the room like Ted Sorensen, who thought about it completely differently. They thought about it in terms of a piercing insight, that on the other side of the divide were other human beings facing the same reality. They recognized that the way back from the very edge of disaster was to realize everyone on both sides just wanted to survive the confrontation. That's not a military tactic. That's not a poker bluff. That is a moral insight that sounds so simple and naive but is deeper than what was in anyone else's head. The generals' training led them to: "We're good at bombing things, so let's go bomb. That's our role." It took wise leadership—I would even say idealistic young leadership—to say, "Yes, of course, that's your job, but our job is to reflect on the human stakes. We're more than tactical decision makers. It's our job to understand the demands of common humanity." That's how they intuited that [Nikita] Khrushchev had the same pressures, constraints, and insights they had. That basic insight was, "They don't want war, and we don't want war; we just need to diffuse this." John and Robert Kennedy understood this.

One of the realities of John Kennedy's administration, which I've studied at length, is that the war engine was always revving. Eisenhower, among others, warned us about this. The real responsibility of the president almost all the time has been to say no. It takes a lot of knowledge, insight, and courage to do that. I like President Obama, and I voted for him twice, but that war machine was always revving. He had his foot on the brake a lot of the time, but when he took it off, we ended up in a war in Libya that was completely unnecessary. We stirred up a war in Syria. Some of the worst aspects of American governance that your father and President Kennedy grappled with are still with us today. It worried President Truman that when the CIA was created in 1947, it had a contradictory and dangerous double mandate. It was to be both an intelligence agency, which we very much needed, and a covert army. Truman asked, "Why give both jobs to the CIA?" He was absolutely right, as history has shown us through the last seventy years. President Kennedy learned it when the Bay of Pigs became one of the big debacles of his administration.

This has happened frequently in our history. I hate it when there are covert operations to destabilize other countries and overthrow their governments. We have special ops in the military, too, which are similarly covert, unexamined, and under the control of people I don't trust for a moment to control such things. John and Robert Kennedy knew how important it was not to let the military and the covert parts of the government run amok.

Kerry Kennedy: *Yes, a great deal of my father's time as attorney general was diverted to trying to gain control over the CIA. After the Bay of Pigs, the CIA engaged in a series of truly harebrained schemes to assassinate Castro, from planting an interesting poisonous shell somewhere he might see while scuba diving, to stealing his shoes and placing a poison* in them that would cause his beard to fall out, on the theory that this would make the people of Cuba reject him. They were inept and ridiculous. When Daddy found out about it, he was furious. He hated communism and was against the Castro regime, but he was morally opposed to assassinating heads of state. He was later accused of trying to kill Castro and said, "Actually, I saved his life."

In Cape Town, Daddy spoke with students about four dangers faced by young people who want to accept the responsibility of creating a better world. The first of them was futility, the belief that there's nothing one person can do in the face of the enormity of the world's ills; then expediency, timidity, and comfort. These are all ills that you've given your life to curing. Many people ask, "How can I do anything about global warming?" but you got the entire United Nations to say, "We are going to stop global warming." People ask, "What can I do about disease?" You helped create PEPFAR, which does so much great work to stop HIV/AIDS. How do you find that kind of belief and commitment in yourself? Where does it come from? How do we get more people to feel, "I have a role to play; I can make a difference?"

JS: The essence of your father's approach to public service was that idea from George Bernard Shaw he often cited: "Some see things as they are and ask why? I see things that never were and ask why not?" When he faced a problem he went to work figuring out a way to solve the problem. That's what made him a leader. In President Kennedy's American University speech in 1963, he talked about how many Americans believe peace is impossible, that it can't be achieved, but then he says this is a defeatist view; our problems are man-made, and therefore they can be solved by man. This was what Robert Kennedy stood for. When you see problems, you try to solve them. It drives me crazy to see problems that I know are solvable but are not being solved. I spend most of my days saying, "Are you kidding? There's no excuse for not doing something about that." You have to understand the issues in sufficient detail to grasp what can be done, and it was also a characteristic of both John and Robert

Kennedy that they had wonderful advisers, really smart people, and they sought those people out for help in understanding problems.

I was working on AIDS in Africa for a while when the anti-retroviral cocktail was just being developed and having positive results in the United States. I asked, "Why aren't we doing this for other countries?" Answer: "There's no budget for it. It costs $10,000 per person. It's out of the question." Well, I looked into it and found out the retail price of the medicine was $10,000, but the actual cost of production was maybe, in those days, $300. So I said, "Don't charge them $10,000; charge them $300." Answer: "Well, that's a little bit tricky." I had to pull apart the challenge to identify what could be done. This is where futility can kick in, so I had to think, "Of course we're going to do this! I'm an economist; I can fill in the numbers. This doesn't cost very much money. We should segment the markets. Why don't we have a global fund? We can put the pieces together." It happened, not as quickly as it should have, but it came together. A lot of good happened when resources were applied to these challenges. Once you understand the problem, you can figure out the solution, and then you can get the money together. It starts with knowing the problem can be solved. We can do a tremendous amount of good in this world. We shouldn't accept things as they are. We should solve the problems we see. You have to start with the belief that there *is* something you can do. There's something every person can do. Every problem can be solved. Maybe there are problems that can't be solved, but you'll never solve problems unless you believe you can. No effort is futile. That's how you do it.

KK: *One of my memories of my father is right after Dr. King died. We were at Hickory Hill, our family home in Virginia. When you walked into the house, immediately to the left there was a den, which we called the TV room because it was dominated by a huge television. I was eight years old and was sitting there with him, watching the news. We were watching Washington burn. My father said, "I've got to go there." Forty-five minutes later I'm still sitting there, still watching the TV, and suddenly the camera pans and there is Washington in flames and there is Daddy standing in* *the midst of it. Right there on the screen. "There's a problem, I'm going: I have a role to play, I'm going to fix that situation."*

The challenge is getting people out of the role of watching TV and into the role of stopping the flames.

JS: I will forever remember the night Martin Luther King was killed and your father went straight into the crowd. He had a depth of feeling and empathy that made it possible for him to connect with people who were brimming with grief and anger, and he had the confidence, and he had the belief that he could make a difference. That's what it takes.

I was lucky to grow up in a caring, loving family, and I had a wonderful father who had social justice innately embedded in his character. He grew up in a working-class immigrant family that worked day and night to be able to get him an education. He became a labor lawyer and represented the trade unions in Michigan. He was one of the leaders of the Detroit ACLU and very much involved in civil rights in the city. We went to see Cesar Chavez in 1968, when he came to Detroit to talk about the farmworkers' movement. That was the atmosphere I grew up in. My mother and grandparents were also role models for me; they had the same basic sense that these are not issues to debate but simply what it means to be a normal, good person. As a child when you see this, it definitely has an impact. I didn't grow up in a religious way, but there is a Jewish idea, a very powerful idea, that I've always loved and taken to heart: It's *tikkun olam*, which means "to heal a wound in the universe." Every human being has the responsibility of trying to heal the world in some way. It's a very beautiful idea. It's not complicated. It's just two words. It seems self-evident. What are you supposed to do? You're supposed to help heal the world. When you're young it's just lucky to have examples like that.

KK: *My father became attorney general when he was thirty-five, the third-youngest ever. He was always intent on reaching out to young people. He sought out young people in the United States and around the world. He spoke about young people in all his speeches. He said, "Our answer is the world's hope; it is to rely on youth." He believed in the next* *generation. As an educator, you've also shown a great commitment to the next generation.*

JS: I've been in school, as a student and as a teacher, for the last fifty-seven years. From kindergarten through college and graduate school, I loved education. I became a professor in 1980 and have been a professor ever since. The remarkable and exhilarating essence of the university for me is that I still have the utter joy of working with young and idealistic people in formative moments of their lives. I believe that idealism is the most realistic attitude in life. It's not some dreamy state of affairs; it's a practical orientation to the kind of problem solving we've been talking about. I learn from my students every day. I started as a real academic doing the classic academic things, publishing articles and writing books. I was lucky enough to get tenured at a young age. I knew I wanted to do practical things; I had learned from my father to value the idea of professionalism, which meant mastery of a useful skill. I always believed that economics should be a useful art. It was in 1985, after I'd been teaching for five years, that I was asked to solve a real problem: an economic crisis in Bolivia. They had massive hyperinflation, 24,000 percent over the previous twelve months, and it was accelerating. It was a crazy situation. The fifty-peso coin, which was then worth practically nothing, was still the coin you needed to use in the pay phone booths, and you had to pay something between 5,000 and 10,000 pesos to get one fifty-peso coin. I was only thirty-one at the time; I brought assistants with me who were in their early twenties. In Bolivia they called them Sachs's Angels, because of *Charlie's Angels*, I suppose. People thought it was a little bit shocking to bring twentysomethings, but I believe it's good to give responsibility to young people. They need guidance and mentorship, but they have energy, determination, and idealism.

Mentorship isn't the norm in academia. We give lectures, students write papers, and they graduate. In medicine or crafts, for example, there's more mentoring, and that serves to transmit the professionalism, spirit, and ethics of the profession. It's important to have young people taking the lead in problem solving. You want people to participate in building their future, so they have to learn the skills and also how to take responsibility. You want to inspire them. You want to empower them. Education and practice are empowering. When you trust people, they rise to the occasion. This is something your father knew.

What goes with that, of course, is the idea of actively building the future. With youth, you're probably building on idealism rather than on cynicism, and that's important. As Jack Kennedy said, "We would trade with no other generation." He and your father saw themselves as part of a young generation on a mission to solve their generation's problems. Your father said, "It is from the numberless diverse acts of courage and belief that human history is shaped."

He warned against "the danger of futility: the belief there is nothing one man or one woman can do against the enormous array of the world's ills—against misery and ignorance, injustice and violence." He said: "Few will have the greatness to bend history itself; but each of us can work to change a small portion of events, and in the total of all those acts will be written the history of this generation."

I would like the future to say of our generation—these are my words—that we sent forth mighty currents of hope, and that we worked together to heal the world.

JOE SCARBOROUGH

⟨∞⟩

The former Florida congressman and longtime Republican conservative Joe Scarborough recently switched his affiliation to Independent. He is the cohost of Morning Joe *on MSNBC. As a member of Congress, Joe Scarborough worked with my brother, Congressman Joe Kennedy, to name the Department of Justice building after Robert F. Kennedy, a position that put him at odds with many of his Republican colleagues.*

Despite being on separate sides of the political divide, I have always considered Joe a friend, and he has been consistently supportive of the work of RFK Human Rights.

Joe Scarborough: I've read just about everything ever written about your dad, and I've never been able to confirm this quote, "Question initial assumptions." That saying was attributed to your father somewhere, and I ran with it. I posted the quote on my office door when I was in Congress so every time I would leave my office for a vote on the House floor, I would be reminded to "question initial assumptions." It has remained a guiding principle in my life through the years and all these years later, I don't really care if he said it or not. Few phrases would better sum up his legacy of service than that.

When I was first elected to Congress in 1994, my freshman class had campaigned on the Contract with America agenda. Though I have never been much of a joiner, I signed the contract belatedly and voted for most of its key provisions. Many were political softballs that Democrats supported as well. Many of us voted for term limits, a balanced budget amendment, a bill that made Congress abide by the same laws they passed, and limits on the years chairmen could run committees. Most were easy calls politically. But when it was time to pay for our proposed tax cuts, Newt Gingrich suggested that we pay for those cuts with spending cuts in Medicaid. I remember the speaker standing in front of the Republican caucus and telling us we could sell $270-billion cut in Medicaid by framing the program as medical welfare. As a small government conservative, I was always looking for federal programs to cut or eliminate. But even in those ideological days, I knew that this was a step too far. That's when everything stopped for me and I started questioning the assumptions that had guided my short political life.

Anyone who has been to an emergency room at midnight knows that for too many disadvantaged Americans, the ER is the primary care provider for the poor. And to make the political argument that the poorest among us are somehow gaming the health care system when they receive inferior care at almost every turn is as deeply offensive now as it was then. I grew up in the Southern Baptist church, but any good Catholic would also know as well that Jesus told his disciples that they would all be judged by how they treated the poor, the sick, the hungry, the imprisoned, and the hopeless. Those words in Matthew 25 were more important than the words in the Contract with America, and I stepped back in that instance and remembered what I had learned growing up because I followed the charge of always questioning my beliefs at every turn.

Many have written about how Bobby Kennedy evolved from a tough, take-no-prisoners conservative to a progressive champion. He used his power on the Senate committee and as attorney general in a way that caused concerns to civil libertarians on both sides of the ideological divide. But that makes his remarkable transformation from November 22, 1963 to June 6, 1968 all the more breathtaking. From his moral leadership inside the Senate, to Cape Town, to Indianapolis to California, the arc of your father's life shows how we can continue to grow while in public service.

Kerry Kennedy: *I agree that one of his great strengths was his ability to evolve, something which few adults do.*

JS: The 1968 campaign was like nothing that has ever happened in modern American history. His transformation was made all the more extraordinary and moving because it was the hardened Bobby Kennedy who both his friends and critics saw transforming in front of their eyes. Even if you disagree with historians' take on the tough and ruthless Bobby, the magnitude and significance of his growth as a human being while still in office remains inspiring 50 years later.

If we want to consider the meaning of his life, why he is still relevant to us today, I think of the dust cover of Arthur Schlesinger's book, which says: "The story of Bobby Kennedy is a story of our times." When conservatives ask me why I admire Bobby Kennedy so much and why your father is the reason I got into politics, I tell them that your fatuher was conservative with a "small-*c*." Both Edmund Burke and Russell Kirk believed conservatism was both the party of preservation and the party of progress. If you are a conservative with a "small-*c*," you look at the challenges of your times and ask, "Is now the time to preserve the existing order or push for change?" The answer to that question in Trump's time is to push back to preserve our constitutional values, push back to preserve our cultural norms, and push back the best of our historical heritage. Now is the time to preserve.

Today, Americans must fight to preserve their governmental institutions, their constitutional traditions, and the cultural norms that have held Washington together for centuries. We are a nation of immigrants that has striven to be more culturally inclusive. But Trump undermined these traditions during his campaign and during his time in the White

House. It is troubling that so many members of Congress have remained compliant even as Trump undermined the rule of law by attacking the legitimacy of federal judges and slandered the free press as "enemies of the people." These elected leaders are complicit because they fear attacks from talk radio and twitter. They cower at the thought of crossing their political base while your father seemed fearless in the face of the greatest challenges. He would deliver the same message to a group of Wall Street bankers that he would deliver to a gathering of West Virginia miners. His audience might change but his speech never would. That was another example I tried to take from his life and use it as a guide for my own public career.

Many saw your father as a tough-as-nails conservative when he worked for his older brother in the Senate and as his attorney general before President Kennedy's assassination. I always thought of your father as a tough liberal who would dare to dream and then fight to make that dream a reality. But because he was a romantic realist, I have no doubt that he would also have been the first to scrap ineffective liberal programs even if doing so upset party leaders. I also read that he had little use for political leaders whose heart wasn't in the fight. I think that Americans have elected too many of those type of leaders in the early part of the 21st century.

We seem to keep electing people to the highest office in the land who aren't completely invested in the nation's capital or its long and winding history. Public service was your father's lifework. It was President Kennedy's lifework. Washington was Lyndon Johnson and Richard Nixon's town. For better and for worse, these men lived and breathed politics, focused completely on government work and made their work in Washington their life. The outcomes were not always spectacular but those in charge of the levers of power were as qualified as anyone alive to sit in the Oval Office. LBJ and Nixon blew through too many constitutional red lights but were still constrained by their limits of power. When the Supreme Court told Richard Nixon to turn over the Watergate tapes, Richard Nixon complied immediately even though he knew it would mean the end of his presidency. Nixon was a tragic figure, in part, because his personal flaws eclipsed his political genius. LBJ was also terribly flawed as a man but his ability to push forward the civil rights agenda of President Kennedy remains his greatest legacy. And he could accomplish that Herculean task because he knew how Washington, DC, worked as well as anyone alive at that time.

This century we have elected George W. Bush, who openly disdained Washington and seemed to be driven to run by family motivations as much as any others. There are many things I admire about Barack Obama, but he too had little use for Washington and even less patience for figuring out how to make it work in his favor. And now we have an old reality TV star as president who didn't even expect to be elected. His campaign run was nothing more than a marketing ploy. Despite anyone's personal feelings for all three 21st century presidents, it is an inescapable fact that not one was prepared to be president and not one has any use for Washington. Bobby Kennedy thought public service was the highest of callings and he lived his life in a way that proved it was. For Bobby, governing wasn't an afterthought. Working to make people's lives better was why you were supposed to run for office in the first place.

As I was growing up with RFK as my hero, my conservative family members asked me: "Why do you like Bobby Kennedy so much, Joey? He was a tough son of a bitch." I even heard the same from my favorite liberal history professor in college. "Why do you like Bobby Kennedy?" he asked. "He's a son of a bitch."

After hearing it a second time, I thought: "It takes that kind of toughness to stand up to bullies, to stare down Hoffa, to challenge the Teamsters even as they were threatening his own family, to stand up to business interests who were exploiting workers, to stand up to segregationists in the South when that was a tough thing for a Democratic attorney general to do." That's one of the things that drew me to your father's legacy. His inner toughness so often made the difference in his effectiveness. Where did it come from?

The answer? I have my ideas about it. I think he was the good son. I think he was the good Catholic. I think as a younger child, he thought that's how he could be a good soldier for his dad. You always read that Joe Jr. was the golden child. You read that when his Choate headmaster asked JFK why he wasn't a particularly good student, he said "My older brother's got that down. He's done that. I don't want to do what he does." Maybe it was that same logic for your father. Maybe by the time he looked around and surveyed the landscape before him, he decided what he could do best was serve his father and brothers. I'm the youngest of three children and my older siblings came of age in the chaos of the late 60s and early 70s. By the time I got into high school, I wanted to be the good son who didn't cause his parents any trouble.

KK: *He was the seventh child, and I was the seventh child. As a younger child in a large family, you understand the benefits of having fair rules that apply to everyone; you don't want to see people who are smaller or weaker get picked on. He was physically smaller. He was also tough. He learned to be. But I think he had a very healthy relationship with his dad. Grandpa was a great father—he was fully engaged, and highly opinionated, and he expected his children to be that way, too. They respected one another. As a child Daddy was very sweet but had no tolerance for bullies.*

JS: He could relate to people in a way I suppose his oldest brother, Joe Jr., never could. Joe Jr. looked like a model; he was a great student and a great football player, everybody's all-American. It's very hard for a guy like that to look at someone who's hurting the same way someone in your father's position could.

KK: *Exactly. When he went to school he was always the kid who fought to protect the little kids. When he got into public life he already had a long history of being on the side of the underdog. He was always able to connect with people who were vulnerable or hurting or broken.*

JS: The things he stood up for then, many are still fighting for now. Racial justice has taken great steps forward over the past fifty years, but the past year has been filled with bitter setbacks. Your father visited the poor and oppressed that lived across the Mississippi delta and in other challenging areas. The rise of Donald Trump shocked so many because too many stayed isolated in Manhattan and Washington and all the places where elites live and vacation. After Trump got elected you had media types announcing, "I'm going to middle America!" They would drive thirty miles through Pennsylvania. And I guess that was good enough because anyone wanting to get a read on how much Americans were hurting didn't need to drive to Kansas to see what was happening. They could just take a cab down to Wall Street and then jump on the Staten Island Ferry. After walking around the Walmart, getting dinner and spending an hour in a Staten Island bar, any decent reporter would figure out quickly just how much trouble Hillary Clinton's campaign was in.

I learned a similar lesson driving from New York to Scranton, Pennsylvania, for a relative's wedding. It was the summer of '16 and as I was driving out, I had to find an ATM because I didn't have my E-ZPass. I finally spotted a Target about twenty minutes west of Nyack right off of the Hudson River. I got my money out of the ATM, I looked around, and I pulled out my phone and called Mika.

"I think Trump is going to win." This came as no surprise to Mika since she had been predicting as much for months but still asked, "Why do you say that? I'm in this Target about twenty-five miles outside of Manhattan and I might as well be in Wyoming. Everybody in this store is going to vote for Trump. He's going to win."

I just got the sense that these were people we hadn't bothered talking to. What was remarkable about that moment was realizing how much of a bubble we were all living in. Your father went to the Mississippi delta when none of his political advisers thought that made sense, went to South Africa when nobody wanted him to go to South Africa, visited disadvantaged and forgotten communities and I read how he would come home to your dinner table and tell everyone assembled there, "Let me tell you what I saw yesterday." Then he told their sad story to the rest of America.

People listened to him. They related to him. They could tell right away. "This man understands me, he's on my side. It's not that he looks like me; it's deeper than that." Your father had an edge to him that I could really relate to. Others like George Wallace had an edge as well, but used it to undermine American values. We saw Donald Trump do the same as Wallace in the New Hampshire primary. I looked up in the stands and there were working-class guys in there, and you could tell that they pulled their one dress jacket out of the closet that they probably hadn't worn in fifteen years. But they put it on to come out and listen to Donald Trump. That moment proved to me just how much Washington had let down working-class voters through the years. I still believe this country never really recovered from what happened in 1968 with the passing of your father.

Deindustrialization, globalization, and automation have combined to drive real wages down on average since 1973. It seems like the economic realities of the past half century have conspired against most American works. I had a 95 percent conservative rating while I was in Congress, but even I don't believe you improve the challenges facing our country's workers by cutting taxes for the richest 1%. Our leaders are in a race against time and unless they start challenging all of their initial assumptions, we will face an ugly economic and political reckoning all too soon.

The challenge for future leaders is to figure out a way to respond to that challenge and confront the fact that the rich keep getting richer and the poor keep getting poorer. Your father was already sounding the warning bells on this issue back in the sixties, when the challenge was far less great.

KK: *People are suffering. Daddy always cared about their suffering, even if they disagreed with him on every other matter. He was authentic in*

his empathy, and he was authentic when he challenged those with whom
he disagreed. People respected him for that.

JS: Here's the great irony: When you go out and speak your mind, when you stand up and say, "This is what I believe in. If you like it, great. If you don't like it, vote for the other guy," people respond to that with great hope and enthusiasm. They just want to be told the truth. And that is exactly what your father did.

FOLLOWING PAGES: Robert Kennedy campaigning
in California, June 1968 (Steve Schapiro/ Fahey Klein Gallery)

"It is indecent for a man on the streets of New York City or Cleveland or Detroit or Watts to surrender the only life that he has to despair and hopelessness."

—Robert F. Kennedy

HOWARD SCHULTZ

❦

Howard Schultz was born and raised in Brooklyn, where his family lived in public housing. He went to Northern Michigan University on an athletic scholarship and in 1975 became the first person in his family to earn a college degree. In 1982, he got a job working for a small coffee company called Starbucks. He soon left and started his own coffee company, then bought Starbucks, and in 1992 took it public. In 2011, he was named Fortune *magazine's Businessperson of the Year.*

He has been much honored for the social activism he has spurred both through his efforts as CEO of Starbucks and through the Schultz Family Foundation, which supports two national initiatives: Onward Youth, which promotes employment for young people between the ages of sixteen and twenty-four who are not in school, and Onward Veterans, which helps post-9/11 servicemen and women make the adjustment to civilian life.

Howard received the RFK Ripple of Hope Award in 2016 for leadership on social activism as a CEO. We met in his office in Seattle, where he started our conversation by showing me a photograph he keeps of Bobby Kennedy.

Kerry Kennedy: *You've said that Robert Kennedy was someone you identify with and you've quoted from his speech in South Africa as an inspiration.*

I'm interested in what you think about the process of turning those ripples of hope into action.

Howard Schultz: Robert Kennedy spoke for the oppressed and those in need, and he did that at times when it took a lot of courage to do. He believed in equality, and he had compassion for people, and was never afraid to communicate that. He showed us that each person can lead in his or her own life, whether it's in business or through volunteering or in whatever way someone gets involved.

Robert Kennedy's example inspires us to do what he was trying to do, and that's why it's so important to remind younger people about what he said and what he did. Those of us who are older haven't made it easy for the next generation, but if we can point to leaders who've made a huge contribution and a huge difference, young people will see the possibilities for change. Robert Kennedy was one of those leaders who showed a way that can be done.

As you know, I grew up in public housing; we moved there in 1956, when I was three. It was a diverse community, and in a sense we were all captives there, a condition that gets imprinted on people for life, especially if you're very young. We were all different colors, we had very different life experiences, and you had to get along with everyone there, despite all the differences. Like so many other people, I watched and will always remember the famous speech your dad gave from the back of that flatbed truck in Indianapolis on the evening Martin Luther King was assassinated. That was an example of leadership I've never forgotten. So when I watched and thought about what's been going on in recent years, with young African American men being murdered, and the lack of empathy and compassion among different communities, I felt compelled to see if Starbucks could do something to elevate the national conversation. I started having town hall meetings with our people, and there were two very powerful moments. An African American young man in Ferguson said, "I'm eighteen years old and I don't know if I'll make it to nineteen living in Ferguson." And someone in Seattle said, "Racism is like humidity. You can feel it, but you can't see it." I don't know if you knew this, Kerry, but I played the Ripple of Hope speech at a companywide meeting, from beginning to end, because I wanted to show the people who worked at Starbucks that those words from fifty years ago are just as relevant today as they were then. We have an individual and collective responsibility to embrace one another. We must reject the hatred and bigotry, and it will help us all to remember the courage, the leadership, and the power Robert Kennedy showed when he spoke out with a force and conviction we seldom hear today. When the recording of your father's speech ended, there was such a deep silence; people were incredibly moved by what they had just heard. I think this showed how people are longing for truth, longing for authenticity, and longing for the kind of leadership that your father displayed.

KK: *As CEO of Starbucks, you have made an effort to advance the national dialogue on race, an issue which has plagued our country since our founding. The fallout fom your Race Together initiative is indicative of why people consider race the third rail.*

HS: People have a longing for human connection. I see this because Starbucks is a place where millions of people gather—almost a hundred million people a week come into our stores all over the world, and they're not coming just for the coffee. They're coming in for the community, to be with other people. When we decided to get people thinking together about racism in America by writing "Race Together" on our cups, we did take a lot of criticism in the media, mostly social media, which kind of hijacked the narrative very quickly. In spite of that, it was one of my proudest moments at Starbucks. We had decided as a company to do it, and our doing it arose from our core purpose and reason for being, which was to try to lift up the lives of our own people and our customers and to try from time to time to use our widespread resources for good. And that was a defining moment of saying, "This could be misinterpreted, we could have people very angry and upset," and we did, but we decided it was the right thing to do to address the issue in the most respectful way we knew how and see if we could elevate the national conversation around empathy and love for one another. I think we will continue to challenge the status quo in ways that we think are appropriate and necessary.

KK: *Howard, in a recent speech you talked about how a company can have aspirations that are not exactly the same as making money. You talked about achieving the balance between making a profit and having social impact. And you describe Starbucks as a "performance-driven organization through the lens of humanity."*

That's the way I was raised—a combination of drive and impact blended with compassion. As a society, we don't usually think of these qualities—competitiveness and compassion—together, and I think that might be because we associate empathy with vulnerability, while winning means beating the opposition without mercy. So I'm very interested in how you, as a CEO, can combine those qualities that don't seem naturally to operate together. How do you make a company competitive and humane?

HS: Well, Starbucks is a public company, and we have a duty to stockholders to perform as well as we can financially. But I believe we have another responsibility, which is a higher one. We have to ask ourselves, "What is the right way to conduct our business?" You can't do business alone. Like almost everything we do in life, business requires other people; it's a team sport. So within the company there has to be a sense of purpose that unites everyone; we have to be confident that we're all in it together, that we are sharing a common endeavor. At Starbucks we have 350,000 employees worldwide. We have to be a community. Every business decision can't be an economic one. In fact, our success is due to many decisions that were not economically in our interest. We provided comprehensive health care to all of our employees almost thirty years before the Affordable Care Act; we provide free college tuition to every employee—no other company does that, we're the only one. We don't do these things because we're a charity or because we're trying to be benevolent. We do these things because we believe that, even though we don't win financially because of these decisions, ultimately our success is because of the way we treat the people who work at Starbucks.

So, viewing our performance through the lens of humanity means that we have to define our core purpose, our reason for being, in terms of human beings and pursue our financial success with that purpose lighting our way. We are very competitive, we want to win, but we want to win in such a way that when we leave the field, we'll be proud of how we conducted ourselves. Most people want to join with others in pursuit of something more important than their individual desires, and that's not because of something that you tell them or something that's written in the handbook but because they believe what they're doing has value for themselves and for other people.

I've thought about and spoken about the role and the responsibility of a public company today, and I believe strongly that the rules of engagement have changed, in large part because the government has become so polarized and dysfunctional that businesses and business leaders need to do more for their people and the communities they serve. I also think companies have a moral obligation today, not necessarily to be political but to be determined to stand up for important human values. So when we announced that we were going to hire ten thousand refugees globally after the president announced his ban, we did that because we believed it was dictated by our principles. I do think of Robert Kennedy in this context. He stood up many times for what he thought was right and just, and it was not always politically convenient. That is leadership, and it's a lot easier to lead when you have the wind at your back than it is when you're confronting powerful opposition.

I never saw your father when the cameras were not on him, the way he was when you saw him, in private, but I know that he didn't play for the crowd, he didn't play for the cameras. He was doing what he had to do to elevate people whose lives were hopeless, people who were in despair, who were powerless. I think he understood that this was his calling, to help those people, and I know it wasn't politically convenient.

KK: *Well, you're right; my father was very much the same off camera. Probably a little more laughter and fun . . . My question is: How do you put that humanity into the culture of your coffee shops?*

HS: Let me give you another example: I mentioned the fractured politics, the lack of trust, the polarization in Washington. Over the last year and a half, we've been talking inside Starbucks about the responsibilities of a public company today. They've changed. And to respond to that change, we have a responsibility to use our platform, raise our voice, and harness the worldwide extent of our potential influence for good.

We talked not about profit and loss, not about growth and development, not about the stock price or shareholder value. We talked about our conscience: our collective conscience as a company. We said to ourselves, "Eighty, ninety million people a week are going through our stores. Let's do everything we can to try to elevate the national conversation about how people treat one another." We asked ourselves, "How many more times are we going to allow ourselves to look at the news and the television and see one injustice after another, just because someone has black skin?"

So we took it on. And Robert Kennedy, despite the fact that he has not been with us since 1968, was the catalyst for me. I remembered his courage the night Martin Luther King Jr. was assassinated, when he spoke from his heart and calmed angry people and comforted an entire nation. I always remember what he did that night, and it frequently helps me figure out what I need to do. I try to inspire my company to follow his example too.

What we did was we opened a store in Ferguson, Missouri. We opened a store in Queens, New York. We opened a store in Englewood, Illinois. People said, "Englewood, Illinois? Starbucks is going into the charity business?" No, it's not charity. It's not charity. It's our values. It's our guiding principles. Just about a year ago, in the same week we were opening in Ferguson, we were opening a store in Johannesburg, South Africa.

I had never been to South Africa, and I didn't realize when we were in Johannesburg that there were preparations taking place in Cape Town for the fiftieth-anniversary commemoration of Robert Kennedy's speech there in which he talked about ripples of hope.

What I did realize, when we were opening a store in Johannesburg, was that a terrible thread of misfortune connected Ferguson, Missouri, and Johannesburg so far away. That thread was a lack of hope, a lack of opportunity, and prejudice. I sat down with these kids, about fifty of them, who were getting ready to open our two stores in Johannesburg. And I learned that none of them had ever had a job in their entire lives. And I went to visit them in the townships where they live. And I saw poverty like I'd never seen before.

But I also saw joy: when they put on their green aprons, you could see the swelling of pride, self-esteem, hope, self-respect. It was exactly the same as what we saw in Ferguson. The kids we hired in Ferguson had never had a job. The people who were supplying us with food didn't have any resources. As I sat down with these kids in South Africa and heard their personal stories and walked the townships with them, I kept hearing over and over again a word I had never heard before. "*Ubuntu. Ubuntu.*" Finally I got up my courage and asked, "What is that word you keep saying? What does it mean?"

It was like they had been bursting to tell me. It means, "I am because of you." I almost began to cry when they were explaining it to me: a sense of shared humanity that comes from recognizing other people and acting with compassion, solidarity, and regard for community. They were telling me that we were together in the knowledge that we don't exist as individuals but as interdependent parts of the world. We achieve our humanity through mutual recognition and compassion for one another.

"Or we can make an effort, as Martin Luther King did, to understand and to comprehend, and to replace that violence, that stain of bloodshed that has spread across our land, with an effort to understand with compassion and love."

—Robert F. Kennedy

MARTIN SHEEN

⌘

Ramón Antonio Gerardo Estévez, stage name Martin Sheen, is an American actor who first became known for his roles in the films The Subject Was Roses *(1968) and* Badlands *(1973), and later achieved wide recognition for his leading role in* Apocalypse Now *(1979).*

He also appeared in Gandhi *(1982),* Gettysburg *(1993),* The Departed *(2006), and* The Amazing Spider-Man *(2012), among many other movies.*

Sheen has played President John F. Kennedy in the miniseries Kennedy; *Attorney General Robert F. Kennedy in the television special* The Missiles of October; *fictional White House Chief of Staff A. J. MacInnerney in the film* The American President; *White House Counsel John Dean in the television miniseries* Blind Ambition; *and the fictional Democratic president Josiah "Jed" Bartlet in the acclaimed television drama* The West Wing.

Sheen is known for his social justice activism, and has been arrested over sixty times for civil disobedience, much of it against US military intervention in Latin America.

Sheen serves on the board of directors of Robert F. Kennedy Human Rights.

Martin has appeared across the globe in the theatrical adaptation of the book I wrote, *Speak Truth to Power*, and we have had long talks about social justice and Catholic faith. Martin invited me to watch him shoot an episode of one of my favorite shows, *Grace and Frankie*. I interviewed him in his trailer afterward.

Kerry Kennedy: *Martin, you've said Robert Kennedy is a hero. Why?*

Martin Sheen: Back in the early sixties, when so many Americans were still devastated by the murder of President Kennedy, Bobby offered us the hope of healing from that loss. I haven't seen any hope since then that inspired so many people, with the possible exception of the candidacy of Barack Obama. Of course, those two times in history and those two men are connected. The hope and the possibility that we experienced just recently through Barack Obama was reminiscent of what it felt like when Bobby emerged from the darkness after the assassination. When I tell younger people what it was like then, they get it. The slogan "Change We Can Believe In" almost seemed as if it was about Bobby because the idea of change was such a significant part of him. We had known him as a very forceful, straightforward, strong person, but then we saw this extraordinary change. His humanity seemed to burst forth so that it matched his leadership qualities. We had never seen the humanity so vividly before. I'm sure in the family you were in touch with that quality every day, but to so many people, what we saw looked like a transformation. . . . It was like the sunrise of a new day after a long, dark night.

It was so phenomenal that he allowed himself to be so publicly vulnerable. It made us all feel it was OK to share the pain we experienced. It made it somehow possible to be more human. That was the significance of his emergence into the public arena at that time.

I'll never forget when I met him. It was 1964.

There was a rally at Madison Square Garden to save the Brooklyn Navy Yard, which was going to be closed. It would've meant the loss of a lot of jobs in the New York City area, so everyone was for saving the navy yard—the union leaders, celebrities, the politicians—and they were all at the rally. It was a time when the parties overlapped on many issues; there wasn't the sharp conflict or radical positions we see today.

Bobby came in while someone else was speaking. He was trying not to make a fuss, but everybody knew he was in the arena, and everybody's focus was on him. People just whispered, "He's here," and we all knew who "he" was. He was ushered down to his seat. My wife and I were seated right behind him, and somebody on his staff, before he sat down, said, "This is Martin and Janet Sheen." He turned around. It was a moment I'll never forget. He was so shy. I was astonished at how shy he was. He greeted us so softly. He sat down in his chair and looked straight ahead.

Every now and then he would reach into his pocket and take out a note card, and he would write something on it, and he would hand it to an aide, who would disappear for a while and then come back. He did this three or four times while he was waiting, and after a while I thought, "This is embarrassing, they're making him wait here, he must have other appointments—he's the only guy anyone's interested in hearing!"

Speaker after speaker spoke, and Bobby barely moved an inch. You could see his mind working, but his body didn't move. I felt that everyone there had some sense of how deep his pain was, and we wanted him to heal and to help us all heal.

RFK was at that time in a difficult political position. They were calling him the outsider in New York, a carpetbagger. Johnson didn't want him on the ticket. He had left the Justice Department. He was on his own. Yet what he was doing was inspiring to all of us. It was a new day dawning, after the darkness that had descended on November 22, 1963.

Finally Bobby got up to speak, and the place went mad. He spoke very calmly—I don't think he talked longer than five minutes.

He said that if he made it to the Senate he would do whatever he could for the navy yard. At the end he said: "Some men see things as

"A revolution is coming—a revolution which will be peaceful if we are wise enough; compassionate if we care enough; successful if we are fortunate enough—but a revolution is coming whether we will it or not. We can affect its character, we cannot alter its inevitability."

—Robert F. Kennedy

they are and ask why; I dream things that never were and ask why not." The place went wild. Everyone stood up and clapped and shouted; no one wanted to let him go, and that was it.

KK: *I think people were drawn to him in part because of that shared sense of pain. And also because he was authentic. They had seen him tell people things they didn't want to hear—so they trusted him to be true to his word. He wasn't afraid to speak truth to power; in fact, he greatly admired that quality. He said that "few are willing to brave the disapproval of their fellows, the censure of their colleagues, the wrath of their society. Moral courage is a rarer commodity than bravery in battle or great intelligence, yet it is the one essential, vital quality for those who seek to change a world which yields most painfully to change." I know you've thought about moral courage. You've described it as requiring actions that draw rejection from the crowd and satisfaction from the heart.*

MS: It's an emotional thing when you challenge the status quo. Where it's most difficult is with those you love and who love you, when you feel you're risking their disapproval. You know it's got to cost you something because anything important costs you something. Part of the journey is accepting the wrath or the disapproval of people you love or a culture you're a part of, and that includes your family. That's the hardest thing to do.

For me, it was going against the Catholic Church. I love the faith, but the organization itself has sometimes been an obstacle for me, and I think for a lot of Catholics. I'm talking about the church hierarchy. The rule makers, the authorities in the church, have been generally conservative and dogmatic. I love my faith, but I've very often had to challenge the status quo inside the Catholic Church, and this is particularly true when it's an issue of war and peace. The Catholic Church has supported the theory of Just War, but I believe all war is immoral, and the current pope has been very encouraging in that direction. But during all my life growing up, the Just War theory was a given, and in New York we had Cardinal [Francis] Spellman, who was an outspoken supporter of the

Vietnam War, and he was the military chaplain. In the eyes of the hierarchy, Catholics who disapproved of the war were not good Catholics.

I've had trouble with other church dogma, the abortion issue particularly. I'm personally opposed to abortion, but I can't make that judgment for anyone else because I'm not a woman; I've never been pregnant,
and I never expect to be. So I'm pro-choice. I would never council anyone not to have an abortion; I wouldn't judge anyone who did have one;
but, of course, the church is very opposed to abortion. It's a difficult
issue for me.

KK: *As an activist you've been arrested so many times. I've read that
it was sixty-six times, but who's counting? You're a public figure and you've
had a lot of public criticism. I think of Michael Jordan saying, "Republicans buy sneakers, too." What's your attitude toward the personal cost of
speaking out?*

MS: I've always resented the extreme right-wing talk radio people!
They make so much money on their politics, and my beliefs have been
very expensive for me.

KK: *You're laughing, but you've never stopped speaking out and taking action—and you've been at it for a long time. The first time you organized a strike you were fourteen years old. You were a caddy, and you
organized the caddies at the club where you were working, and you were
fired. What did you learn from that experience?*

MS: What I learned was, if you believe in something, and that belief
is based in your fundamental values, and it *doesn't* cost you something,
you need to question those values. I learned a lot about organizing too.
I was the leader, and all the caddies supported me. I wasn't sure I was
going to be able to get everybody behind me, but it was a total walkout.
There were thirty kids, and some of them were older than me—one of
them was my older brother. The union only lasted for forty-eight hours.
They fired us, but then they called us back because we were so skilled and
they needed us. I didn't even have to promise we'd never strike again.

KK: *So you also learned that if you're skilled enough they're going to want you back, even if you cause trouble?*

MS: I've often been asked whether my activism cost me in my career. I don't like to think about it that way, but when I do, I have to say I probably got as many jobs as I lost. There were probably as many people who supported me as rejected me because of my positions on issues. And in the acting business it was mostly, "Let's get him in there; he knows how to play this kind of part." I think that's generally been true. The real lesson is that, as Daniel Berrigan—who's one of my heroes—always reminded us, the activists, the peacemakers, can never be confident of success. You can never expect to achieve your goals, but you must never stop trying.

The only success you can be sure of is that you showed up and were willing to accept whatever came your way. As long as you're willing to accept whatever happens to you for showing up and doing what you have to do for what you believe, and you stick it out, that's the only success you're entitled to. You can't expect to get any further reward, whether it's a reduction in nuclear weapons or whatever it was you were hoping for. You know going in that's probably not going to happen. You always hope.

I was arrested once at the Pentagon and they took us inside, and mind you, we just blocked an entrance, we didn't throw anything; we prayed, we didn't even raise our voices. And their big issue was, "Do you advocate the overthrow of the US government?" I said, "No, I have some issues with the Reagan administration, but I love the country." "Do you advocate violently overthrowing it?" I said, "No I never thought of that before. No, no, that's not it. I'm very nonviolent." That was their big concern, "Why don't you like us?" kind of—you know that attitude—and these are just the guys who guard the Pentagon, and I guess there were some civilian guys there too, maybe they were FBI, I don't know, but that issue seemed so important to them: "What do you have against us? You know, you really should explain yourself. We're a good country, we do a lot of things, and you ought not—" and I said, "No, I love the country; I love it enough to risk its wrath by drawing attention to the things that are not good about it." The areas of injustice and cruelty and violence, that's where we have to focus some attention. We've got to be peacemakers first, among ourselves.

Once I interviewed Jimmy Carter when Reagan was president. I said, "It must be very painful for you personally to watch the slow unraveling of your administration now under Reagan," and he said, "Well, no, I didn't do it alone, and nothing is ever lost." And I think that's right. Nothing is ever lost if you act with moral courage. For you and your children, with me and my generation, and all of us, nothing is ever lost.

KK: *What drove you? Theodore Roosevelt talked about the man in the arena, and Robert Kennedy often quoted him:*

"The credit belongs to the man who is actually in the arena . . . who knows great enthusiasms, the great devotions; who spends himself in a worthy cause; who at the best knows in the end the triumph of high achievement, and who at the worst, if he fails, at least fails while daring greatly, so that his place shall never be with those cold and timid souls who neither know victory nor defeat."

MS: Yes. I've had this sense all my life, and I've felt it very deeply, that I had work to do. I always knew I had a purpose. I couldn't always see beyond acting, but I knew there was something more. I just had to be—I guess the only word I can think of is *responsible*. I couldn't be lazy.

KK: *A calling?*

MS: There's a guy in our parish, he's Croatian, and up until a few years ago, he seemed OK. Then he started to look like he wasn't taking care of himself. Clothes are dirty, and he's unshaven, and he's bumming around and asking for money and so forth. So I said to him one day, "What's happened to you?" Well, he's fifty years old, he's been here for twenty years, and he's undocumented. He has a passport from the

1980s, he's got no Social Security card because he was with this family, stayed with them for twenty years, and they were nice to him, and he just lived there, but now they've gone, and he's on the street. So we found a place for him to stay, under an apartment building in the neighborhood where they all still know him, and they said it'll be OK as long as he gets in there before dark, because they didn't want the tenants to see him. So he said OK, fine, he's good with that.

He's kind of testy, and he complains a lot, saying things like "Why doesn't God strike me dead?" and "My life is useless," so I talk to him and I keep him on a regular cycle, and he's not always grateful. I spoke to my confessor about it, and he said, "Never make him feel less than human. Never let anybody see you give him anything." So I always shake his hand, and that's it, and I've been doing this for years. That's my . . . You know what I mean—my cup. I've been doing that kind of thing most of my life. I can't help myself.

KK: *Don't you feel overwhelmed sometimes by how much need there is, by how many people there are who need so much?*

MS: All the time. Sometimes I just weep. It's hard to look at TV; you look at what's going on now in Syria, and you see how many people are going to be dead by the end of this week, from war and starvation and disease. . . .

I don't have any illusions about changing anything or about even helping my poor Croatian friend. I don't have any illusions at all, but I know what I can do now. That's my responsibility. Reverend King, your father, they had that sense of commitment. They were in the fight. They were in the arena. You can't be happy if you don't accept that cup. You have to accept that cup as offered, and you can't alter it. We try to alter the cup all the time. Oh, take a little of that out, spill a little, could you please put some sugar in it, but eventually you're going to have to take it exactly as it comes. We have to accept the cup as offered, not altered.

---------------❧---------------

*"There are people in every time and
every land who want to stop history
in its tracks. They fear the future, mistrust
the present, and invoke the security of the
comfortable past which, in fact, never existed."*

—Robert F. Kennedy

---------------❧---------------

Robert Kennedy, 1968 (Steve Schapiro/ Fahey Klein Gallery)

---------------- ∞ ----------------

"We who are educated, who are healthy and
well fed, would remember the justice of the
Incas—who punished nobles more severely than
peasants for the same crimes.

For the failing of inaction—in the case of poverty
and ignorance and injustice—we will deserve
greater punishment as well. For to us is put the
great question of our time: whether our heritage
of freedom can survive in an era of sweeping
technological change—whether revolution can
succeed without destroying the very humanity
in whose name it is carried on."

—ROBERT F. KENNEDY

---------------- ∞ ----------------

ROBERT FREDERICK SMITH

Robert Frederick Smith, born and raised in Denver, Colorado, is a chemical engineer by training and an investor and philanthropist by conviction and passion. His ancestors were Cherokees forced to walk the Trail of Tears, and escaped and newly freed slaves who met and formed a community in Southern Colorado.

Robert is the son of two educators who instilled in him an appreciation for the power of learning and the moral obligation to apply our unique skills to change society for the better. He is the first and only African-American to sign onto the Giving Pledge and was named by Forbes *as one of the 100 Greatest Living Business Minds. Smith is the Founder, Chairman & CEO of Vista Equity Partners, Chairman of Carnegie Hall, and Chairman of the Board of Robert F. Kennedy Human Rights.*

Robert has been a mentor, a friend, a brother to me. He possesses a boundless heart and is the most generous person I know, in all the ways generosity truly matters. He is a problem solver and a visionary, and he is constantly determining how to help people in need. For

Robert, it's not just about giving, it's also about doing. It's personal for him. I was inspired to learn that every Christmas, he brings scores of kids aging out of foster care to spend the holidays with his family at his ranch in Colorado.

Kerry Kennedy: *Robert, you've said that Robert Kennedy has been a great influence in your life and work. What is it about my father that inspired you?*

Robert Frederick Smith: Robert F. Kennedy is a reflection of all that is hopeful about America and all that continues to drive our optimism for the future. I wasn't there when your father gave the speech in Indianapolis after Martin Luther King Jr. was killed, but I've studied that speech, and it was remarkable. It took great courage to speak the way your father did to an angry crowd. He appealed to people to stay calm and he spoke about compassion, responsibility, and community. He expressed his hope that people wouldn't act based on racial animosity. He reminded people to consider what obligations we all have to our brothers and sisters and to our divided country, and he did this in the face of intense grief and anger.

During that dark time for America, I was part of school desegregation in Denver, Colorado. I was six years old, and I recall how intense a time it was for me and for the community I lived in. I was one of about twenty-five African American first graders who were bused to the elementary school across town. The previous years, I had been in an all-black kindergarten; now I was in first grade at an integrated school with a whole bunch of people who didn't look like me. I remember it was spring, which is always a time of hope and optimism after a cold Colorado winter, and we were finishing our first year at the new school trying to make sense of it all. Why would they kill Dr. King?

We lived in a middle-class black community. My father was principal of the elementary school around the corner, the one I wasn't going to. My mother was a fourth-grade teacher. The parents in our neighborhood were professionals—doctors, dentists, teachers. I shoveled the driveway of a guy who was one of the founders of the Pullman Porters Union, and our next-door neighbor was George Brown, who held the highest office of any black person in any state government at that time—he was lieutenant governor of Colorado. In our neighborhood, we shared our celebrations and setbacks, we relied on each other, and our "extended family" was there to look out for us. The pioneering spirit in Colorado translated into a resourcefulness and resilience that made us stronger together.

My father was chairman of the board of the local YMCA. That's where we all played and learned to swim and learned to do all the things children did. It was the center of our community. We did fund-raising for it, sold candy or hosted events, whatever it was, as we had to provide significant community-based funding in order to make it accessible to all members of our community. We invested in our community: as educators, my mother and father were very active in bringing the Head Start program into Colorado. My parents lived what they preached. It was so clear to them that education was the way we were going to lift up our community. My parents instilled in us the value of striving to get the best education possible. That's why they fought for desegregated schools. And while my aunt was very active in the Black Panther party back on the East Coast, this passion for the African American community, the belief in integration, and the belief in education, was central to my upbringing.

KK: *Apparently your upbringing prepared you for a good career. You're one of the most successful people in the private equity field. The way we usually hear that presented is that you're the wealthiest African American man.*

RFS: I'm fortunate to have achieved success, but it's been a long journey. And I feel like I'm just getting started.

I'll tell you a story that's almost funny, but is not. We've been the top-performing private equity firm in the world since 2000, and we've never lost a dollar of institutional capital for going on eighteen years. Until recently, despite this track record, I couldn't raise money from some institutional investors managing state pension funds. The only reason for this is because of their unspoken biases. And yes, that's unfortunate for me and for Vista, but it's also sad to think that the people who are invested in state pension funds—the teachers, firefighters, nurses, and so many others—aren't getting the most of their money because the people responsible for managing those funds in certain states won't work with the best-performing funds. I'm glad to say that slowly, some of these states are changing their ways.

I remember one time not long ago, I invited the CEO of a very large financial institution out for dinner. When the check came I reached for it, and the guy says, "No, thank you. I can't have a black man buy me dinner." He thought he was being nice! And this isn't ancient history, it's today, and there are still a lot of people with issues about a person's race, in spite of all the work that's been done, the words that have been shared, the terrible experiences of your father's times and also of the last few years. This is something we have to continue to work on.

This is why I go back to that speech: April 4, 1968. Your father said we have a choice: we have to ask what kind of nation we are and what direction we want to move in. If we're black, we can be filled with bitterness, with hatred, and with a desire for revenge. As a nation we can move in the direction of polarization, black against white, filled with hatred toward one another. Or we can make an effort, as Martin Luther King did, and as your father called on all of us to, to replace the violence and bloodshed with compassion and love. I certainly believe, as he did, that the vast majority of white people and the vast majority of black people want to live together, want to improve the quality of all our lives, and want justice for all human beings who are part of our American community.

America's not always going to be perfect. There's going to be violence and lawlessness, there are going to be gang issues, but we have to harness the moral courage within our own communities, which is what it comes down to. We have to say we're not going to condone this; instead we're going to embrace respect, and we're going to create a more peaceful existence.

KK: *Many of the divisions Daddy talked about still exist, and while some things have improved, there are also new divisions. What do we do to heal the divisions that exist today?*

RFS: The disunity and pessimism that pervades our country today is real; but it is not unique. Today does bear striking similarities to 1968. Then, as now, millions of Americans felt as though they were throttling headfirst toward a future that was alien and beyond their control. Now, as then, the solution is to reach across divides and remind ourselves that we are all in this together. And that hope always conquers fear.

One factor that makes our divisions today different from those in 1968 is the role of technology. Technology has enormous power to unite, but it can also alienate. It can amplify, but it can also disenfranchise. It can tear down barriers, but it can build up walls. What just a few years ago took a factory and 40 workers can now be done by one engineer with the right equipment. This is progress. But there's a downside if technology lifts up the few and leaves behind the many. The future doesn't have to be a zero-sum game, but we need to re-skill and skill-up. We can begin to heal many of the economic and cultural divides in our country if we get to work training and retraining people to operate the technology platforms that will be the job engines of the future. I'm focused on creating on-ramps for inclusion of all people—no matter what their race, gender, or religion – in the workforce of today and the future.

We can either choose to harness technology as the greatest equalizer and wealth creator in human history, or we can choose to let it victimize, minimize, and fracture our communities. The important thing to remember is that we do have a choice in the matter. We must choose to invest in the thinkers, the doers, and the leaders who won't follow the arc of history, but bend it.

KK: *You've done something in that spirit at your Vista investment fund. You've made a concerted effort, without looking at race, to find a fresh way of discovering merit and potential. You've hired people who were gas station attendants, who'd done all sorts of things, if you thought they showed an aptitude for your business.*

RFS: That's the way America should be: Opportunities should be available to the people who have an aptitude and want to work hard. My job is to provide that platform. I provide a place where you can become your best self, and I cast a wide enough net to catch all those people who want that opportunity. I look to every community–every race and gender—for people I'd love to "catch." I'm a fly fisherman, you know; I love to fish, and that's how I think about this.

Recently I was giving a speech. I was with some top developers and programmers, and I told them how we have to catch promising people we can train to make a contribution to our business. We find the most creative and capable people, and we get them to work in our organization for as long as possible. We have to do everything we can in the organization to support that; it's our job to develop people; it's our job to develop a pipeline.

We have a session once every month on a Saturday, and we bring in the inner-city kids and teach them how to program. Not all of them are going to be programmers, but we're going to expose them to it, and this year we'll have had fifteen thousand come through the process, and next year we can do it twice a month so it'll be at thirty thousand, and then keep going. We just have to cast our lines and hook on as many prospects as we can. It's a systemic process based on things I learned as a kid, that you have to develop the preschoolers and the kindergarteners so they can do well in school. That's why Head Start is so important, and the after-school programs and the development programs and the extra sessions for kids who didn't have that culture of learning as part of their family fabric. Many of them didn't because they're the first generation that even has a chance of going to college and becoming professionals. It takes time to weave that fabric into the community so those children can see there are real possibilities for them. That's taking responsibility for your community. That's taking action to lift people up.

It all comes back to this: What your father stood for was taking responsibility for your community—I have a responsibility to do the best I can for my community—that's for the people I grew up with, the people in the city, the state, and the country I live in. That's my community. So I will do as much as I can for those people, for as long as I can.

KK: *You mentioned city, state, and country, but your community orientation doesn't end at the borders of the United States. When the girls kidnapped in Nigeria by Boko Haram escaped and went home, you offered those girls the chance to go to college.*

RFS: It's all part of the fabric of being a human. It's in your father's phrase: "To tame the savageness of man and make gentle the life of the world." To work for that is the job of every human being. When I saw those little girls kidnapped for going to school, I saw the savageness of man. Those little girls were kidnapped, forced into sexual slavery, some killed, just because their parents wanted them to get an education. They were taken simply because they went to school that day. It's my human responsibility to make life gentler for those girls. Perhaps sometime later they'll say, "Yes, these savage things happened, but there was some good in this world that found me." Maybe inspiration will spark those girls to improve the part of the world they live in. We have some of the girls in America now, and they say, "I want to become a doctor, I want to become a human rights worker," and it's spectacular to see how far they've come. There's a light in them, and the light is hope for the future.

I'm a chemical engineer by education and training, but I love to read, and I read a lot. I read Walt Whitman, and I read James Baldwin, and I read Maya Angelou. I've been reading Ta-Nehisi Coates. I want to expand myself and expand my reach. The point of my reading is that I never wanted to be a prisoner of my own life. That's one of my central principles. I've never wanted to be categorized as X and then have to be a prisoner of X so I measure up to some expectation of someone else. I try to let my spirit tell me if this problem in front of me is a problem I can solve, and I take that problem on.

It would be a disservice if I didn't do that because that's part of my calling. We're all here for just a short period of time, so you might as well do all you can. What are you going to get done in this short time? How are you going to make this a better place? I'm not interested in people knowing my name two hundred years from now because I won't know about it anyway. What I'm interested in is pushing more good into the hearts of more people more often. If I can do that, I'll feel pretty good about the contribution I've made.

I teach my five children Zoë, Eliana, Max, Hendrix, and Legend that there are three important things to remember in life.

The first thing to remember is: You are enough—to do the things you want to do and become the person you want to become. That's an affirmation that's true no matter what difficult circumstances you might be in. The second thing is to discover the joy in figuring things out because there's not much in life that's better than identifying something that's wrong and figuring out how to fix it so it works. The third thing is that love is all that really matters. Those are the three things I want to leave my children.

Robert Kennedy calls us to these things. His vision is more important now than ever before. We have new tools now that we can use to help us deliver his inspiration to our communities. I'm optimistic that we can make the progress we have to make. We all need to hear Robert Kennedy's clear voice now even more than we did in 1968.

GLORIA STEINEM

❦

Gloria Steinem is a writer, lecturer, editor, and feminist activist. She was a cofounder of the magazines New York *and* Ms. *She has written many books and received many awards for her journalism. In 2013 she received the Presidential Medal of Freedom.*

Someone sent my brother Joe a subscription to *Ms.* magazine, and, as a young adolescent I used to snatch it from the mailbox, race to my bedroom on the third floor of our home, and read it. Growing up in a society dominated by men (watch a few *Mad Men* episodes to see what it was like) in a single-parent household with a mother who espoused traditional roles for women but was mightier and more fun than all the men in her orbit, *Ms.* provided a source of insight and relief from confusing, mixed messages. As a human rights activist, I came to understand that the suppression of women and girls is the single greatest threat to justice and peace in our world. Gloria is the icon of women's empowerment, and a kind, engaged, and loving friend.

Gloria Steinem: The first time I saw your father, he was attorney general, and he was speaking to a large group in Washington. He clearly did not enjoy public speaking, but he was doing it anyway; he was doing it, I would say, courageously. I never spoke in public until I was more than forty years old, and had devoted much of my life to avoiding public speaking. When I absolutely had to, and I would say to myself, "Okay, if Bobby could do this when he so clearly would rather have been anywhere else, maybe I can do it, too." This is one personal way he was an inspiration to me.

Kerry Kennedy: *I've watched many of his early speeches, and he's clearly miserable in front of a microphone. He hates it; he's not very good at it; he's not charismatic; he can't find the right words. He's a mess. Then he changed.*

GS: Yes, of course, he got much better. The most important thing about his speaking is that he was always authentic. I got the impression that because he cared so much about the subject, he overcame his disinclination to speak and just got out there and did it. His message was clearly coming from inside him. He wasn't thinking about how he looked or whether what he had to say fit neatly into some political strategy. He just wanted to speak the truth—but he would have been just as happy if someone else said it.

The *Village Voice* writer Jack Newfield once confided to me that the secret of interviewing Bobby was to bring along someone who disagreed with him. Otherwise, if you asked him a question and he was aware you already knew the answer, he wouldn't see any point in repeating it to you. I found this to be true when I was interviewing him. He was just so straightforward and practical that he would say, "You know the answer perfectly well." I would say to him, "Yes, I know the answer, but you have to say it. I need quotes from you." But if you brought along someone he didn't know, or who would express an opposite opinion, Bobby would see a reason to explain his own view, and then you could get quotes!

KK: *That does sound like him. You covered Nixon, McCarthy, and my father as a reporter during the primaries in 1968. How would you compare them in the field?*

GS: The styles of the two Democrats, Gene McCarthy and Bobby Kennedy, were polar opposites. McCarthy was distant, cool, above it all, academic, a little disapproving. He very rarely stopped in black or poor neighborhoods. I saw him touch another person only once. He touched a little black kid and then wiped his hand on his pants.

It was truly a profound contrast. Bobby was especially warm with children. He would reach out and gently touch their faces. It seemed to me he always did that. He certainly did it frequently. He was most able to forget his shyness when he was absorbed in what other people needed.

KK: *I remember that everywhere we went on campaigns we brought a football to throw around, and my father connected that way with the kids, through play.*

GS: I don't remember the football, but I vividly remember the touching, and the obvious way he cared about the kids, especially if they seemed to be in any kind of trouble, or if the neighborhood was a poor neighborhood, or if they were black children and vulnerable. Once on a campaign plane, Bobby's staff objected when he wanted to make a stop at an Indian reservation—there weren't enough votes there to make it worthwhile—and Bobby got mad and said, "You don't really give a damn, do you? He made the stop anyway.

Many of the reporters on the campaign loved your father, so I think they overcompensated by writing critically about him. On the other hand, they found Nixon to be shifty and inauthentic, so I think they concealed their feelings by being super objective. The result was that many Americans didn't know who those men really were until it was too late—until Nixon was in the White House—and until Bobby was no longer with us.

KK: *Some journalists came to the campaign with extreme skepticism, and then they would start to admire him and say, "Well, I can no longer be objective, so I have to get a different assignment."*

GS: I think that's ridiculous. It's a fault that grows out of journalism school, for which we're paying the extreme price with Trump. Objectivity is equated with a false equivalency. If you say something negative about one candidate, you have to balance it by saying something negative about the other. You give equal time to lies and to facts.

KK: *Example number one is global warming. A scientist cites the facts; then, in the name of "balance," an oil company hustler gives the "other side" as though there were a valid "other side" from reality.*

GS: It's a tragedy. Issues do not all have two sides. They may have ten sides, or three. It's as if the world is divided into two kinds of people: those who divide everything into two and those who don't. As a philosophical note, this is a function of dividing human beings into masculine and feminine, which is also bullshit because each person is unique, and also shares the human race. Dividing everything into two doesn't allow for uniqueness and continuum and subtlety and individuality. Journalism schools need to cut out that binary thinking. The journalist's responsibility is not to be evenhanded. It's to be accurate.

One time, all the journalists who were following the campaign were sitting in the bleachers overlooking a mass Nixon rally. The "Battle Hymn of the Republic" was associated with Bobby—people knew it was his favorite hymn—and when the band played it, even those reporters who were striving to pretend they had no feelings, even they reacted emotionally because they associated it with Bobby. Someone said, "They shouldn't play that song here. It doesn't belong to them." There was a game some were playing: a dollar for the person who saw the first black face in Nixon's crowd. It was a tough game to win because the Nixon crowds were overwhelmingly white. They were so different from Bobby's crowds.

KK: *Daddy had mixed audiences because he reached out to a wide range of people. He was particularly concerned about farmworkers. You were an advocate for farmworkers in the sixties.*

GS: My connection with the farmworkers started with Marion Moses, who was the nurse for the United Farm Workers union. She came from Delano to New York and she needed a place to stay. Cesar Chavez, in his way, had sent her off with $5 a week and orders to stop the grape shipments to the entire East Coast. She stayed with me, and she organized me, and once you're organized by and for the farmworkers, you stay organized!

Later, Cesar sent an older Filipino man named George Catalan to New York to help with our street demonstrations. Many Filipino men had been imported as farmworkers, but they were forbidden to marry by the antimiscegenation laws of California, so there was a large group of lonely older men who could no longer work. Cesar had managed to construct some housing for them. George volunteered to come to New York because he had no family, and he would cook for all of us strikers in my tiny closet of a kitchen. Marion and I also organized a benefit for the farmworkers in Carnegie Hall, with everybody from Broadway performers to George McGovern. We also used every journalistic and union organizing tactic to get Cesar on the cover of *TIME* magazine, because it seemed that publicity would be his best protection against the violent threats from some of the growers.

Through Marion, who later became a doctor and worked on public health and environmental health as well as farmworkers' health, I became aware that women were coming to the farmworkers' clinic, pleading for contraception or for safe abortions. Cesar was saying no way. I felt he was wrong, and since I was raising money, I began raising it not for Cesar—the United Farm Workers did have support from some other unions—but for women's groups. I think Marion had been secretly providing contraception, but there was no money—the clinic was operating out of a house trailer or some such place. I just directed the money I was raising—we're not talking about big sums here—to support women farmworkers instead of other aspects of Cesar's work.

—∞—

"The classic role of wife and mother as just a wife and a mother is something that belongs to simpler times than ours—and to simpler minds than yours. . . . Consider it imperative, for your own and your husband's and above all your children's sake, as well as the sake of your countrymen, that you continue to make full and generous use of the mind your education has set free.

If only with part of your time and only in the region of your own community, you may find yourself able to work effectively against the forces of darkness around you."

—ROBERT F. KENNEDY

—∞—

KK: *Did you know that the United Farm Workers medical program is called Robert F. Kennedy Medical Care?*

GS: I didn't know. That's great!

I think young people today would benefit so much from knowing more about your father, who he was, what he said, what he did. He was so ahead of his time. The death of President Kennedy was enormous and shocking, he was the first president I had ever in my life felt connected with. Other presidents had seemed distant, unrelated to my concerns and to my entire generation. But the death of Bobby Kennedy was the death not just of the past, but of the future.

Your father had something in common with Buddha. That might sound odd, but I'm thinking of how Siddhartha Gautama left his princely compound, and discovered the real world of poverty and suffering. Your father, through some chemistry of his experiences plus the quality of his heart and mind, empathized with people who didn't have power over their own lives, whether because they were poor, or black, or female, or young, or from another country. That capacity of mind and spirit seemed to have grown in him. I remember reading that when he went to the Soviet Union for the first time and became ill, he was helped by a woman doctor there. That experience changed his whole attitude toward the Soviet Union, away from the rigid anticommunism he knew from Joe McCarthy. If my memory is right, he came back and said, "The trees are not Communist trees." This is a testimony to his empathy, and his ability to change based on what he learned from experience. He was a truly democratic leader because he didn't divide people by empathizing with some and not others. His empathy was universal, not selective. He was deeply democratic.

He embraced a wide range of causes and movements that represented the dispossessed, including the antiwar movement, the Native American movement, the farmworkers, the antiapartheid movement, and others. This was remarkable because he came from such an exalted economic place. I grew up in house trailers, and went to high school in a factory-working neighborhood, then went to an all-white Ivy League college, and lived in India. Your father didn't have the advantage of growing up in different worlds, yet as an adult, he bridged many differences.

It's also very important to remember that during the Vietnam War, he seemed to be the only man in Washington who counted Vietnamese casualties, not just US casualties, as a tragedy.

I hope young people get to know Bobby, they would love him. I'm greatly encouraged by this young generation of women and men, especially women, and especially women of color—in their teens, twenties, and thirties. When I look at them, I think: *I just had to wait for some of my friends to be born!*

These younger people are more daring, and they understand the connections among all the issues. The movements are not separated— the civil rights movement, the women's movement, the environmental movement, they're all connected. Human beings were seen as unique and connected until patriarchy came along with the idea that men should control reproduction, and thus women's bodies, in order to control numbers of workers, and what race they are and what class or caste they are. This means everything from female genital mutilation, in order to enforce virginity and take away all sexual pleasure, to making birth control and abortion a crime. The ways that women had always decided whether and when to have children were taken away from them by patriarchal cultures and religions.

If you talk to older Native American women who weren't deculturized by religious boarding schools—and to young women in Indian country who are rediscovering their cultures—they will give you the whole list of abortifacients, herbs—with these things, and timing, they understood perfectly well how to control reproduction. There was no such thing as an illegitimate child because each child had a place within a matrilocal group of the child's mother, her sisters, and the men they married. Women might be in control of agriculture and men of hunting, but both were equally important. Men might be leaders, but they were chosen and could be deposed by women elders. No wonder Paula Gunn Allen, a great modern native writer, said, "The root of oppression is the loss of memory."

That's true in Southern India and Africa, too. Some years ago or so, when there were more San, the so-called bush people, living in the Kalahari, I went there with a whole group led by a Cherokee friend. The San women took us out in the bush and showed us: "Here's the herb we use for contraception, here's one for abortions, here's one for headaches, here's the one for migraine headaches." They're very sophisticated.

That capability was suppressed quite purposefully, including in Europe. Over 300 years or so, six million so-called witches—meaning women who were healers, who practiced and taught midwifery—were murdered. That's a lot of people, and it was all about putting men in control of women's bodies and reproduction.

The forefront of women's struggle today is the struggle for bodily integrity. That sounds like simple logic, and it is—but it means we are seizing control of the means of reproduction. It's the struggle to say, first of all, that the power of a government stops at our skins. We get to decide what happens inside our own bodies. Some poor or racially powerless men also suffer from forced organ transplants, men also get sexually assaulted and raped. The issue is more acute for women, because of reproduction, but we all need bodily integrity as number one. We know it's the first step toward democracy, and the first step toward authoritarian hierarchical structure is the reverse—controlling reproduction. When Hitler was elected, among the first things he did was to padlock family planning clinics, and declare abortion a crime against the state.

KK: *The first thing George W. Bush and Donald Trump did when they became president was to cut off funding for family planning.*

GS: Right. It's the first step in absolutely every authoritarian regime. And you can also tell the degree of violence in a nation by how polarized the gender roles are. The more peaceful and democratic the society, the more flexible the gender roles. The more violent the society, the more polarized the gender roles. That's because "masculine" and "feminine" is the first step in normalizing hierarchy. If it's normal at home, it's normal everywhere. If we don't have democratic families, we will never have a democratic society.

Men used to raise children; people traveled in small groups and men raised the children, too. Raising children is what enabled men to develop those human qualities wrongly called feminine: patience, attention to detail, empathy.

To go forward, we have to regain control of our physical selves. Now, violence against female infants, girls, and women has brought us to a place where for the first time we know of in history, there are fewer females on earth than males. The biggest indicator of whether a country is violent within itself, in its own streets, and whether it will be willing to use military violence against another country, is not poverty or access to natural resources, not religion, or even the degree of democracy. It's violence against females. The reason is to control reproduction, and the result is the normalization of the idea that one group is born to dominate another.

KK: *At RFK Human Rights, we've worked on post-conflict violence against women in countries around the world. We held a conference a few years ago with the chief justices of the supreme courts of five Latin American and five African countries, all of which had recently experienced conflict, to talk about the role of the judiciary in stopping violence against women in post-conflict situations. One hundred years ago, 85 to 90 percent of the casualties of war were soldiers; and today, 80 percent are civilians, and most of them are women and children. Women and children are targeted during wartime, when there's no justice system and no accountability for the violence that happens. After the war, it takes years for the police and the judiciary to reactivate and prosecute cases, by which time it's been ten, fifteen, twenty years of no accountability for violence against women. A whole generation of people has experienced that reality.*

*It becomes calcified into the culture that such things are OK, that it's OK
to treat women that way, and it goes on and on.*

GS: Yes, and in gender-polarized societies women were getting
beaten or killed by the men at home before the men went off to war. As
of now, we haven't had a war on our territory, not since 90% of Native
Americans were killed by war and imported diseases. But, if you add up
all the Americans who were killed on 9/11, in two wars in Iraq and in
all the years of war in Afghanistan, and then you add up all the women
who were murdered by their husbands or boyfriends in the same period
of time, the number of women killed far outnumbers the total number
of Americans killed in war and terrorism. I don't need to tell you which
deaths more motivate our policies and our spending of tax dollars, yet
if we want to uproot and de-normalize violence, we have to begin in the
home with violence against women.

KK: *I think all these issues—race, women's rights, farmworkers, the
plight of people living in poverty from Appalachia to Watts, are connected.
So, in the end, it's not so important which issue you work on, just as long
as you take up an issue and strive to create change—send forth that ripple of hope. Because, in the end, as Daddy said, it's going to take all of us
working together to bring down the walls of oppression.*

GS: I so wish he were here to say that—but because of you, he is with
us right now.

"Some who accuse others of inciting riots have by their own conduct invited them . . . violence breeds violence, repression brings retaliation, and only a cleansing of our whole society can remove this sickness from our soul."

—ROBERT F. KENNEDY

ALFRE WOODARD

❦

The Tulsa, Oklahoma-born Alfre Woodard has won four Emmys, a Golden Globe, three Screen Actors Guild awards, and has been nominated for an Oscar and a Grammy in her brilliant career in theater, film, and television. A life-long activist, she has worked against apartheid in Africa and against racism and sexism in the United States.

Alfre and I met and became friends during the antiapartheid struggle of the 1980s. She joined me on an RFK Human Rights delegation to Uganda and Zimbabwe on sexual minority rights and Zimbabwe on democratic governance. She has performed in the theatrical version of *Speak Truth to Power* across the globe.

Alfre Woodard: Your father was a rare politician because he was willing to be transformed by the things and people he encountered. He was able to hear and see and bear witness to the full range of the American people, most of whom were not seeing each other then. Through his eyes we all began to see each other and the possibility of a way forward through connectedness. His vision and his words were a catalyst for so many people of our generation; he affected everything I've done with my life since he lived.

From when I was five years old, every day at six o'clock, my father would call us in from outside and say, "It's time for the news." I would stand there with my sister and brother, eleven and nine, all itchy and sweaty, and watch "This is Douglas Edwards with the news." My mother would say, "You smell like outdoors." My father would be eating. When the half hour was over, he'd turn and say, "What did you think about that?" My sister would say, "I don't know. I don't care." He'd say, "You've got to care; you live in the world." His emphasis was always, "You have a responsibility to know what's happening so you can do something about it." I would say, "Well, I think . . ." this or that, and my sister and brother would say I wasn't making any sense, and my father would try to sort out my logic, and he would say, "It's good to have an opinion."

When I was seven or eight, one evening I burst into tears at the dinner table. My brother and sister giggled. I was a little bit of a hysteric about certain things. My mother looked at my dad like, "Be calm with her," and he asked what the matter was. I told him, "Two thousand people died in a flood in India." My father looked solemnly at me and said, "Go wash your face. Do your homework. Maybe someday you'll be able to help some people."

Both my parents grew up rural. The land is a great equalizer. It doesn't care who you are, what you are, what you look like, how you pray. When you put the crop in, it comes up or it doesn't. When it doesn't come up for some other family, it's your responsibility to make sure that family still eats the same as you eat because it could have been you with no food.

It was around that time that the president was shot. Thinking of this still makes me very emotional. The whole elementary school was in a panic. We thought it was the end of the world. All the teachers were weeping; they didn't even care that there were children around. Everybody said, "Okay. They're going to kill all the black people now." Adults thought this was the end. Any hopes we'd ever had were gone.

Two to three years later: There was this group called the Hungry Club—they were the Greenwood Chamber of Commerce. Greenwood was an African American community in Tulsa that was burned down by racists in 1921. They always had a junior high school student address all these black businessmen in Greenwood. It was always a boy, but I told my civics teacher I wanted to do it. My teacher said, "No! It's the top boy in the class," but I badgered them until I was selected to give the speech. My father said to me, "I need you to put some things in there for me. I do business, so I can't say everything out loud, but you can say some things for me." When I realized I could say those things for my father, it gave me this sense of power—to be told I could speak for my father, who was a self-made man with tremendous respect in the community, it fed into a sense of my ability to do things. My father had his opinion on every crisis every nation had. I never really understood what that meant until I studied your dad in interviews. When I saw him I really began to understand that I had a place not only in my community but in the world. My parents always taught me that I belonged in my world as a person. My influence had to include people everywhere in the country and everywhere in the world. I was seeing the connectedness. When I was listening to your father, he reinforced in me what it meant to have personal responsibility. It wasn't that you should just think it or talk about it; it meant walking out your door and doing things that were right and just. For me, your father was a personal call to arms, but it wasn't to arms, it was a call to stand up, to walk, to be active. Every injustice was connected. It wasn't just that people didn't have food, didn't have jobs, and were discriminated against because of the color of their skin; it was that those things were not separate things. Injustice creates injustice; each injustice is connected to all injustices. If you worked on those things, you worked on the full range of it. It takes the transformation of the individual, and it takes a recognition of the connection of each individual to all others. That was the first battlefield, putting your body on the line to work for things. Part of that was transforming people's minds.

When I saw RFK saying certain things, I got excited. Oh, my God, here is this man who is part of the power structure, who is white, who is affluent, who is speaking his truth, who is putting himself on the line. Not only was this a white man with power, who could've been somewhere golfing, saying the things we all said in our houses, he was saying them clearly, out loud on television, about our shared human condition. He was able to put our predicament into words that gave everyone a common language. It was a victory, but it was scary because we knew from experience that when people got close to something truthful and real, they would be taken from us. You know, Malcolm had been killed.

He was taken out because of his transformation. It was dangerous to change—to learn about the connections—but as you start to understand, you become emboldened by the truth. When you stand with the truth, especially when there are repercussions—physical, economic, societal—it makes you a little nervous, but at the same time you feel emboldened. You feel a part of the continuum of people who have told the truth. It's something bigger than you are. It's invigorating to step into that moment when you feel that. It's outside of you. It includes you. The world was on fire in those days. We can talk about what's going on now, but back then the shit hit the fan every day. I don't know why we didn't say, "All is lost. We're going to hell." Maybe it's because we were young and hadn't become jaded or been so often disappointed. There were other people who were standing up with us. Like now, I see kids charged up. Then, I had never heard anybody doing this, except Dr. King. It was the same awareness that RFK brought to southern poverty. I didn't live in a city, and I grew up comfortably. The "ghetto" experience wasn't my experience, but I saw southern poverty, how greedy and choking and strangling that condition is. There were people who looked just like me, and there were also people who looked like the extreme version of poor white people I saw in pictures of Oklahoma and Texas, from the Dust Bowl. It was a world away from power. RFK in his suit and tie brought that recognition back from his visits to those places. Politicians didn't show up in those places. Your father was a politician and he showed up. I'm getting emotional talking about this.

I was in a coed Catholic school, and all this stuff was going on around women demanding to be seen. At first they'd say, "Oh, my God, shut up." Bras were burning, people were lying down in the streets to stop the war, Dr. King was being taken up, Stonewall happened. It was a time of "End this war!" The enemy, the racism and classism, was so strong that sometimes we said, "We can't freaking fix any of this."

All that was happening when I was in high school. We were allowed to start very intense conversations and arguments, and the first was: "What would Jesus do?" We knew what Jesus would be doing. We knew the radical walk of this prophet. You can't be talking to me about the Bible, the life of Jesus, and tell me you don't know which side you need to stand on. The idea was that Christianity had to be active or it was not valid.

At the same time I discovered I was an artist, and I saw the power and purpose of art, the fact that it was also spiritual expression. It all came together, and it was your father—his walk, his ability to embody and demonstrate and articulate not only what our challenges were but also our feelings, without ever alluding to the possibility that it could not be done. We all started to believe. We believed every time we stood up for people, every time we went out with people, every time we had to reach across to people we didn't really get, but still we knew, "Hell. If you're in this too, I'm with you." We hadn't accepted homosexuality in my community, but we all joined hands because we were all feeling poverty and oppression. When you're a little baby and you see another little person walking, you stand up and walk. We do that all the time. You see somebody—they don't even know they're modeling—and you go, "Oh, OK." That's what RFK gave, I would say, to everybody between nineteen and forty. Stand up and walk. This is what's vital and, at the same time, this is how you're forming that more perfect union. This is how you are patriotic. This is love of country. Love of country is reflected in your love for the people of a country. That was the other thing: I had never heard of a politician, a person in power, before RFK, talk about love as a part of the solution.

It would take balls to talk about love now. "I want us to create love. I want everyone in this country to feel loved." The whole idea of feeling personally charged, that's what our activism was. I remember in ninth grade, you would look at the history and the documents and then you would look around you and nothing you saw supported what you had read. You spoke the pledge, you studied the preamble, and all that because it was history and you had to learn it. Your father was the first person in charge—when I say in charge I mean he was the attorney general, he was a senator, he was legitimate, he was a leader—it was the first time I heard a person in his position connect the incredibly horrific conditions and attitudes and situations that a vast number of Americans were facing. He made the connection to us not living up to our principles. Not only is it not right, not only is it inhuman, not only is it not compassionate, it's totally off the court from what the documents say. It's illegal, or it should be; it's unconstitutional. If those laws don't reflect the Constitution, they have to be changed, and you *can* change the whole system.

I think of those contemporary prophets like Gandhi, like Martin, like Malcolm, all of them and all the ones not known, who said it's your obligation as a person who loves this country to change the laws if they go against the founding principles. This is a tough part to talk to you about, Kerry. He just thought everything was possible. I thought then that the whole country saw it. I thought when he was running for president that it was going to be it. We were going to be Americans. We were going to change that status quo. I thought we had succeeded at that point. Then you lost your daddy. We lost our shining big brother. There was a lot of anger, discouragement, despair. It seemed to say: *Anybody who gets close to effecting fundamental change is gone. Just settle down and go along and make the best of your own life.* But once he had ignited that fire, once he called us to our feet, once we walked our walk, there was no turning back.

This is the deal: you're not going to see it happen. But that is the point. You stand up and walk when it's your turn because before that somebody walked for you. People have been walking for generations in this country. You have to know that once you've been transformed, you can't go back on it, because somebody you looked to has paid the price, and even more so after that, you owe it to the continuum to step up.

Sometimes you get tired, sometimes you get discouraged. Some days I'm laughing because it's so ridiculous, but I keep coming back to the power of, "We have seen dark things, and we're going to be the boys and girls who keep standing up because somebody stood up for us and somebody is standing up with us now." Besides trying to create joy, it's our purpose to redefine what it means to be in community, neighbors, a nation, a world.

Things were happening on the front here, in the states, of course. One of the things that Robert Kennedy opened people's eyes to was the fact that America was not an island. Whatever injustices one human being was capable of, all human beings were capable of. Injustice does not recognize borders. As an activist, I realized that the struggles were happening on all the continents. A realization like that opens up the world the same way the internet opens up the world. I was drawn to Africa. I started to bond with like-minded people, trying to be of assistance to them in their struggles. I got to South Africa first. The Ripples of Hope speech that RFK gave in Cape Town was a game changer for those people, those students, because they had been isolated. They were living in a toxic space, and your father brought new life, new energy, there— truth and the possibility of enlightenment. It was a game changer for us too because we got to see him there as well. He was working on many fronts at the same time. That reminds us as progressives and liberals that, instead of bickering, we can all work together. The times demand that we work on all these fronts. I found myself very deeply involved in South Africa, with the South African struggle, and people here would ask me, "Why are you so concerned about the things there?"

When RFK talked about the challenges we have, he always showed us how they were all connected. When somebody's liberties are compromised, all liberties are compromised. When somebody is starving, you are starving, too. We are all part of the community of people who need food to live. Justice is a universal truth, a gift of God. It's what you're born with; it's part of what makes you a human being. If you're standing for that, you have to stand wherever people need you to be. Sometimes it feels like we're all running back and forth, but we have to keep listening to everybody everywhere. We have to open people's minds.

RFK did this by telling his truth and making himself vulnerable. It was his vulnerability that revealed his strength. He saw what most of America wasn't seeing in those days. We have to tell the story, that's the thing. We have to keep telling the story. You have to take the time to tell the story completely. We all think we're new, but we're part of a continuum.

When I get tired, y'all are going to keep going. That's true to RFK's message. Once you've been called to action, you can't rest with it. Once you've been awakened, you know that activism is not a pastime nor is it a luxury but a way of life, as necessary as breathing. You're grateful when somebody asks for help. Ten blocks from your home, no matter where you live, you get to put that awakening into practice. That's where change truly happens.

I always say, "I don't know what I have to bring, but I'll show up." We have our bodies. Your body showing up is powerful. It says, "This person believes your life has value." If you're RFK, you give people the language. "We have common needs." He could've been sailing, he could've been doing anything he felt like doing, but he knew his presence would give people a lifeline. Can you imagine those black dads and grandfathers and uncles, how they felt sitting there when he came strolling through their slave quarters and touching their babies? That's a life changer. Showing up can be a life changer.

We all need to keep inspiring each other, charging each other, emboldening one another. We are our own army. We are peaceful warriors, but we are warriors. We have to be. Justice and peace is as old as mankind. The thing is that we are slowly, slowly winning these battles, but we gotta show up on the battlefield with love and action, or the battle goes another direction.

VICTORIA WRIGHT

❧

Victoria is an eighteen-year-old senior at Freeport High School in Long Island, New York. After learning about Bobby Kennedy while taking the Robert F. Kennedy Human Rights Speak Truth to Power human rights education course, she decided to commit herself to social justice.

Pamela Schmidt, an inspiring teacher who has used the Speak Truth education program from Nepal to Haiti to Long Island, introduced me to Victoria.

Victoria Wright: The first time I heard about Robert Kennedy was freshman year, when my teacher, Mrs. Schmidt, brought the Ripple of Hope quote to one of our class meetings. She discussed some of his work and it was really very inspiring. I told her that hopefully I can be like him.

My take on Robert Kennedy is that he was an insanely giving person. Sometimes when people have so much, they don't think about people in other situations, but he always did, and you can clearly tell that he was genuine and cared for other people. So, over our four years in our effort to be like Robert Kennedy and give back, our Speak Truth to Power club took on a community service project each year.

Our freshman year we sold bracelets made by kids who were trapped in forced labor as carpet factory workers in Nepal. Kailash Satyarthi started the home for those children. We sold the bracelets and then donated the money straight back to the home, to provide more for the kids.

We continued to sell the bracelets throughout high school, but we added other things. Sophomore year we also entered the Speak Truth to Power video contest.

Our video was based on how wasteful we Americans can be. One of our scenes was in the cafeteria. Students were taking food, deciding they didn't like one of the foods on the tray, and throwing away the entire plateful. The message of the film was that maybe you should think about how you are wasting the resources that could honestly be helping someone else. We took third place in the competition.

Our junior year we sold Christmas tree ornaments made by children in Haiti who were orphaned or abandoned by their families because of the earthquake. Many of the kids had intellectual disabilities and were physically challenged. So a home was started for those kids, which our teacher visited.

Kerry Kennedy: *That was started by Loune Viaud, Nancy Dorsinville, Paul Horan, and Paul Farmer from Partners in Health. The home is called Zamni Beni. All the kids were adopted by Loune, so now it's a family—a large family, with sixty or seventy kids, but a family. So you were selling Christmas ornaments for them?*

VW: Yes, and throughout each of the years we had the "Ripple of Hope" wall in our school. Each time someone bought an ornament or bracelet we would put their name on a piece of blue construction paper cut into the shape of a raindrop with the words "I am a ripple of hope" on it, and then we would pin the raindrop to the wall. By the end of the year the entire wall was covered with raindrops. It was very, very nice. We had pictures of raindrops growing on the wall as people donated.

KK: *That must have made everyone feel like they were part of the community, and that they each had a role in making a difference. And then senior year?*

VW: Our main thing this year was reverse trick-or-treating. I was deeply involved in this effort. First we watched a film and learned about the exploitation of children in the manufacturing of chocolate. I had no idea that 70 percent of the chocolate consumed in the United States is made by children in slavery or child labor, working so they cannot go to school. I cried when I learned about the terrible conditions. Sometimes it's like an awakening—people shouldn't have to go through this.

Then we made a plan. We decided to buy fair-trade chocolate—chocolate not made by exploited kids—and to give it to other students ("reverse trick or treat") and explain what we learned about child labor to them. It was my idea to hand out the fair-trade chocolates with cards explaining the problem during the lunch period because that is when most kids are together and available. We handed them out and what was really touching was that usually you get teenagers who just don't care—you just give them chocolate and they walk away. But all of the kids we spoke to actually wanted to know about what we were doing instead of just taking it and moving on. So we ended up actually having conversations in which we explained our project. It was just very touching because you don't expect so many people to actually listen and care about what you are doing.

KK: *Good for you! When you go off to college next year, do you want to continue working on social justice issues?*

VW: Yes! I was accepted to a college program focused on social justice. I enjoy working on these issues and I want to do more. First-year students choose an organization to volunteer with as part of a service project, and for the next three years you can continue to work for that organization. I am excited to choose an organization that I am really passionate about. I don't know which one yet, but I will be continuing my work.

KK: *Come and work with us!*

VW: It sounds amazing. The Ripple of Hope quote says you can touch another person's life and that can lead to another person and that is how change happens. Robert Kennedy believed all of us can change things.

Instead of just focusing on his own life, he focused on making sure other people's lives were better. If we had more of that in the world then we would not see some of these issues that we are seeing. He was a humanitarian, someone who cared deeply about social justice issues. If you are looking for work to follow and someone to be inspired by, look to Robert Kennedy.

"Our answer is the world's hope; it is to rely on youth."

—ROBERT F. KENNEDY

ACKNOWLEDGMENTS

"Each of us can work to change a small portion

of the events, and in the total of all these acts will

be written the history of this generation."

So said Robert F. Kennedy to students at the University of Cape Town, South Africa, on June 6, 1966. Indeed, this book is evidence of the power not of one, but of many working toward a common goal. To all those who played a role in creating this book, I am truly grateful. First and foremost, thank you to the people I interviewed. Their insights fill these pages, and they have left their mark on our country and the wider world, using their gifts to help create equal justice, stronger community, and more beauty, all at personal sacrifice. They are leaders who choose not to sit idly by and critique, but to enter the arena. Their wisdom abounds.

Thank you to Nelson Lewis, on whom I depend every day, for scheduling appointments, keeping track of lists, hunting down photos and releases, getting the recorder to work and the videos to send. He did it all with meticulous detail and reliably good humor, often after hours and on weekends. I cannot imagine a more unflappable, kind, patient, hardworking aide. I am forever grateful.

Thank you to my daughter Cara, who transcribed many of the interviews. Our talks about the content helped hone the process and bring out the best in the work and most of all made writing this book a source of

Robert Kennedy and David Kennedy at Hickory Hill in 1958 (Ethel Kennedy personal collection)

deep joy for me. My daughter Mariah wrote her thesis on Cesar Chavez and Robert F. Kennedy, and we interviewed Dolores Huerta together, which added depth and meaning. Thank you to all the other transcribers, who put such effort into the process. Michaela, I love you!

I spoke with Marc Grossman extensively about the idea of this book, and he helped draft the proposal and researched the background for each of the interviews. Marc worked as communications director for Cesar Chavez for decades, and I deeply appreciate our extensive discussions about the history of the farmworkers' movement and the struggle for justice. For advice and support throughout, thank you to Lynn Delaney. Lynn has devoted most of the last three decades to Robert F. Kennedy Human Rights. Her knowledge about my father, his life, his friends, and all that he stood for informs the work of the organization.

Thank you to Laurie Austin at the John F. Kennedy Presidential Library for helping me find photographs, track down photographers, and determine copyrights. Laurie is a dedicated public servant.

Thank you to the photographers who donated their works to this book—to Harry Benson, who joined us on the Snake River in 1966 and who remains to this day one of my dearest friends, along with his ever-generous manager, whom he had the good sense to marry, Gigi. Thank you to Mort Zuckerman, Eric Gertler, and the New York *Daily News* for the use of their photos. Thank you to Steve Shapiro, who traveled with my parents across Latin America and around much of the United States. And thank you to all the other photographers who documented my father's life.

Thank you to Kate Hartson, my editor at Hachette, for her enthusiasm and insightful suggestions on the book. Kate was kind and generous from day one, and I feel lucky to know her. Jaime Coyne is a terrific associate editor. At Aevitas Creative Management, thank you to David Kuhn, my agent and ever-reliable champion, and William LoTurco, who reminded me of looming deadlines and kept me on track.

A very special thanks to Daniel Zitlin, whose red pen and razor-sharp ability to separate the meat from the fat is evident across the book. Daniel was an absolute joy to work with: easy, reliable, insightful, and fast.

Shannon and Drew Hayden, thank you for a much-needed retreat at your home in Newton—a sharp contrast after seven days in a row of eighty people at each dinner over our weeklong family-and-friends reunion in Hyannis Port. Gail Evertz, thank you, dear friend, for your generosity, huge energy, and gratitude, but especially for your talents as a farmer.

Hope and Robert Smith, the days I spent at your ranch in Colorado served as inspiration: the history of Lincoln Hills as one of the four communities for African American recreation over the last one hundred years; walking the paths of my favorite poets, Langston Hughes, and Zora Neale Hurston; being surrounded by photographs of black cowboys, gold miners, and the great musicians who came there to play and whose photos grace the walls (Armstrong, Fitzgerald, Horne, and more). After several days of catch and release (I would catch, and the fish would release itself), actually landing my first trout on a fly line after fifty-plus years of failed attempts reminded me to never ever give up. A special thank-you to Zoë, Eliana, Max, Hendrix, and Legend, who took me canoeing, hiking, fishing, riding, beat me in Bananagrams, and made me laugh throughout.

ABOUT THE AUTHOR

Kerry Kennedy is the president of Robert F. Kennedy Human Rights. Since 1981, she has worked on diverse human rights issues including child labor, disappearances, indigenous land rights, judicial independence, freedom of expression, ethnic violence, impunity, mass incarceration, women's rights, and the environment. Kennedy founded RFK Compass, which convenes biannual meetings of institutional investors to address human rights violations and investment outcomes.

Kennedy is the author of *Speak Truth to Power* (Crown Books, 2000). *Speak Truth* has grown to include a photography exhibit now traveling on four continents, a play by the Broadway playwright Ariel Dorfman, which has opened in over twenty countries, an award-winning website, a PBS documentary film, and an education program and toolkit-for-action packet now being taught to millions worldwide.

She serves on the boards of the U.S. Institute of Peace, Human Rights First, Ethics in Action, SDG USA, Sustainable Development Goals Center Africa, Health eVillages, and the Kailash Satyarthi Children's Foundation. She serves on the Department of State Advisory Committee on International Economic Policy (ACIEP) as well as several other advisory committees. She is the best-selling author of *Being Catholic Now* (Random House, 2000). A graduate of Brown University and Boston College Law School, she received the Social Activism Award from the World Summit of Nobel Peace Prize Laureates (2017) along with many other awards and honorary degrees.

Kennedy is the mother of three daughters, Cara, Mariah, and Michaela.